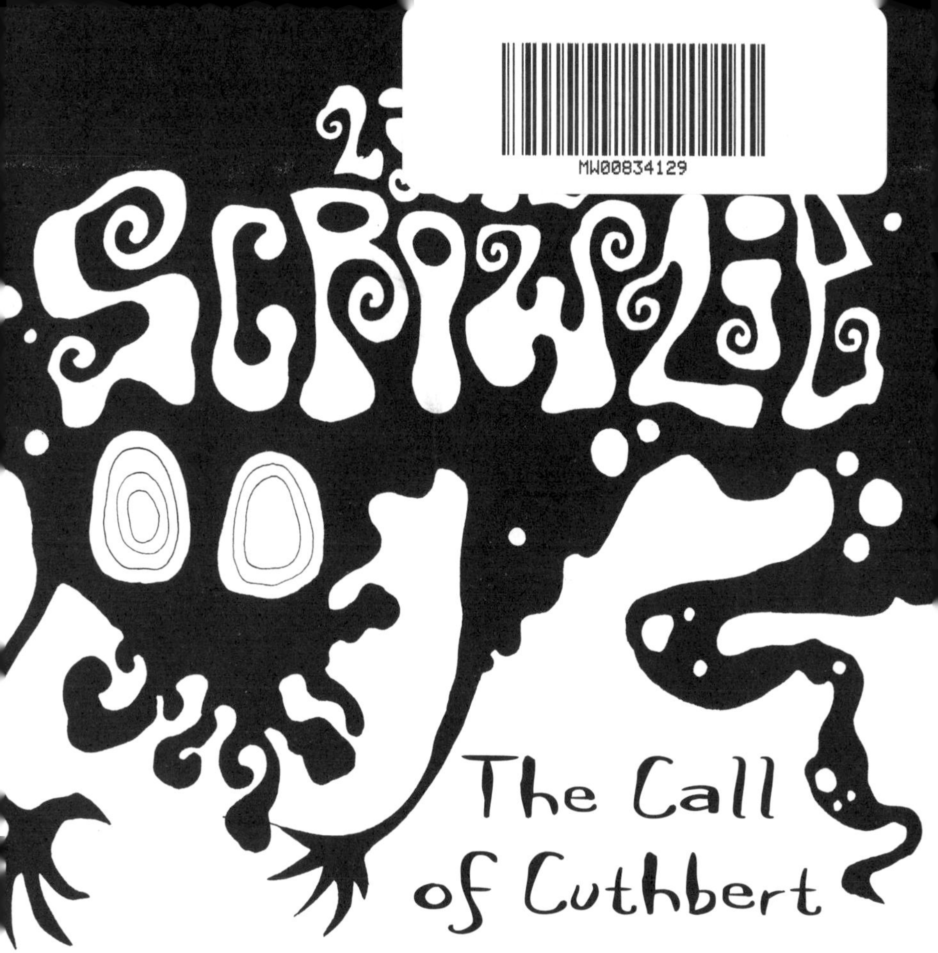

The Call of Cuthbert

by
Jennifer Feinberg
&
Todd Meister

Little Scrowlie

The Call of Cuthbert

drawn by
Jennifer
Feinberg

written by
Todd
Meister

indroduction by
Serena Valentino

pin-ups by
Black Olive
Christopher
FSc
Derek Hunter
Tommy Kovac
Diana X. Sprinkle
Eddie Perkins

Published
by SLG

President/Publisher
Dan Vado

Editor-in-Chief
Jennifer de Guzman

Director of Sales
Deb Moskyok

P.O. Box 2642
San Jose, CA
95159

Little Scrowlie: The Call of Cuthbert
collects issues #1-4 of the SLG Publishing
series Little Scrowlie.

First Printing:
September 2004

ISBN 1-59362-000-4

Introduction

by Serena Valentino

"Come little kittens, and I will show you weird things...."

Enter if you will the spookirific world of *Little Scrowlie*. A cute little ghost will lead you through a wicked-looking door where you will creep down a dark, dank stairway leading you on a wild adventure where you will be invited to a strange party by a befuddled landlady and her tea-serving Cuthbie Beastie.

This is but a fraction of what lies ahead in this imaginatively written story. The writing is hilarious and satirical and the art is stylistic, swirly and magical. I love everything about this comic, and I am so thankful my sister introduced me to this sparkly little treasure; it was love at first sight.

For years I hunted down Jen and Todd at local comic conventions in hopes of getting a new issue of *Little Scrowlie*... and they were ever so patient with me when I pouted and stomped my little feet when they didn't have a new issue out yet — I needed my Scrowlie fix after all!

And then one day something magical happened.... SLG announced they would be publishing one of my favorite comics. I can't express how pleased I was when I learned Jen and Todd would be joining the SLG family – and now not only is it easier to get my grubby little paws on their enchanting comic, it has given me the opportunity to get to know two amazingly sweet creators whose work I enjoy immensely. I am truly honored they have asked me to write the introduction to their wonderful first collection — I just hope I am adequately expressing how well I love *Little Scrowlie*.

I think it's also worth noting that I would willfully become a fashion zombie if it meant Jen designed clothes for stores like Hip Gothic — one of the many things I enjoy about this comic is Jen's clothing designs... though I think willingly becoming a fashion zombie goes against the social commentary Jen and Todd are making in this charming little gem you have in your paws.

Speaking of paws, I cannot conclude my introduction without gushing a bit about how much I adore the kitties in this story. Scrowlie and the voluptuous white cat are more than welcome to come over to my place for tea anytime they please; for that matter they may bring James and a lick-monster over as well; I think we'd all have a lovely time.

Make yourself a cup of coffee, curl up in a comfy chair and if you have a kitty, let her snuggle up on your lap and enjoy the magic of *Little Scrowlie* — I know I do.

Squishings,
Serena Valentino

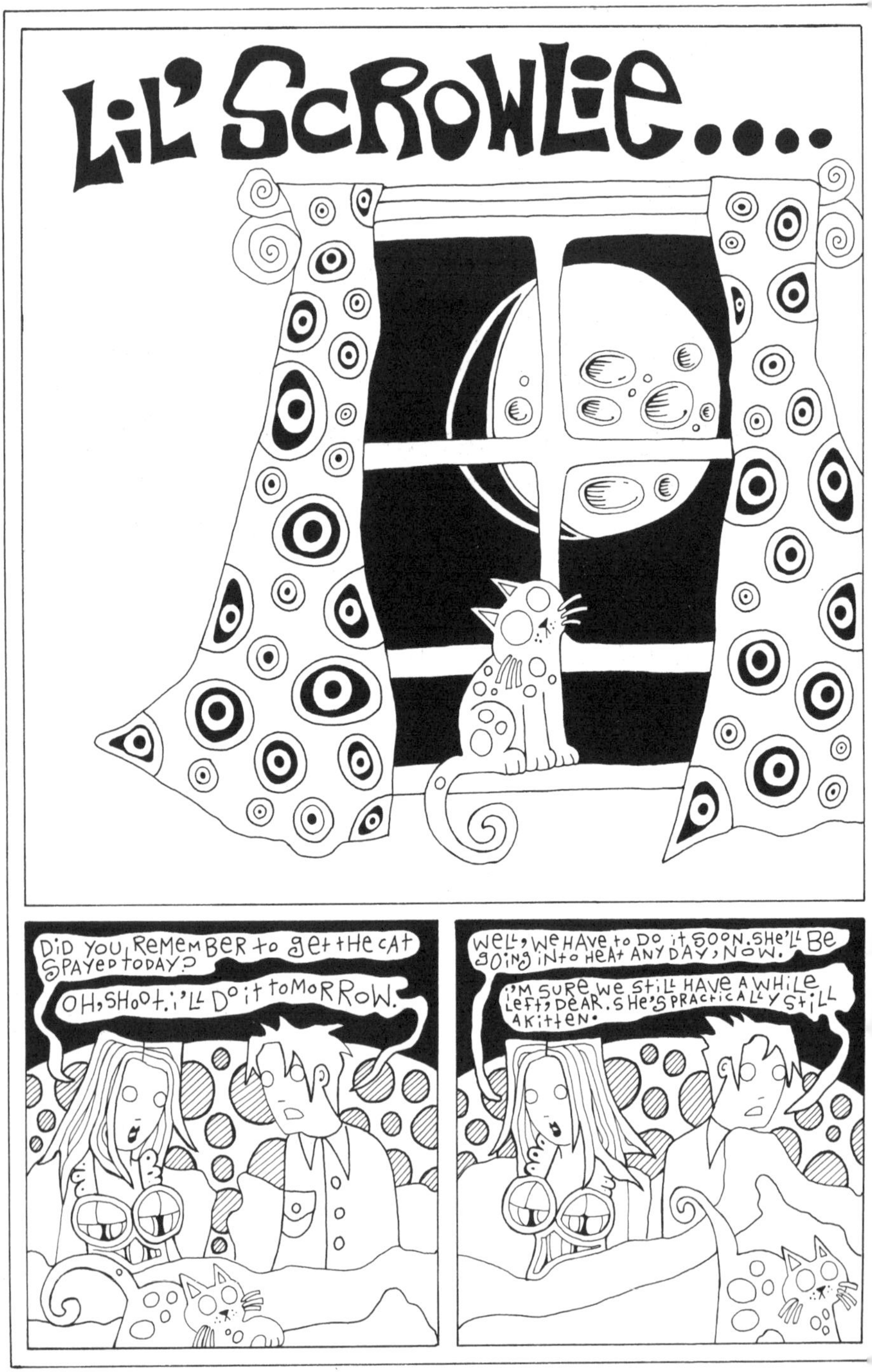
LIL' SCROWLIE....
DID YOU REMEMBER TO GET THE CAT SPAYED TODAY?
OH, SHOOT. I'LL DO IT TOMORROW.
WELL, WE HAVE TO DO IT SOON. SHE'LL BE GOING INTO HEAT ANY DAY, NOW.
I'M SURE WE STILL HAVE A WHILE LEFT, DEAR. SHE'S PRACTICALLY STILL A KITTEN.

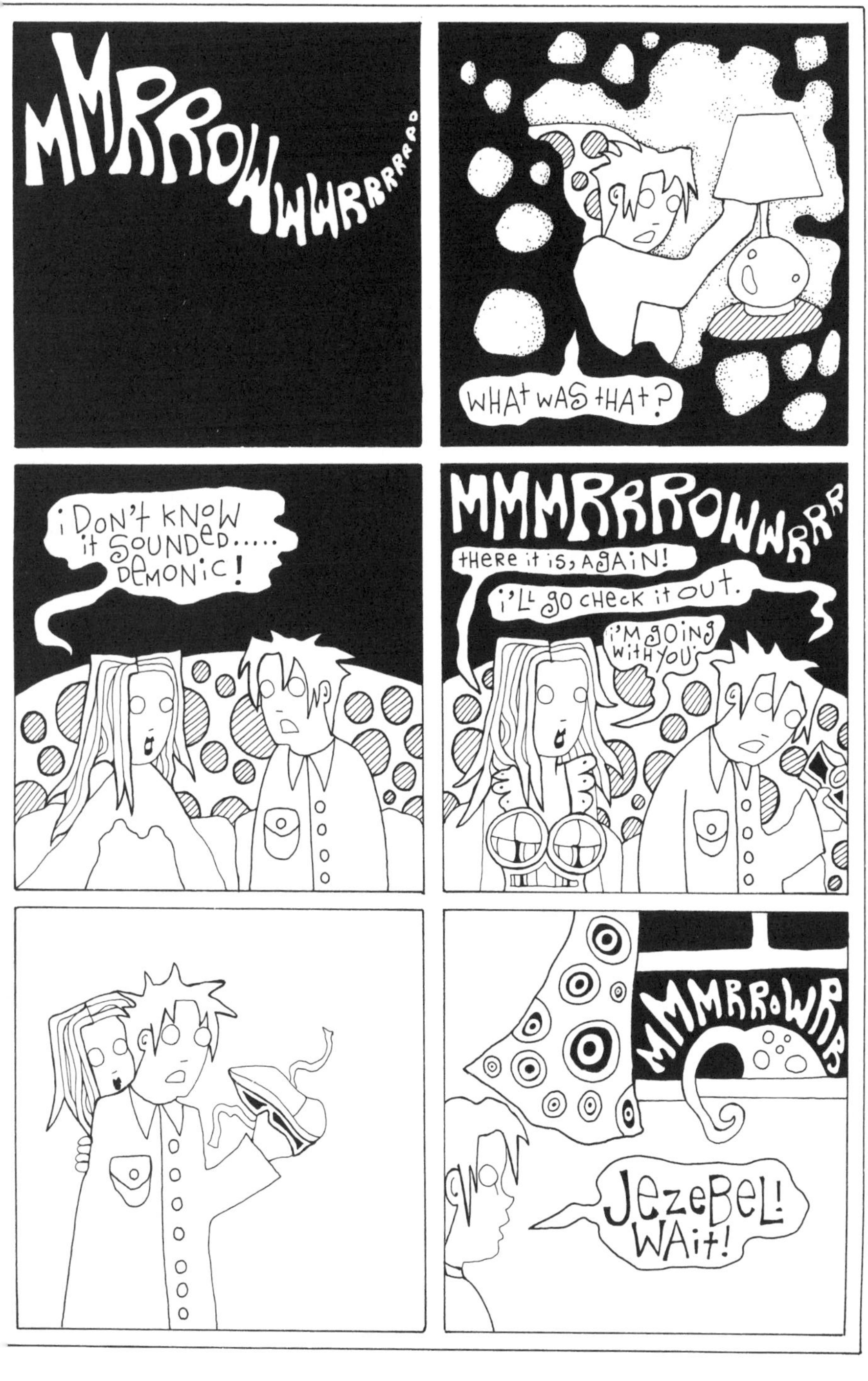
MMRROWWWRRRRRO
WHAT WAS THAT?
i DON'T KNOW it SOUNDED..... DEMONIC!
MMMRRROWWRRR
THERE it iS, AGAIN!
i'LL GO CHECK it OUT.
i'M GOING WITH YOU.
MMMRROWRR
JEZEBEL! WAit!

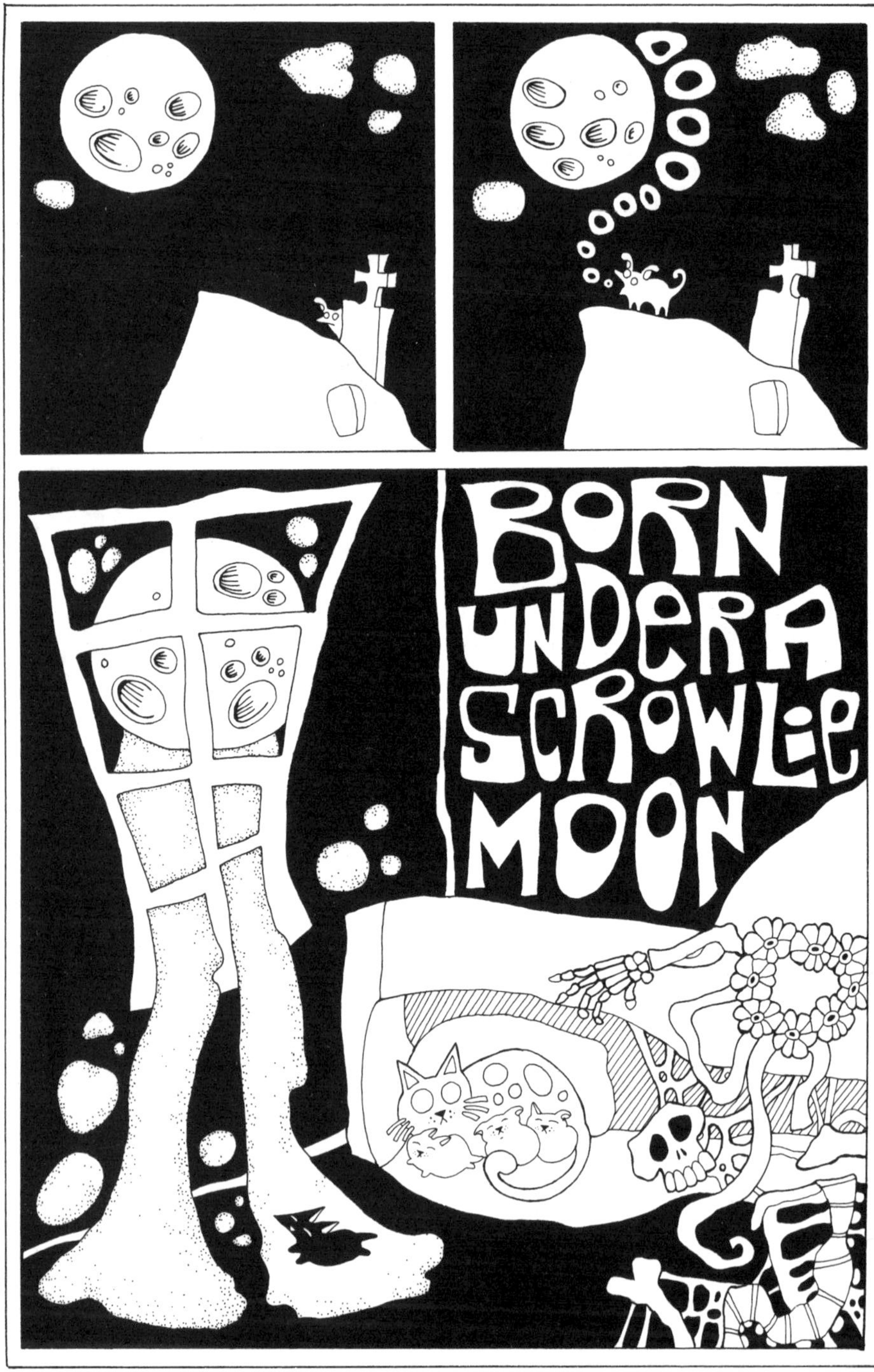
BORN UNDER A SCROWLIE MOON

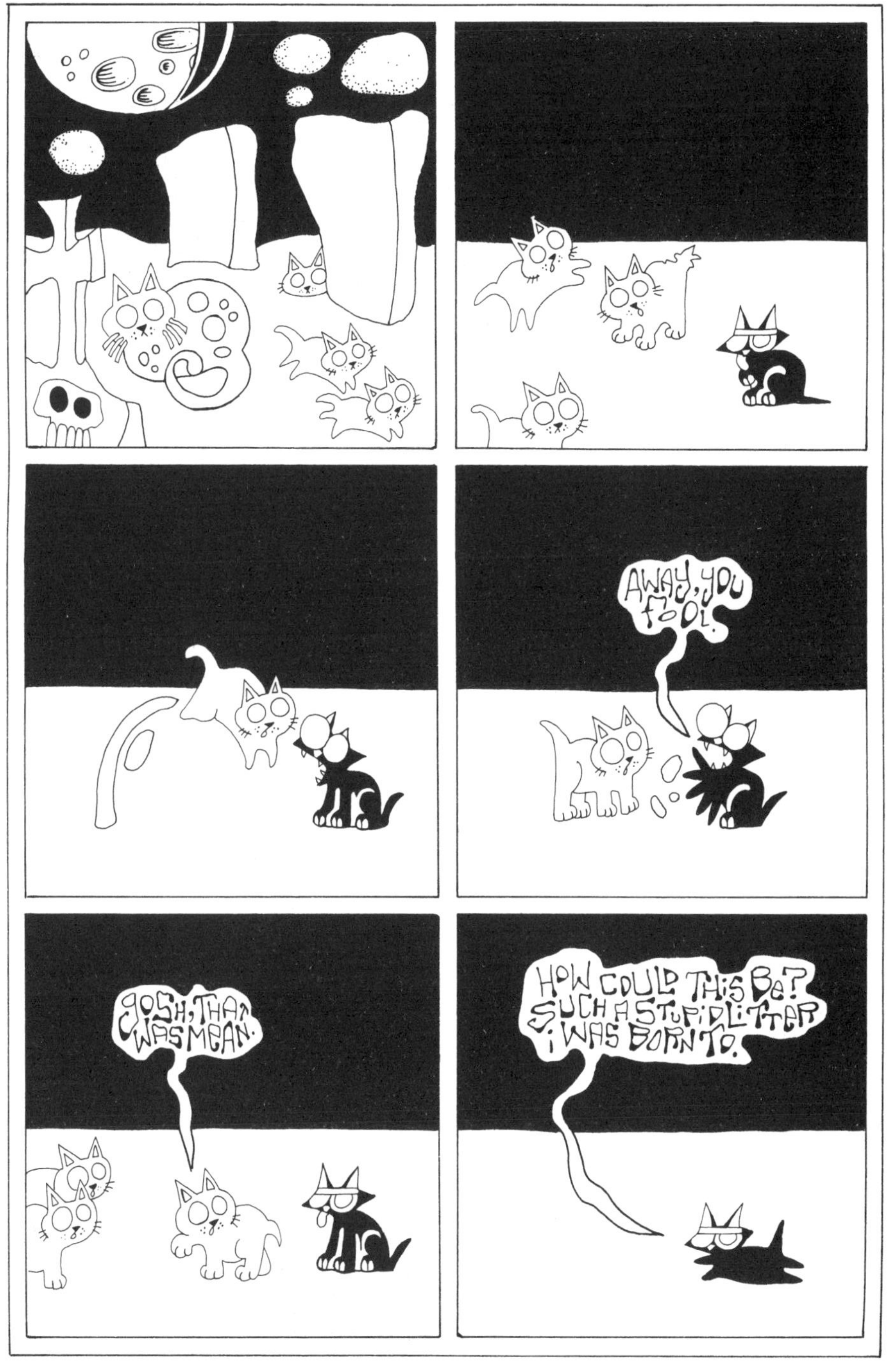
AWAY, YOU FOOL.
GOSH, THAT WAS MEAN.
HOW COULD THIS BE? SUCH A STUPID LITTER I WAS BORN TO.

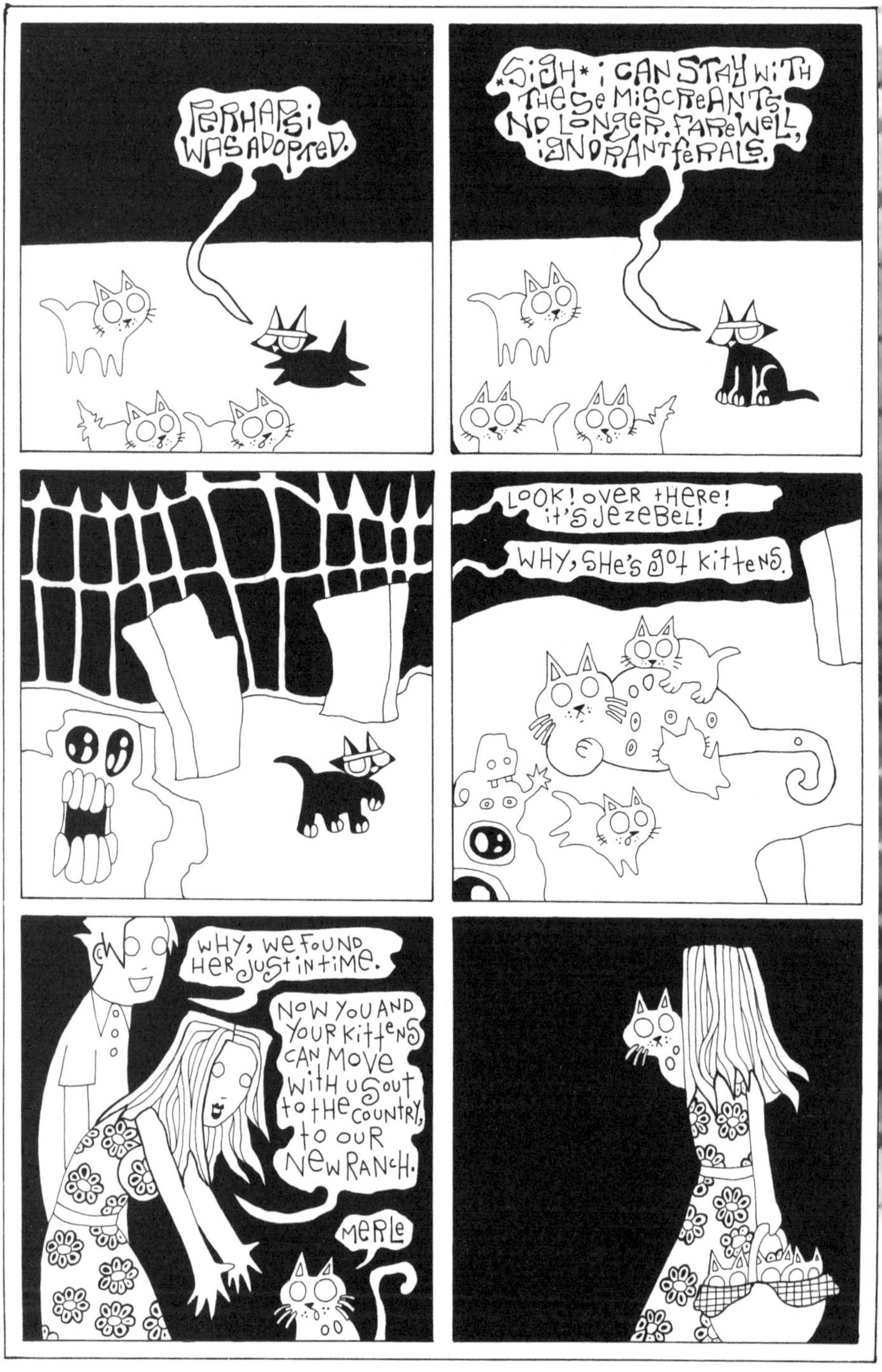
PERHAPS I WAS ADOPTED.
SIGH I CAN STAY WITH THESE MISCREANTS NO LONGER. FAREWELL, IGNORANT FERALS.
LOOK! OVER THERE! IT'S JEZEBEL!
WHY, SHE'S GOT KITTENS.
WHY, WE FOUND HER JUST IN TIME.
NOW YOU AND YOUR KITTENS CAN MOVE WITH US OUT TO THE COUNTRY, TO OUR NEW RANCH.
MERLE

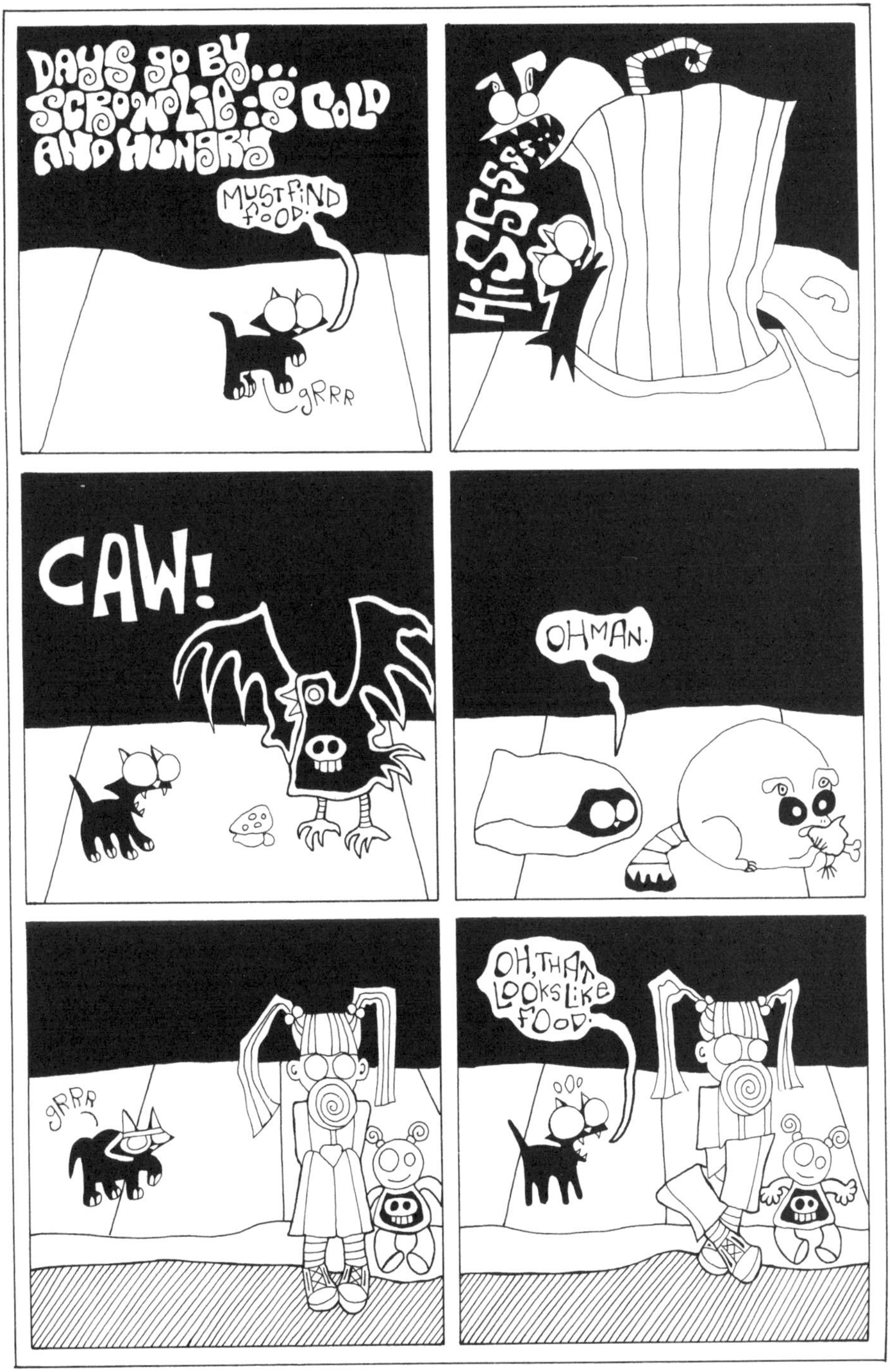
DAYS GO BY... SCROWLIE IS COLD AND HUNGRY
MUST FIND FOOD.
gRRR
HiSSSSS
CAW!
OH MAN.
gRRR
OH, THAT LOOKS LIKE FOOD.

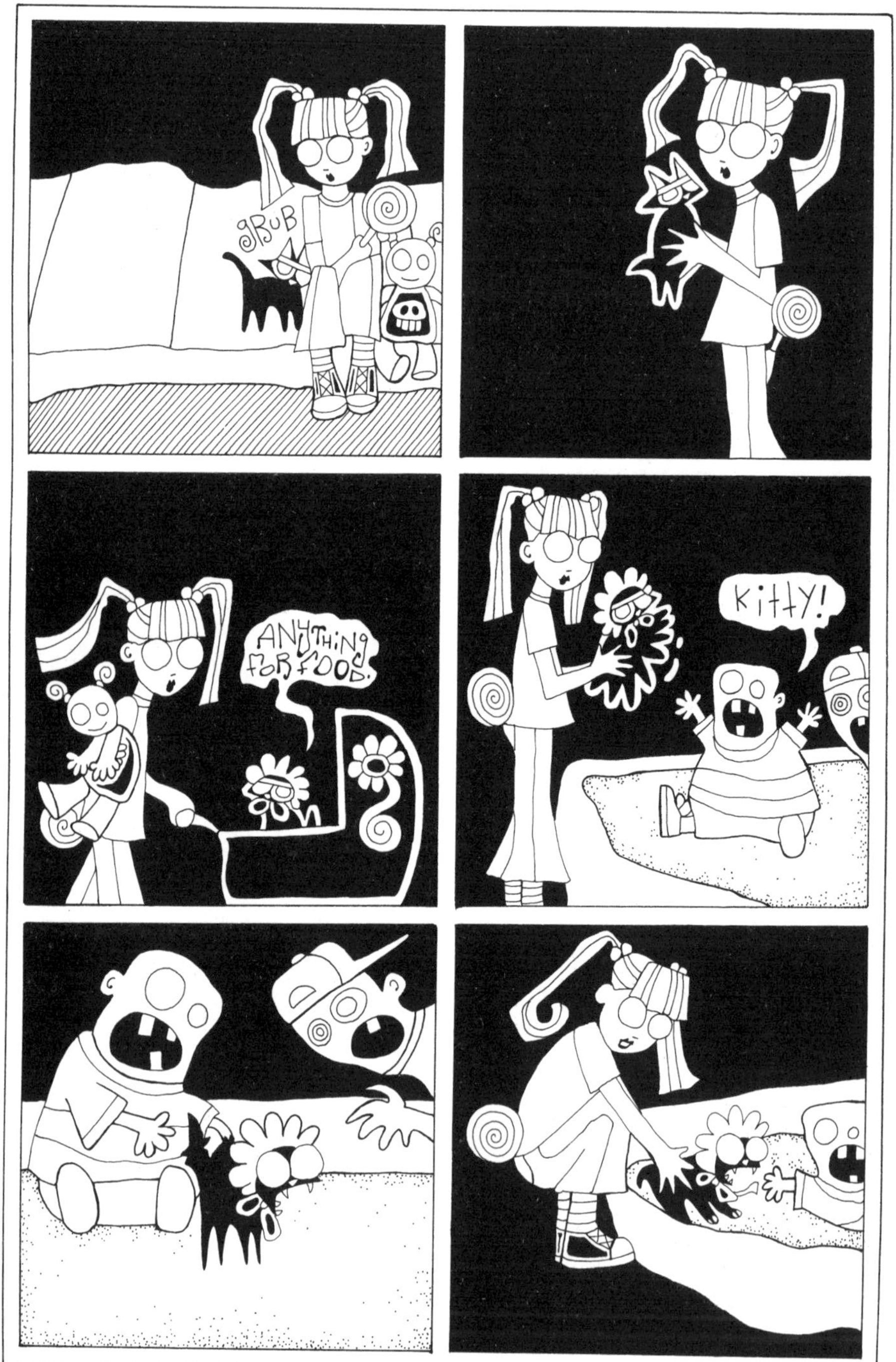
gRuB
ANYTHING FOR FOOD.
Kitty!

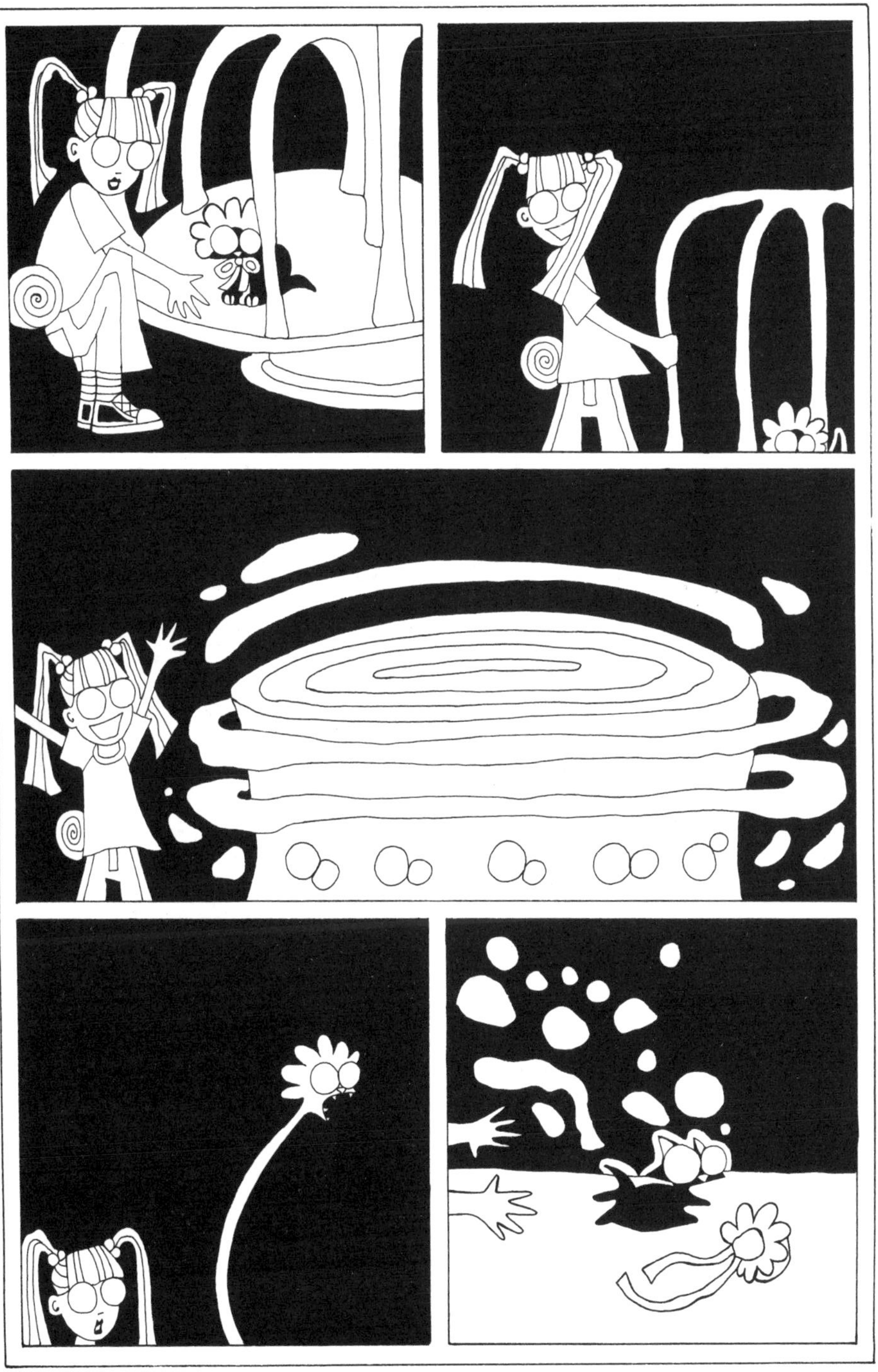

AND SO LIL' SCROWLIE REMAINED ALONE AND HUNGRY, DOOMED TO WANDER THE STREETS IN SEARCH OF CAT FOOD AND COMPANIONSHIP. EVENTUALLY SHE WOULD FIND THAT FOR WHICH SHE SEARCHED, AND HER DREAMS WOULD BRING WITH THEM, THEIR OWN PARTICULAR HARDSHIPS.
BUT THAT IS ANOTHER TAIL, TO BE TOLD ANOTHER TIME...
THE END

1

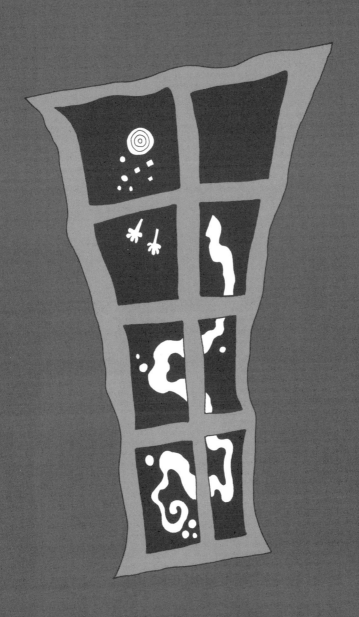

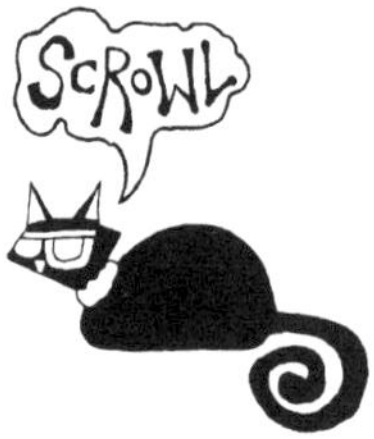
SCROWL

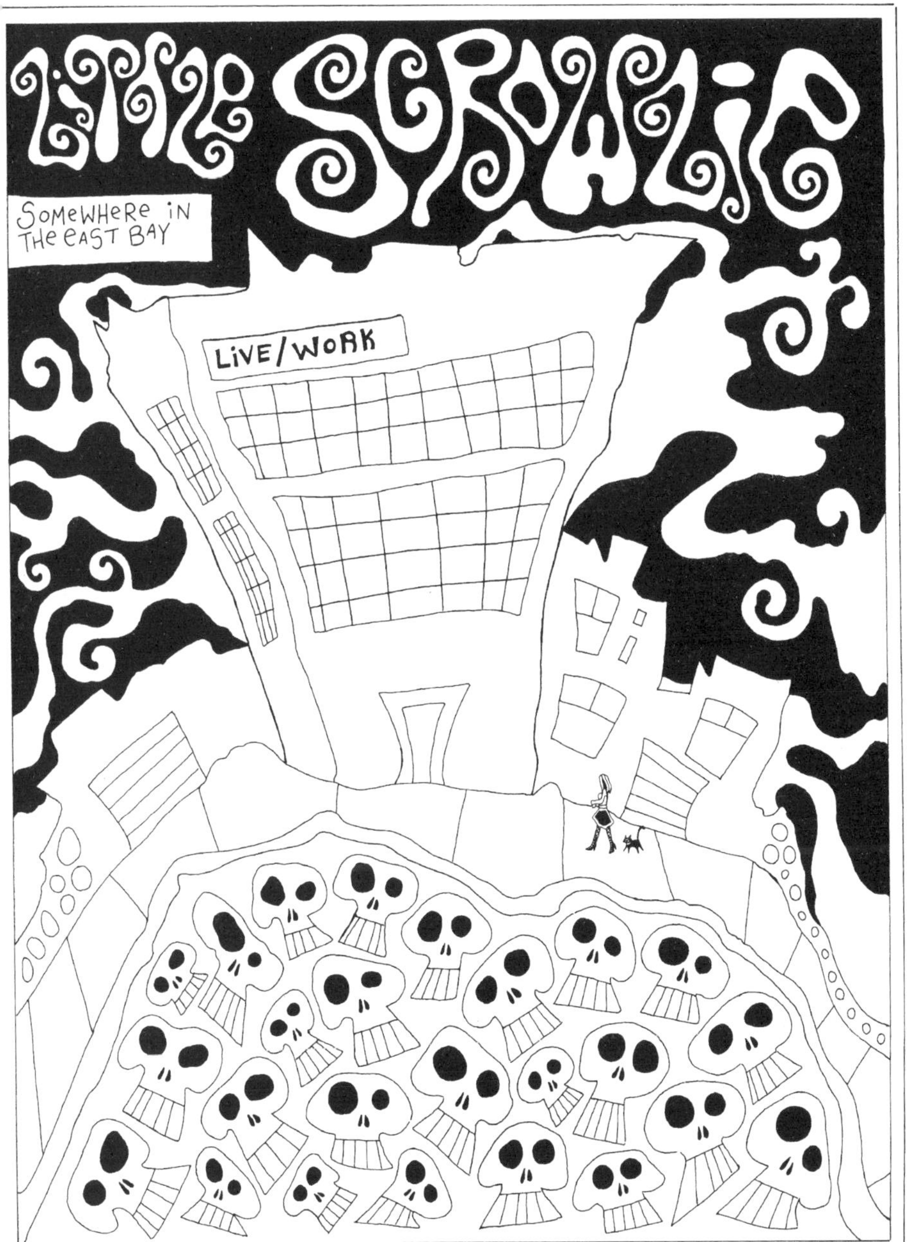
SOMEWHERE IN THE EAST BAY
LIVE/WORK

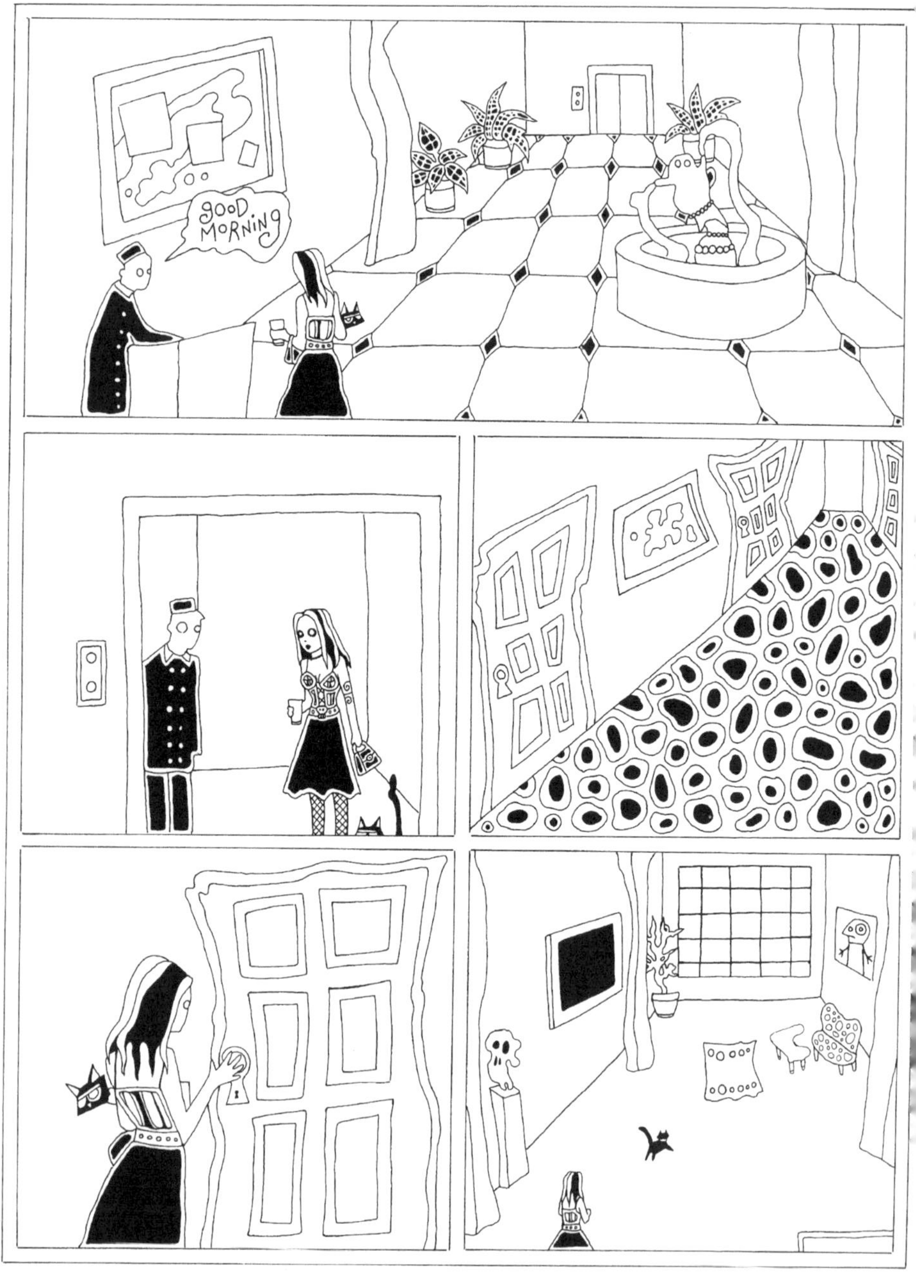
GOOD MORNING

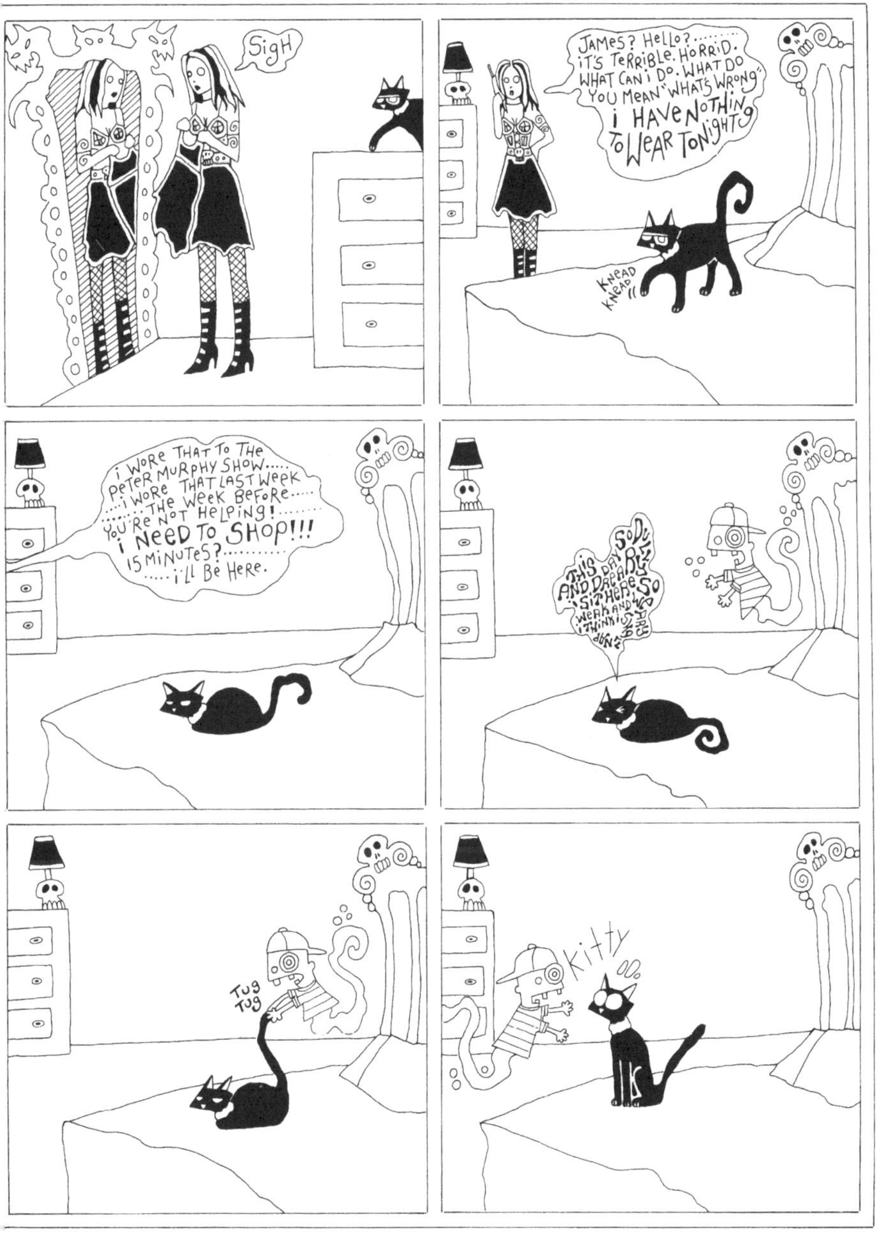
SigH
JAMES? HELLo?........ iT'S TeRRiBLE. HoRRiD. WHAT CAN i Do. WHAT Do YOU MeAN "WHAT'S WRoNG". i HAVe NoTHiNG To WeAR ToNiGHT
KNeAD KNeAD
i WORe THAT To THe PeTeR MURPHY SHOW..... i WORe THAT LAST Week ....THe Week BeFoRe..... YoU'Re NoT HeLPiNG!........ i NeeD To SHoP!!! 15 MiNUTeS?............ .....i'Ll Be Here.
THiS DAY So DULL AND DReARY So i SiT HeRe WeAK AND WeARY i THiNK i SHAll NAP
TUG TUG
Kitty

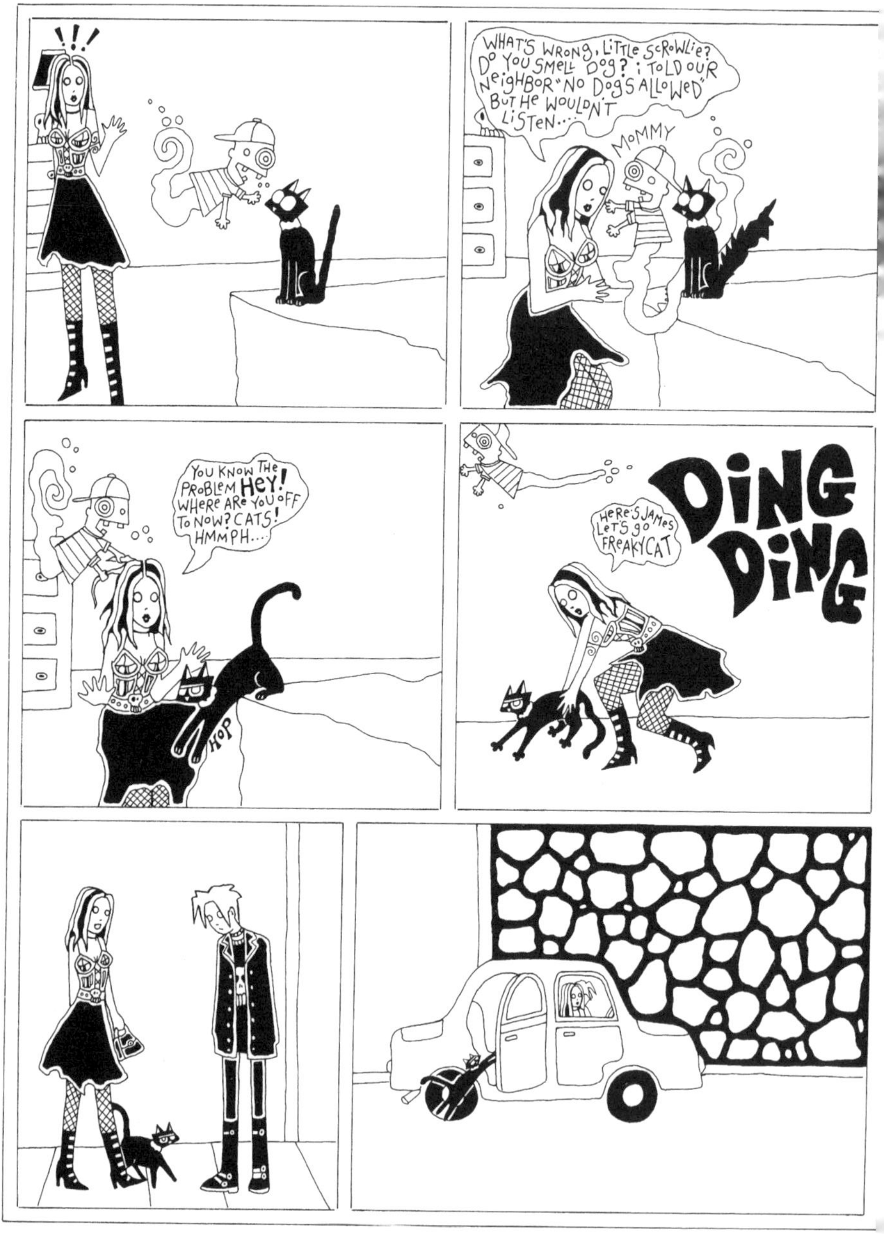
!!!
WHAT'S WRONG, LITTLE SCROWLIE? DO YOU SMELL DOG? I TOLD OUR NEIGHBOR "NO DOGS ALLOWED" BUT HE WOULDN'T LISTEN....
MOMMY
YOU KNOW THE PROBLEM HEY! WHERE ARE YOU OFF TO NOW? CATS! HMMPH....
HOP
HERE'S JAMES LET'S GO FREAKYCAT
DING DING

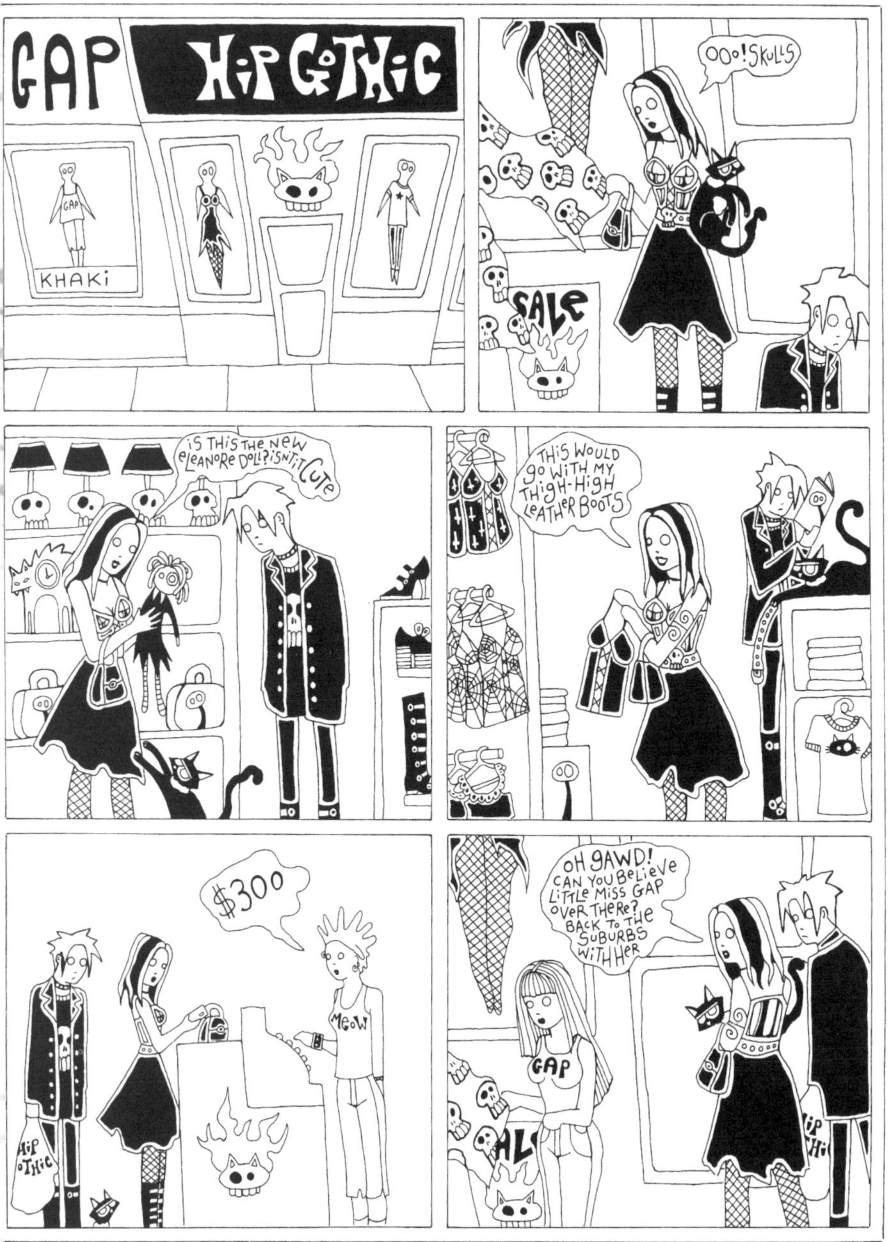
GAP
HIP GOTHIC
GAP
KHAKI
OOO! SKULLS
SALE
IS THIS THE NEW ELEANORE DOLL? ISN'T IT CUTE
THIS WOULD GO WITH MY THIGH-HIGH LEATHER BOOTS
$300
MEOW
OH GAWD! CAN YOU BELIEVE LITTLE MISS GAP OVER THERE? BACK TO THE SUBURBS WITH HER
GAP

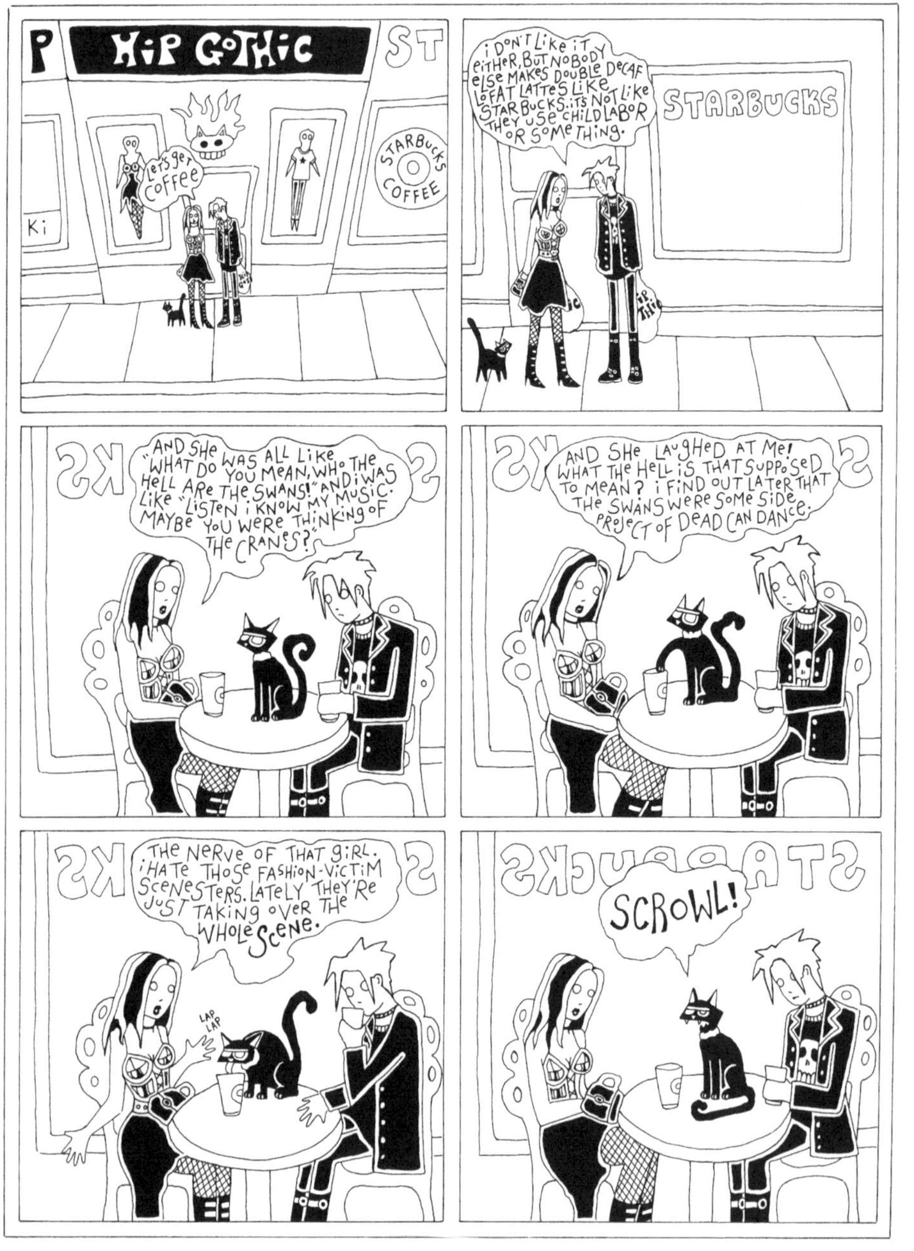
P
HIP GOTHIC
ST
LET'S GET COFFEE
STARBUCKS COFFEE
KI
I DON'T LIKE IT EITHER, BUT NOBODY ELSE MAKES DOUBLE DECAF LOFAT LATTES LIKE STARBUCKS. IT'S NOT LIKE THEY USE CHILD LABOR OR SOMETHING.
STARBUCKS
"AND SHE WAS ALL LIKE "WHAT DO YOU MEAN, WHO THE HELL ARE THE SWANS!" AND I WAS LIKE "LISTEN I KNOW MY MUSIC. MAYBE YOU WERE THINKING OF THE CRANES?"
AND SHE LAUGHED AT ME! WHAT THE HELL IS THAT SUPPOSED TO MEAN? I FIND OUT LATER THAT THE SWANS WERE SOME SIDE PROJECT OF DEAD CAN DANCE.
THE NERVE OF THAT GIRL. I HATE THOSE FASHION-VICTIM SCENESTERS. LATELY THEY'RE JUST TAKING OVER THE WHOLE SCENE.
LAP LAP
SCROWL!

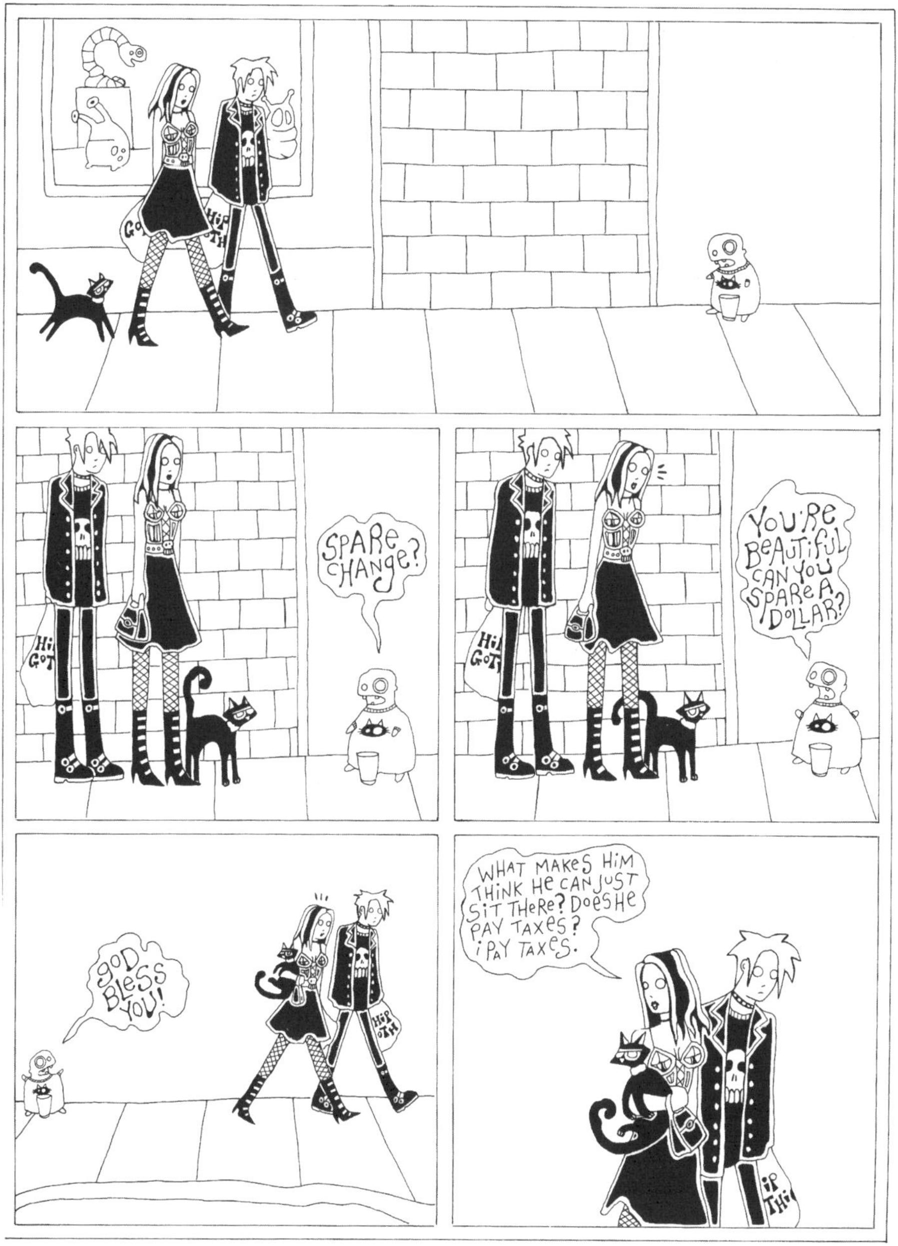
SPARE CHANGE?
YOU'RE BEAUTIFUL CAN YOU SPARE A DOLLAR?
GOD BLESS YOU!
WHAT MAKES HIM THINK HE CAN JUST SIT THERE? DOES HE PAY TAXES? I PAY TAXES.

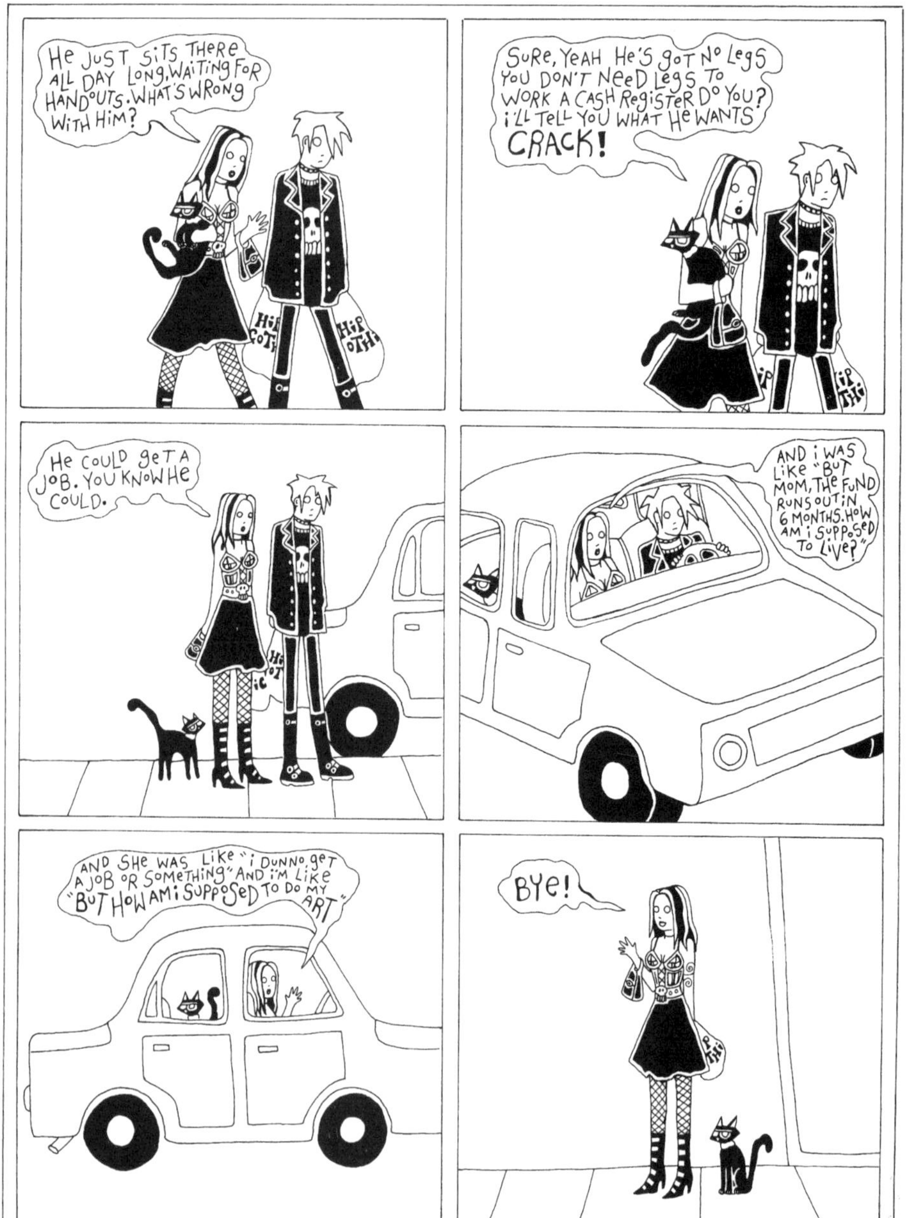
He JUST SiTS THERE ALL DAY LONG, WAiTiNG FOR HANDOUTS. WHAT'S WRONG WITH HiM?
SURE, YEAH He'S goT No Legs YOU DON'T NeeD Legs To WORK A CASH RegiSTeR Do YOU? i'LL TeLL YOU WHAT He WANTS CRACK!
He COULD geT A JOB. YOU KNOW He COULD.
AND i WAS Like "BUT MOM, THe FUND RUNS OUT iN 6 MONTHS. HOW AM i SUPPOSED TO Live?"
AND SHe WAS Like "i DUNNO, geT A JOB OR SOMeTHiNg" AND i'M Like "BUT HOW AM i SUPPOSED TO DO MY ART"
BYe!

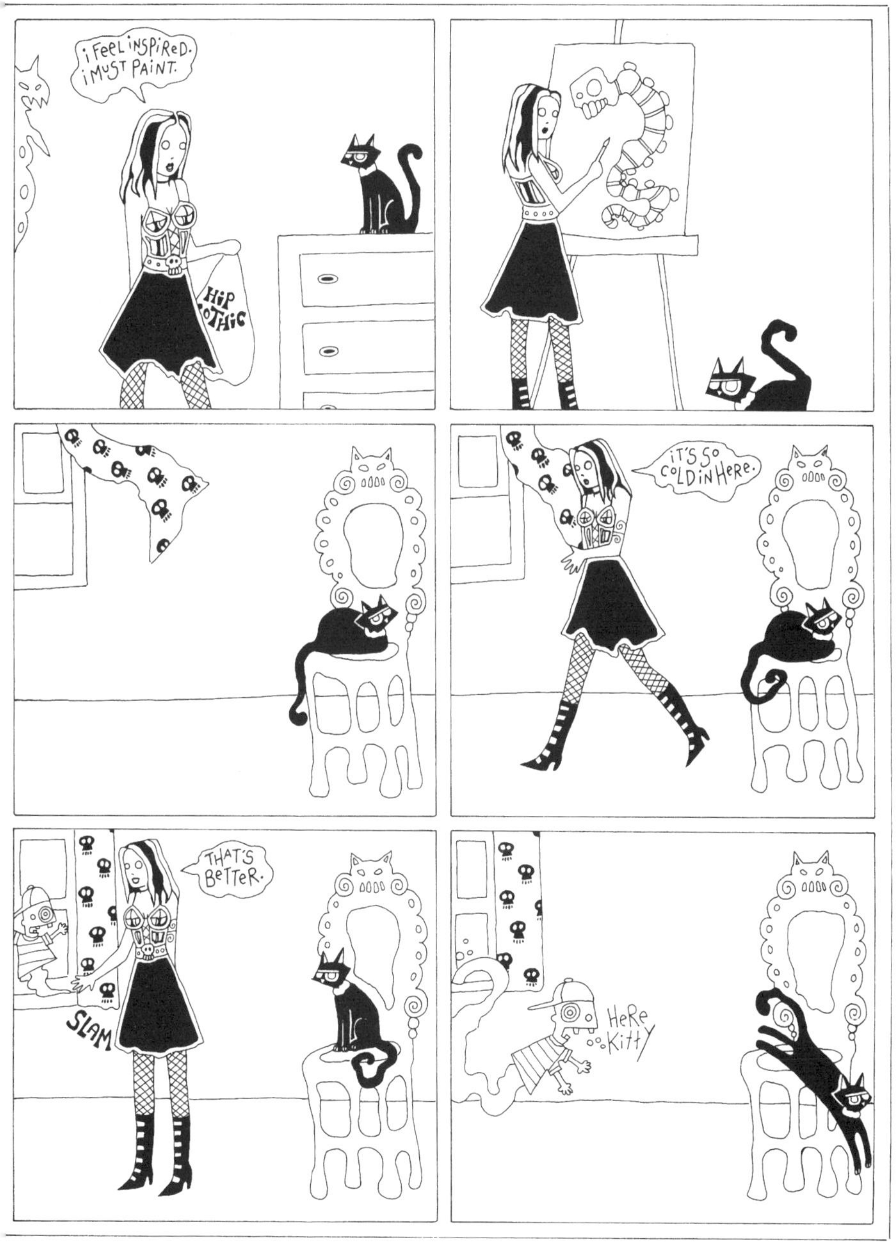
i Feel inspired. i MUST PAINT.
HiP GOTHIC
iT'S SO COLD iN HeRe.
THAT'S BeTTeR.
SLAM
HeRe Kitty

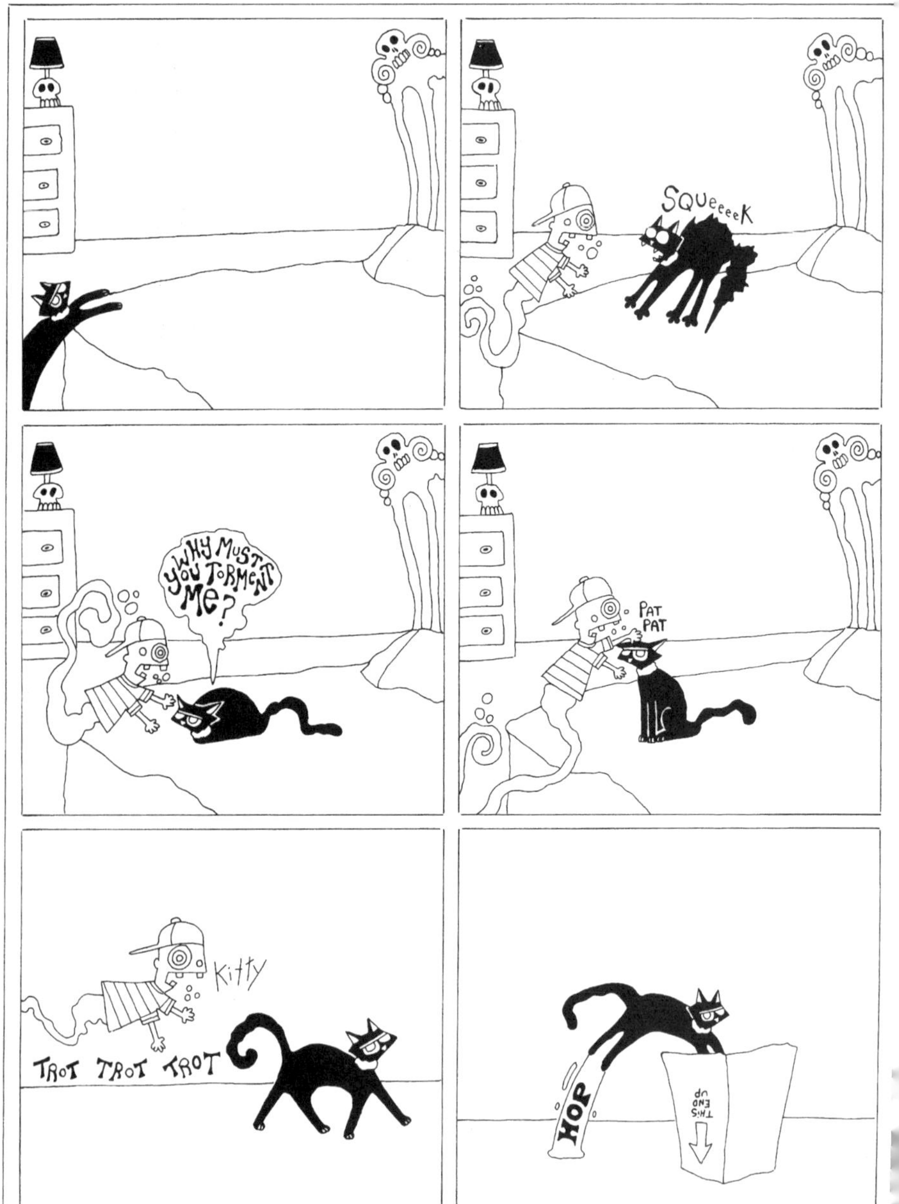
SQUeeeeK
WHY MUST YOU TORMENT ME?
PAT PAT
Kitty
TROT TROT TROT
HOP
THIS END UP

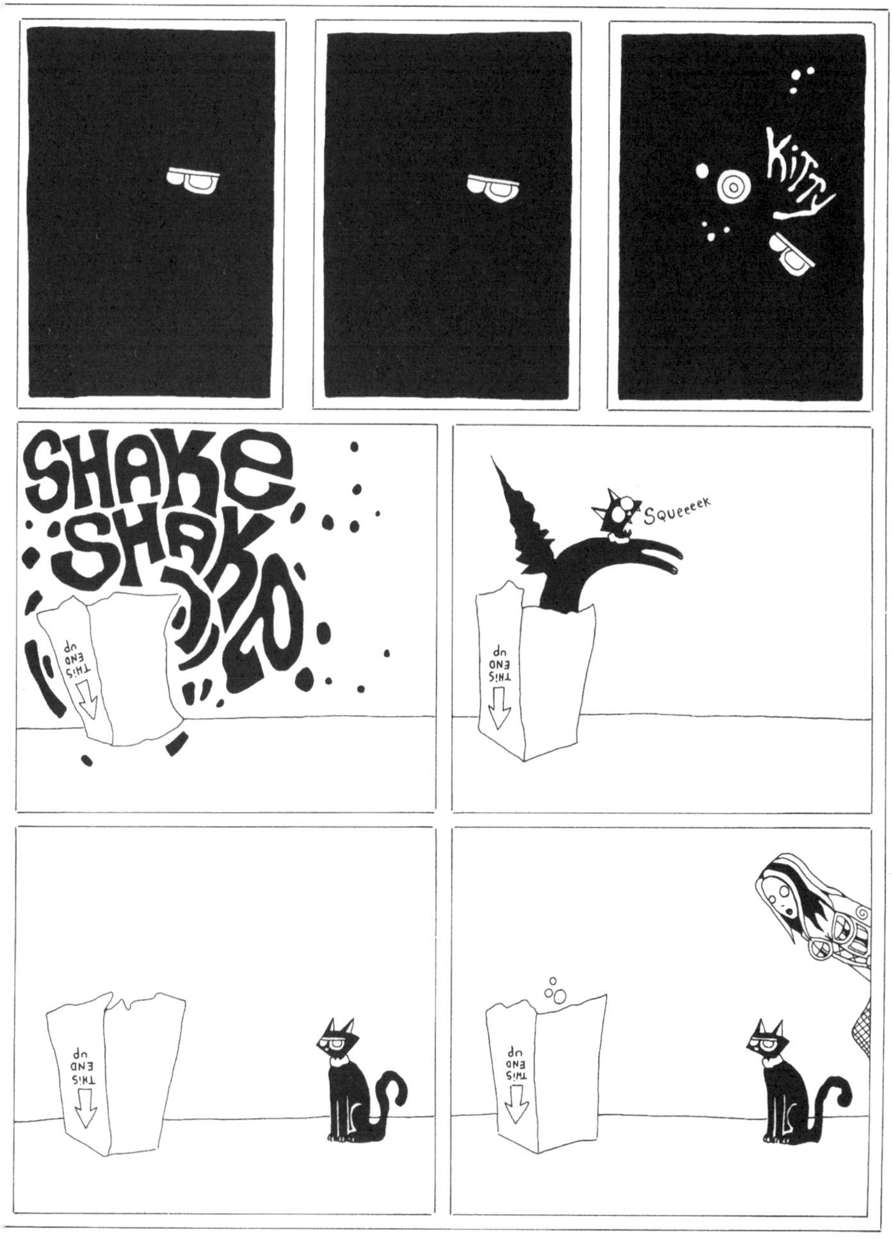
KiTTY
SHAKE
SHAK
THIS END UP
Squeeeek

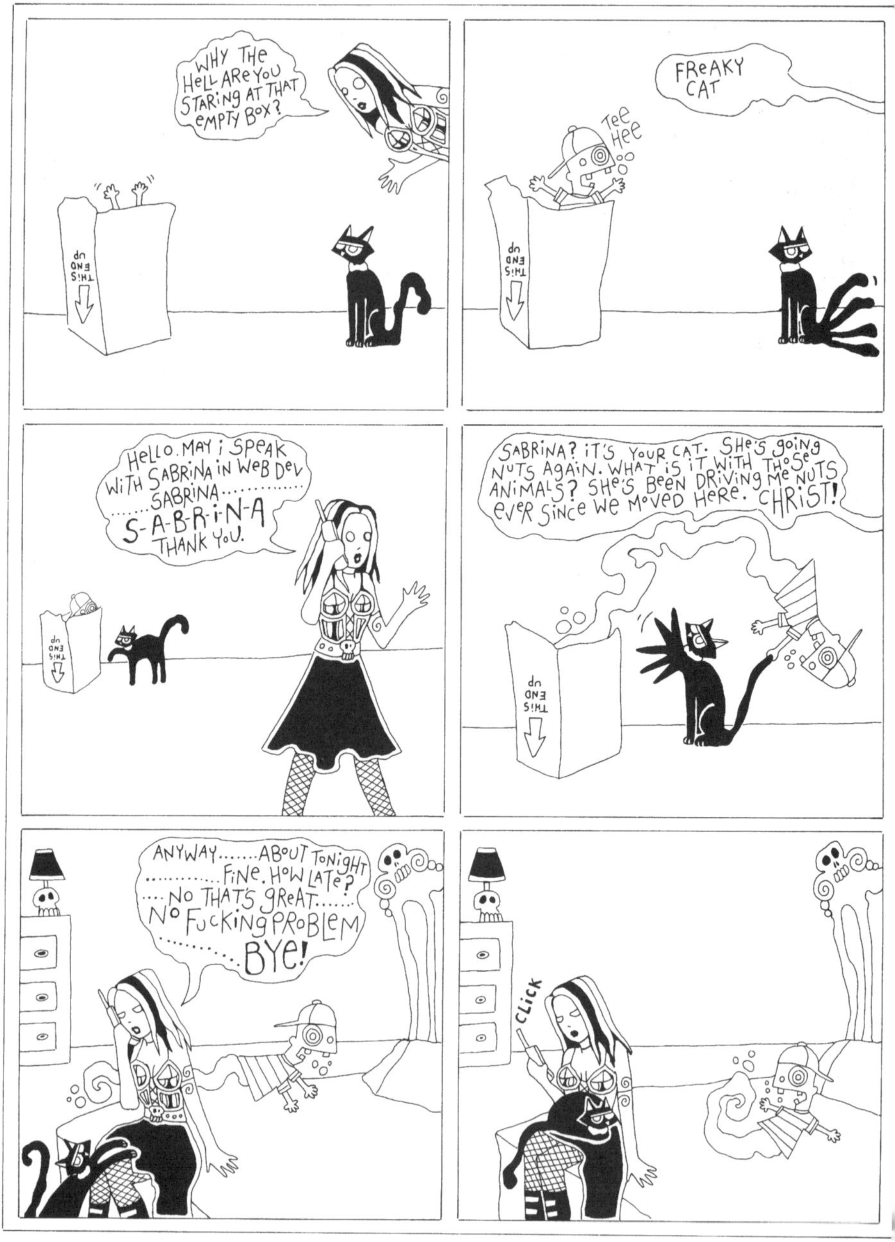
WHY THE HELL ARE YOU STARING AT THAT EMPTY BOX?
THIS END UP
FREAKY CAT
TEE HEE
THIS END UP
HELLO. MAY I SPEAK WITH SABRINA IN WEB DEV
SABRINA..............
.......SABRINA
S-A-B-R-I-N-A
THANK YOU.
THIS END UP
SABRINA? IT'S YOUR CAT. SHE'S GOING NUTS AGAIN. WHAT IS IT WITH THOSE ANIMALS? SHE'S BEEN DRIVING ME NUTS EVER SINCE WE MOVED HERE. CHRIST!
THIS END UP
ANYWAY.......ABOUT TONIGHT
...........FINE. HOW LATE?
....NO THAT'S GREAT.......
NO FUCKING PROBLEM
...........BYE!
CLICK

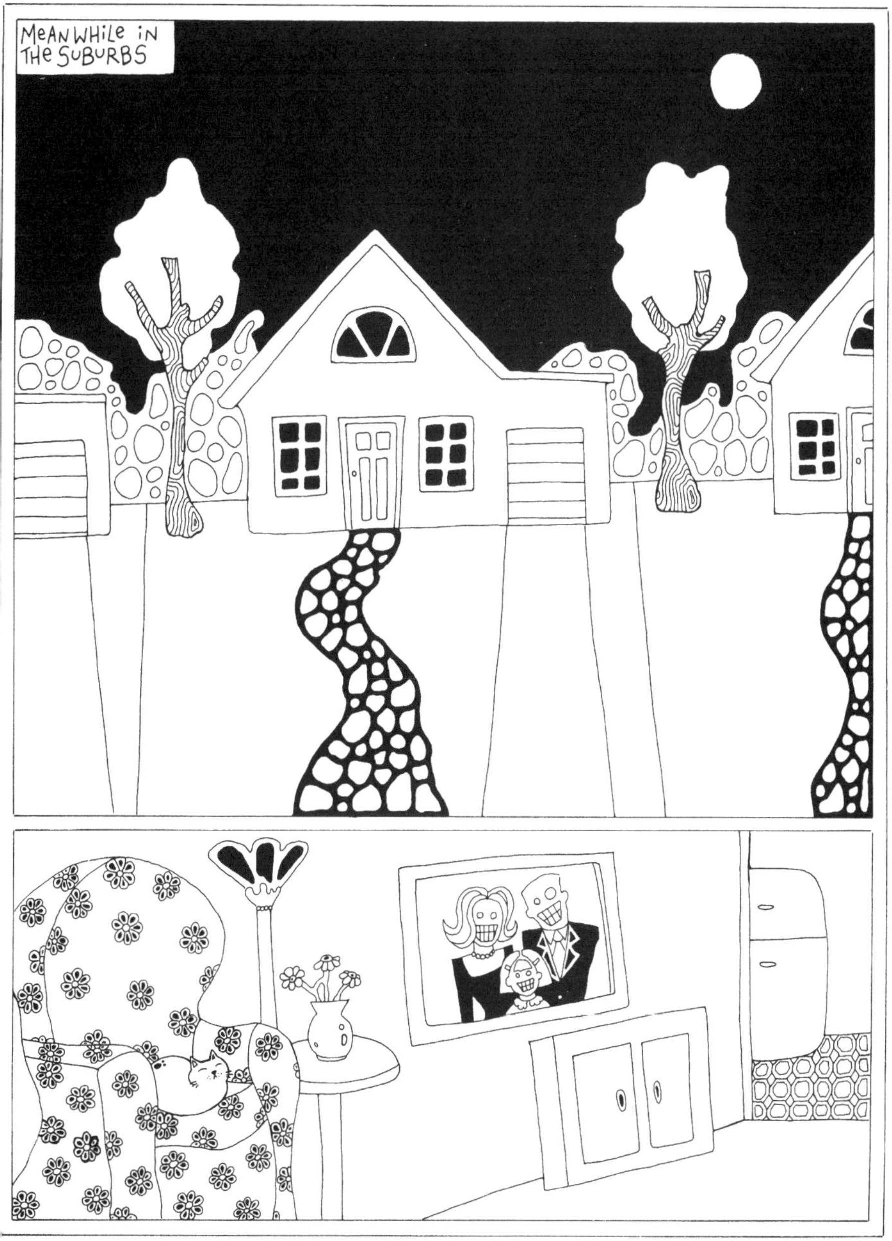
MEANWHILE IN THE SUBURBS

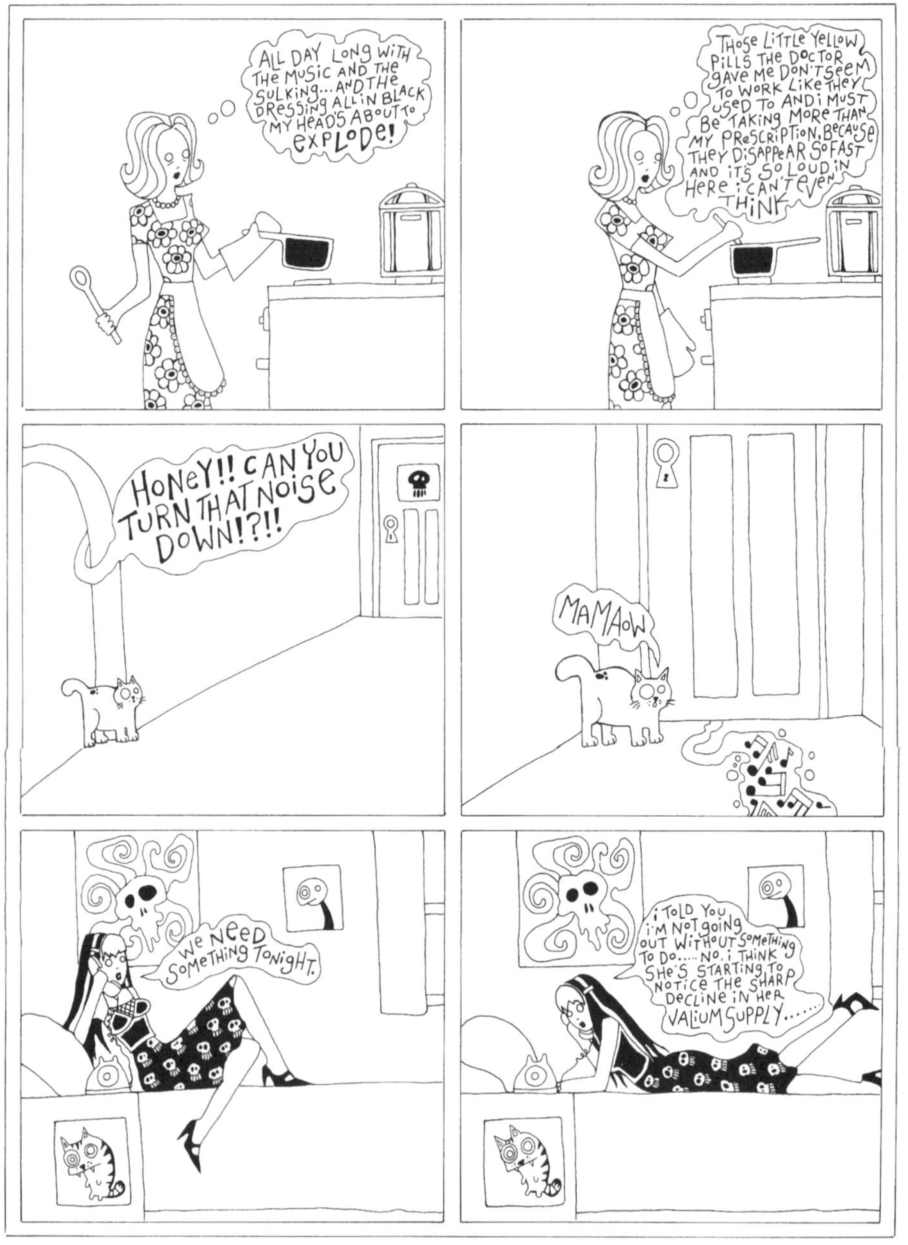
ALL DAY LONG WITH THE MUSIC AND THE SULKING... AND THE DRESSING ALL IN BLACK MY HEAD'S ABOUT TO EXPLODE!
THOSE LITTLE YELLOW PILLS THE DOCTOR GAVE ME DON'T SEEM TO WORK LIKE THEY USED TO AND I MUST BE TAKING MORE THAN MY PRESCRIPTION, BECAUSE THEY DISAPPEAR SO FAST AND IT'S SO LOUD IN HERE I CAN'T EVEN THINK
HONEY!! CAN YOU TURN THAT NOISE DOWN!?!!
MAMAOW
WE NEED SOMETHING TONIGHT.
I TOLD YOU I'M NOT GOING OUT WITHOUT SOMETHING TO DO..... NO. I THINK SHE'S STARTING TO NOTICE THE SHARP DECLINE IN HER VALIUM SUPPLY......

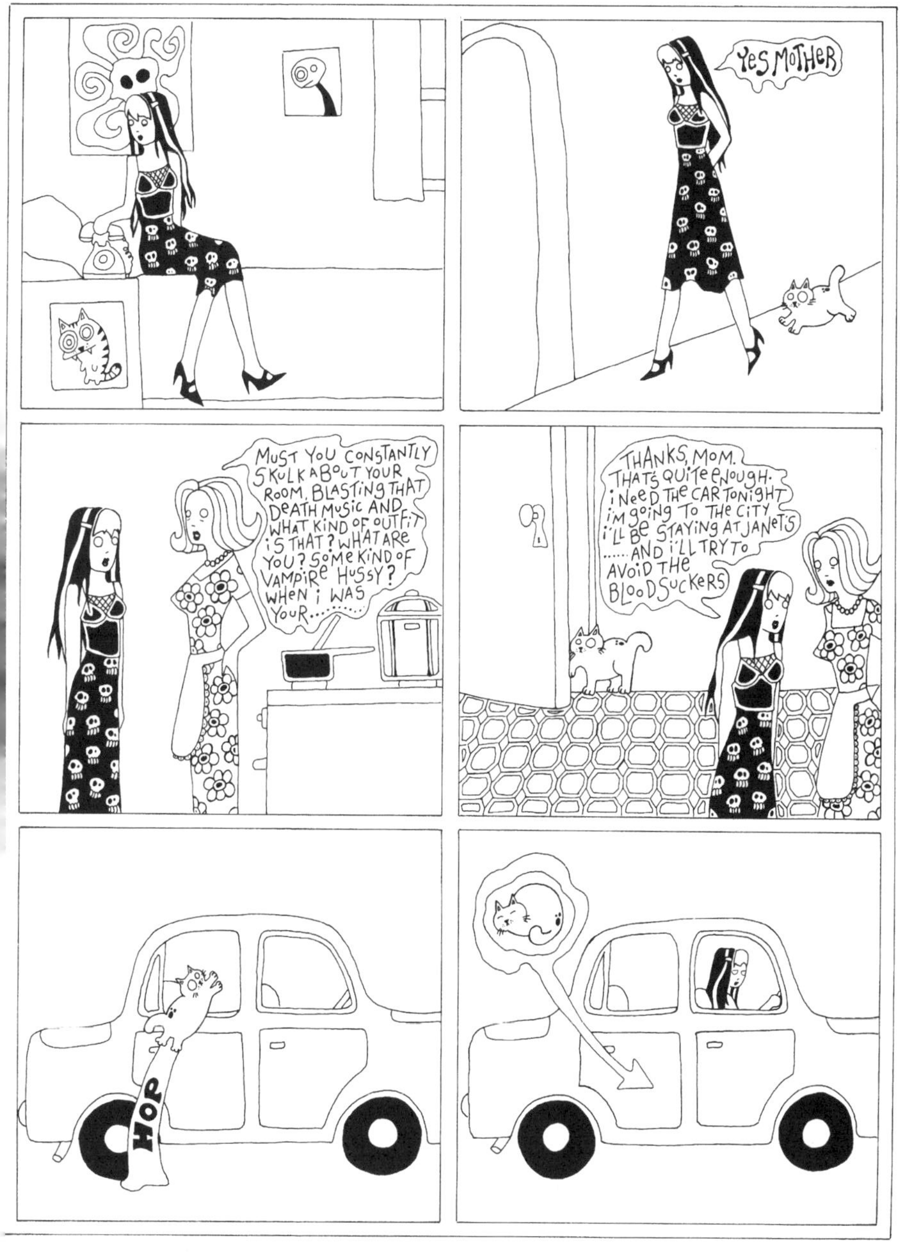
YES MOTHER
MUST YOU CONSTANTLY SKULK ABOUT YOUR ROOM, BLASTING THAT DEATH MUSIC AND WHAT KIND OF OUTFIT IS THAT? WHAT ARE YOU? SOME KIND OF VAMPIRE HUSSY? WHEN I WAS YOUR.........
THANKS, MOM. THAT'S QUITE ENOUGH. I NEED THE CAR TONIGHT I'M GOING TO THE CITY I'LL BE STAYING AT JANET'S ......AND I'LL TRY TO AVOID THE BLOODSUCKERS
HOP

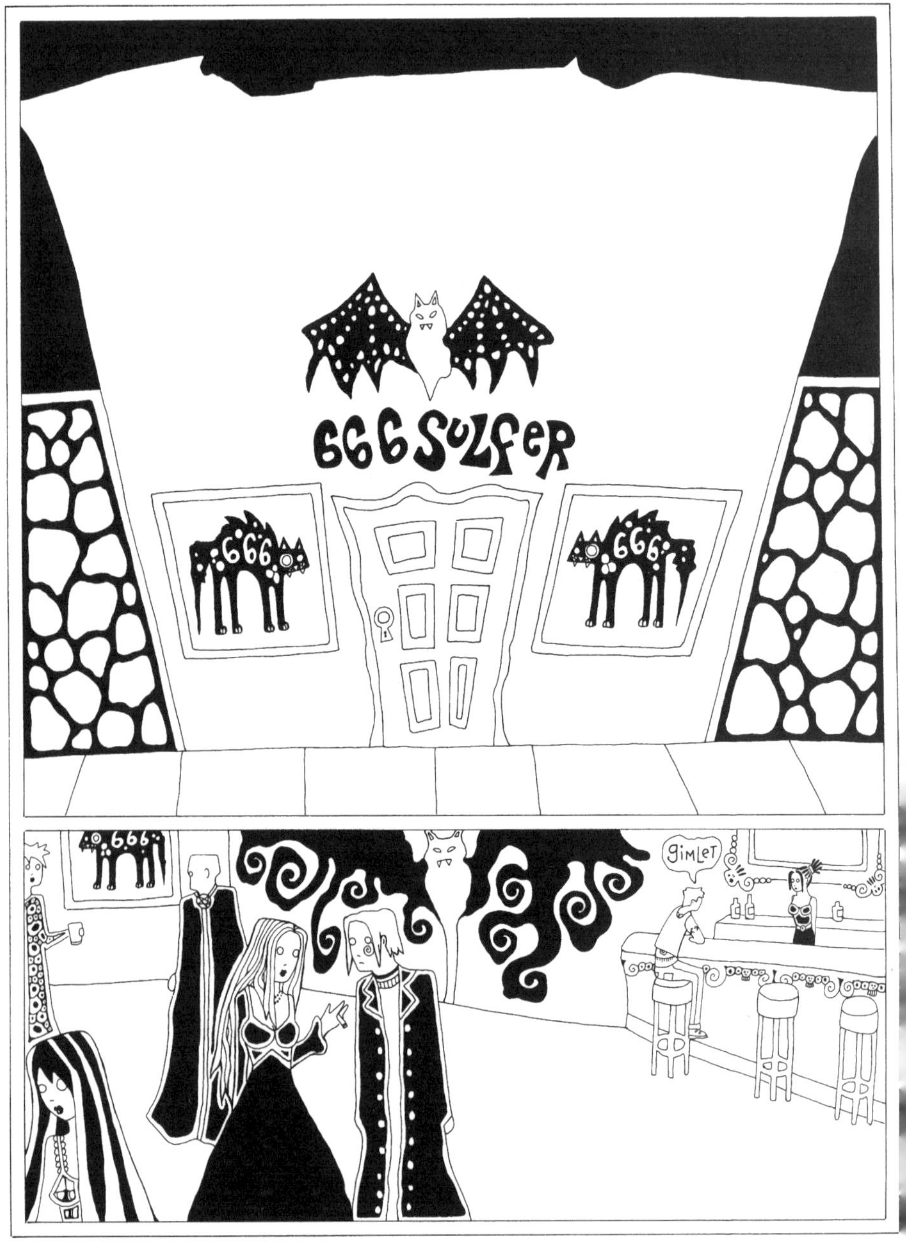
666 SULFER
666
666
666
gimlet

POINTLESS LIKE THERE'S SOME HUGE PRESSING WEIGHT CRUSHING THE LIFE OUT OF ME..... DESTROYING MY WILL TO LIVE. SAPPING MY......
SHUT UP
OF COURSE NOBODY UNDERSTANDS HOW HARD MY LIFE IS. THE TRIALS I GO THROUGH, THE DIFFICULTY INHERENT EVEN IN SO SMALL A TASK AS GETTING OUT OF..........
SHUT UP
..AND ELEANOR LEFT ME. I JUST FELT LIKE GIVING UP THE WALLS CLOSE IN ON ME AND I.....
SHUT UP
SIGH
IS THIS STOOL TAKEN?
SO TELL ME SOMETHING I'M PRETTY IGNORANT AND ALL, BUT IT SEEMS LIKE ALL YOU GOTH TYPES ARE DEPRESSED ALL THE TIME. IS THAT TRUE?
GIGGLE

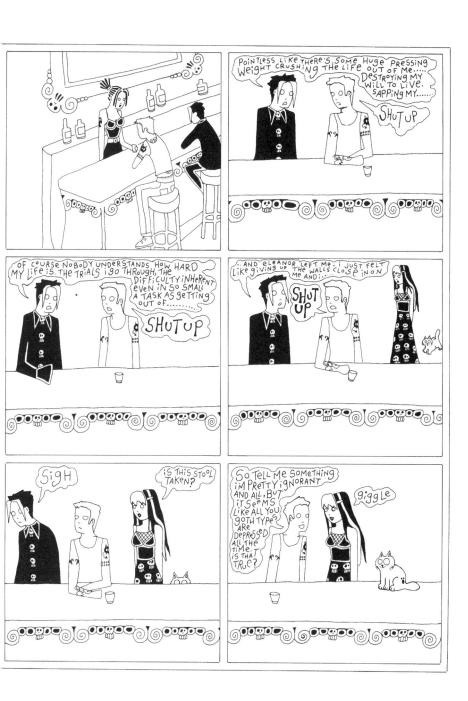

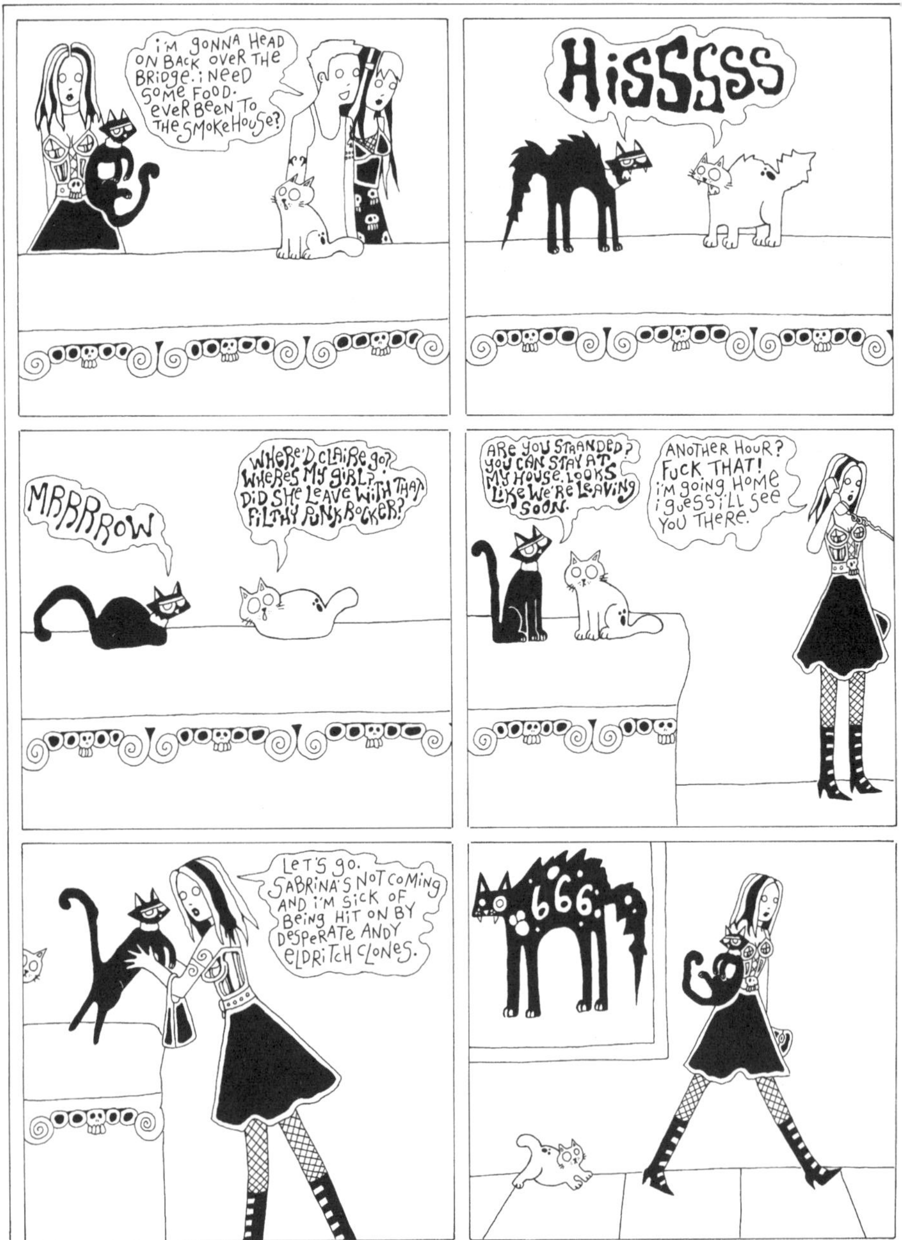
I'M GONNA HEAD ON BACK OVER THE BRIDGE. I NEED SOME FOOD. EVER BEEN TO THE SMOKEHOUSE?
HISSSSS
MRRRROW
WHERE'D CLAIRE GO? WHERE'S MY GIRL? DID SHE LEAVE WITH THAT FILTHY PUNK ROCKER?
ARE YOU STRANDED? YOU CAN STAY AT MY HOUSE. LOOKS LIKE WE'RE LEAVING SOON.
ANOTHER HOUR? FUCK THAT! I'M GOING HOME I GUESS I'LL SEE YOU THERE.
LET'S GO. SABRINA'S NOT COMING AND I'M SICK OF BEING HIT ON BY DESPERATE ANDY ELDRITCH CLONES.
666

WHO'S YOUR LITTLE FRIEND? WELL SCROWLIE. ANOTHER MOUTH TO FEED. LOOKS LIKE IT.
MAMAOW
NEARLY MIDNIGHT. AND STILL NO SABRINA. HOW MANY HOURS CAN YOU SIT IN FRONT OF A DINGY MONITOR BEFORE YOU GO CRAZY?
SCROWLIE
TIME FOR YOU TWO TO SCROWL OFF TO BED
SLEEP TIGHT AND DON'T LET THE HIDEOUS GHOULS BITE.
KNEAD KNEAD
WAKE UP KITTYS
IS THAT A GHOST? WOW! WE DON'T HAVE GHOSTS IN THE SUBURBS CAN WE PLAY WITH IT?
!!!

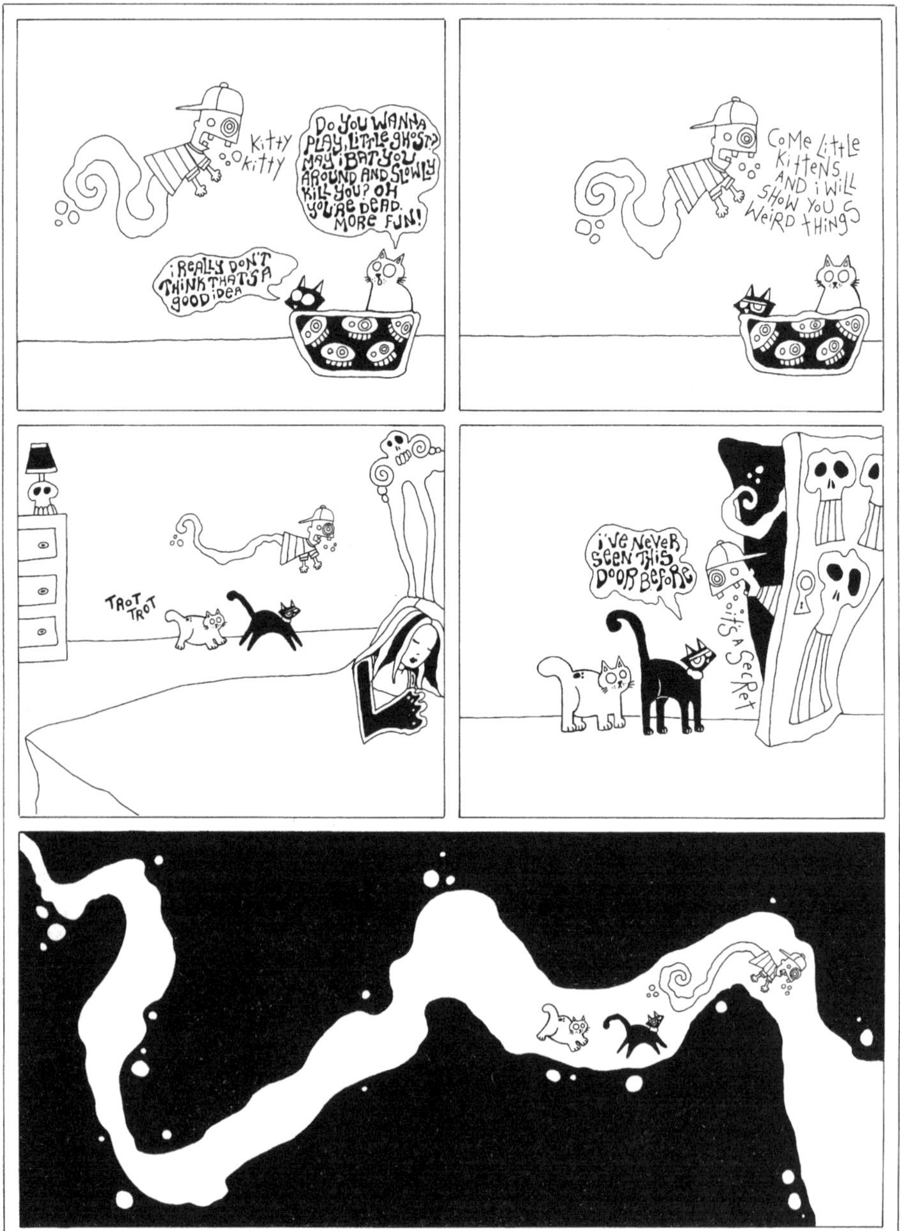
Kitty kitty
DO YOU WANNA PLAY, LITTLE GHOST? MAY I BAT YOU AROUND AND SLOWLY KILL YOU? OH YOU'RE DEAD. MORE FUN!
i REALLY DON'T THINK THAT'S A GOOD iDEA
Come Little Kittens and i will show you weird things
TROT TROT
i've never seen this door before
it's a secret

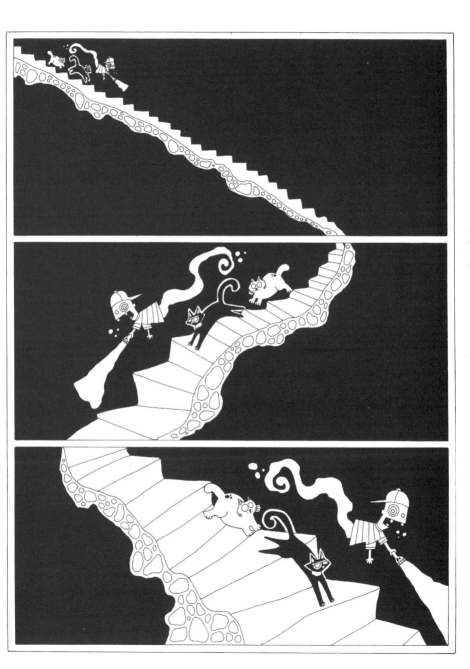

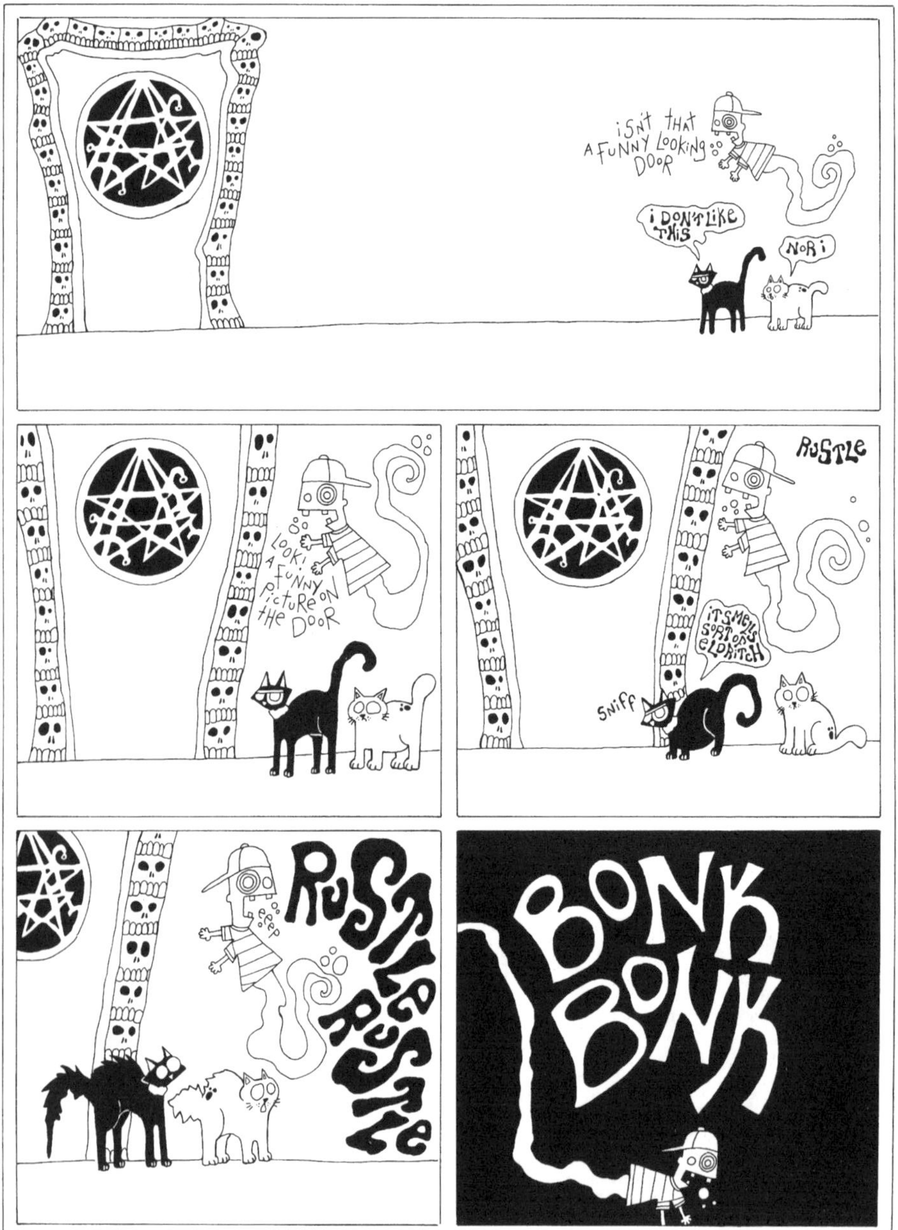
ISN'T THAT A FUNNY LOOKING DOOR
I DON'T LIKE THIS
NOR I
LOOK! A FUNNY PICTURE ON THE DOOR
RUSTLE
IT SMELLS SORT OF ELDRITCH
SNIFF
RUSTLE RUSTLE RUSTLE
EEEP
BONK BONK

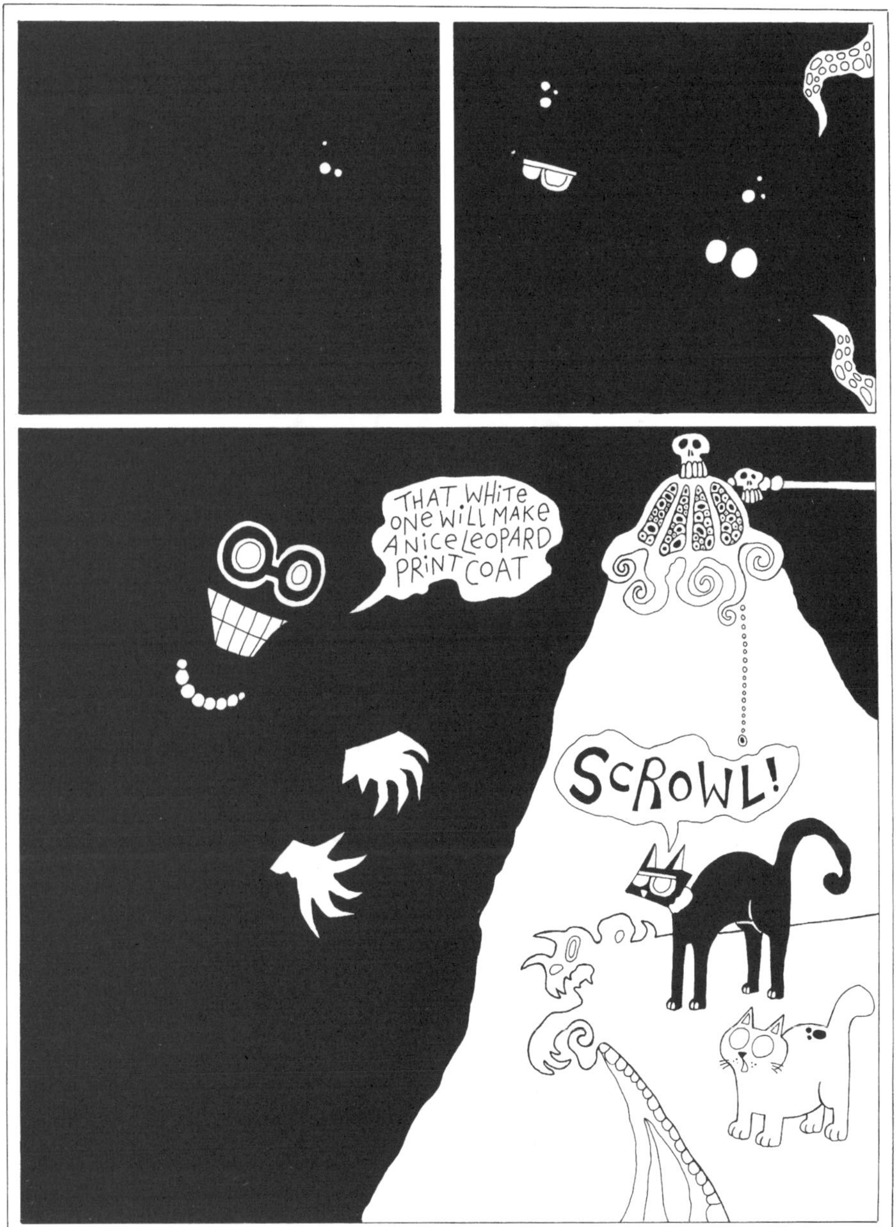
THAT WHITE ONE WILL MAKE A NICE LEOPARD PRINT COAT
SCROWL!

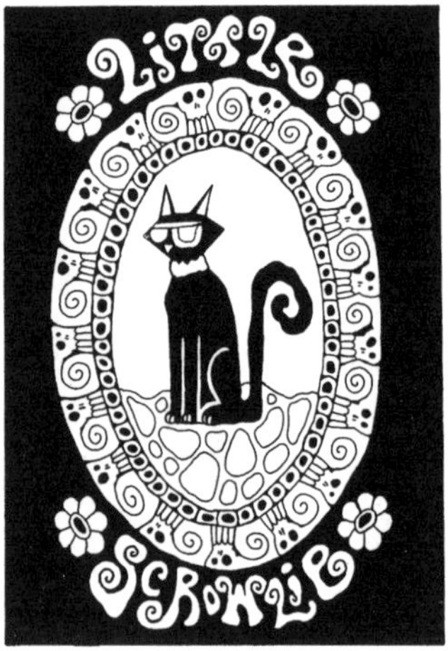
Little
Scrowlie

2

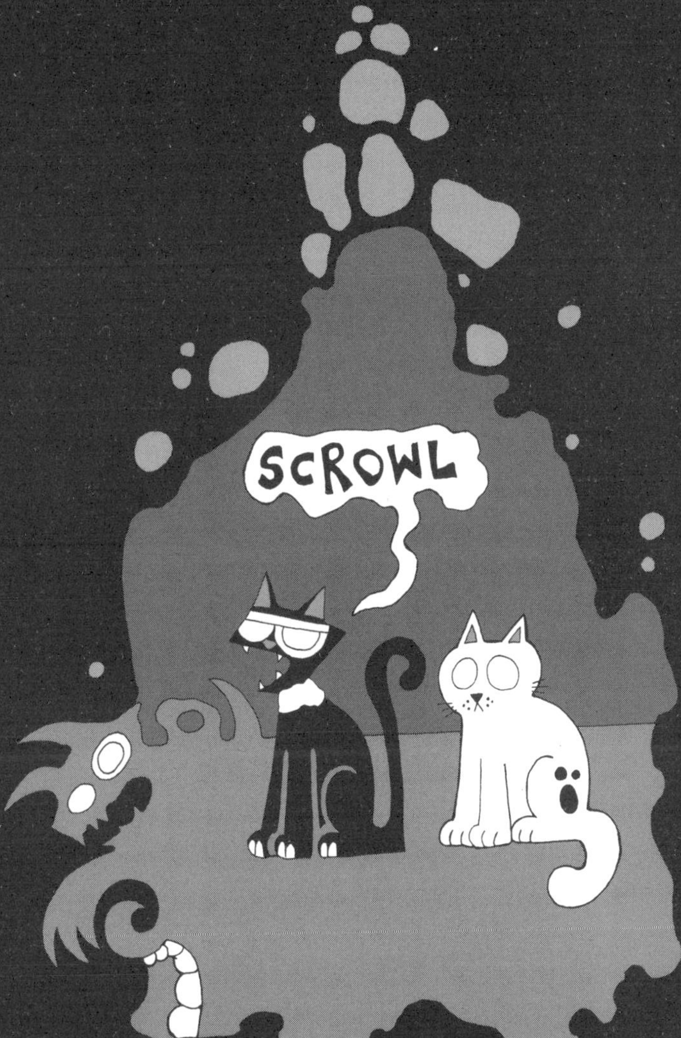
SCROWL

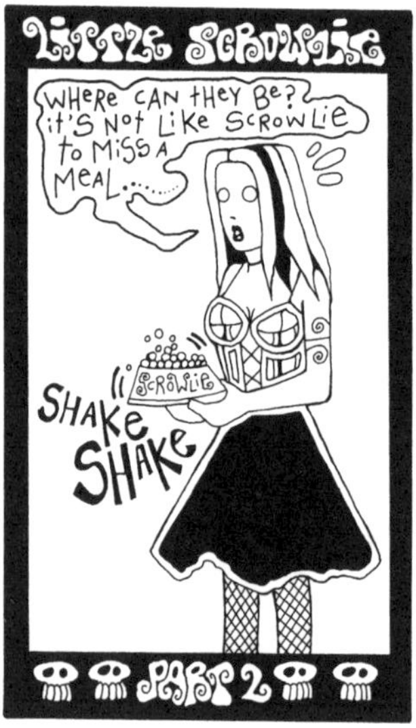
LITTLE SCROWLIE
WHERE CAN THEY BE? IT'S NOT LIKE SCROWLIE TO MISS A MEAL.......
SCROWLIE
SHAKE SHAKE
PART 2

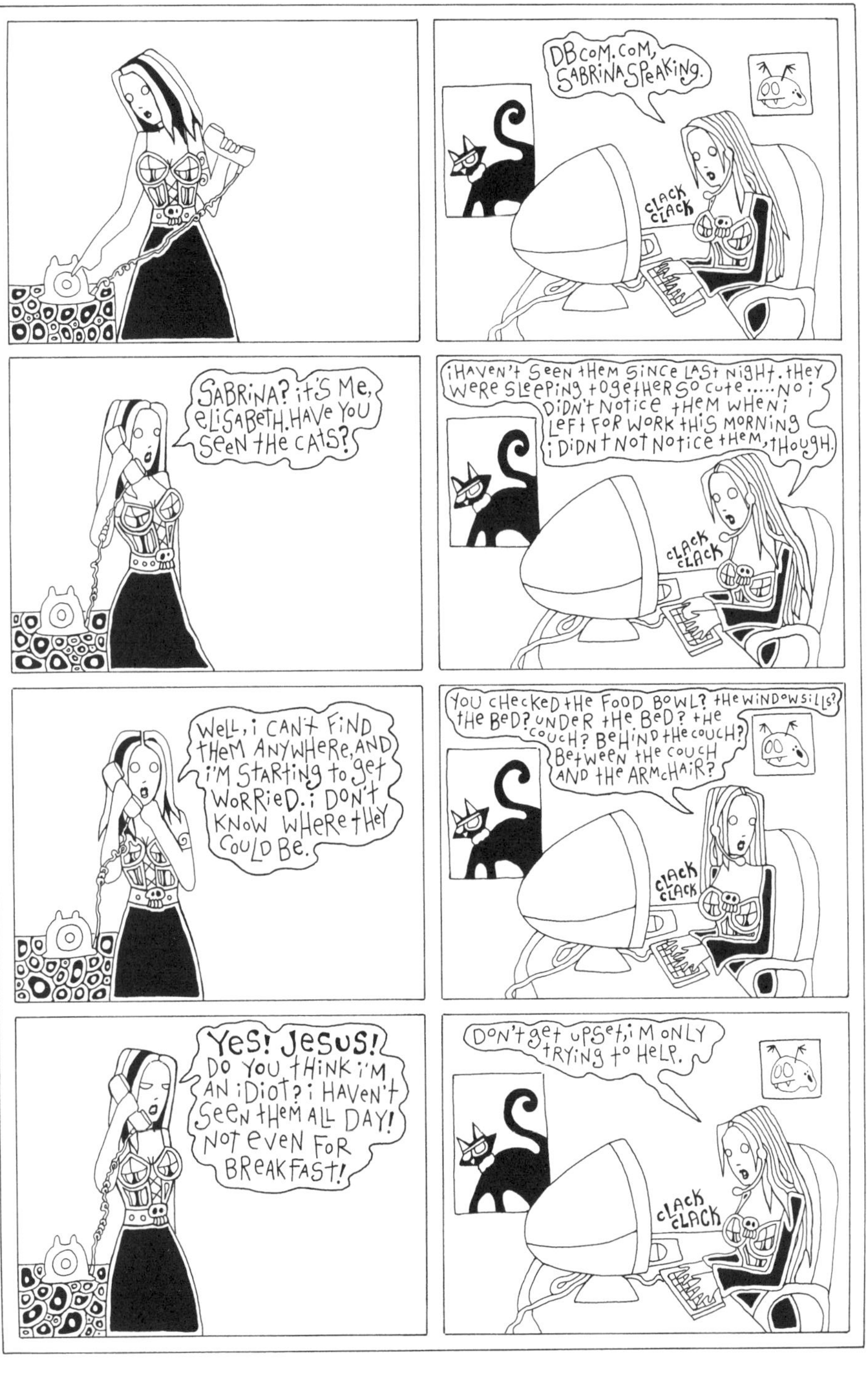
DBCOM.COM, SABRINA SPEAKING.
CLACK CLACK
SABRINA? IT'S ME, ELISABETH. HAVE YOU SEEN THE CATS?
I HAVEN'T SEEN THEM SINCE LAST NIGHT. THEY WERE SLEEPING TOGETHER SO CUTE..... NO I DIDN'T NOTICE THEM WHEN I LEFT FOR WORK THIS MORNING. I DIDN'T NOT NOTICE THEM, THOUGH.
CLACK CLACK
WELL, I CAN'T FIND THEM ANYWHERE, AND I'M STARTING TO GET WORRIED. I DON'T KNOW WHERE THEY COULD BE.
YOU CHECKED THE FOOD BOWL? THE WINDOWSILLS? THE BED? UNDER THE BED? THE COUCH? BEHIND THE COUCH? BETWEEN THE COUCH AND THE ARMCHAIR?
CLACK CLACK
YES! JESUS! DO YOU THINK I'M AN IDIOT? I HAVEN'T SEEN THEM ALL DAY! NOT EVEN FOR BREAKFAST!
DON'T GET UPSET, I'M ONLY TRYING TO HELP.
CLACK CLACK

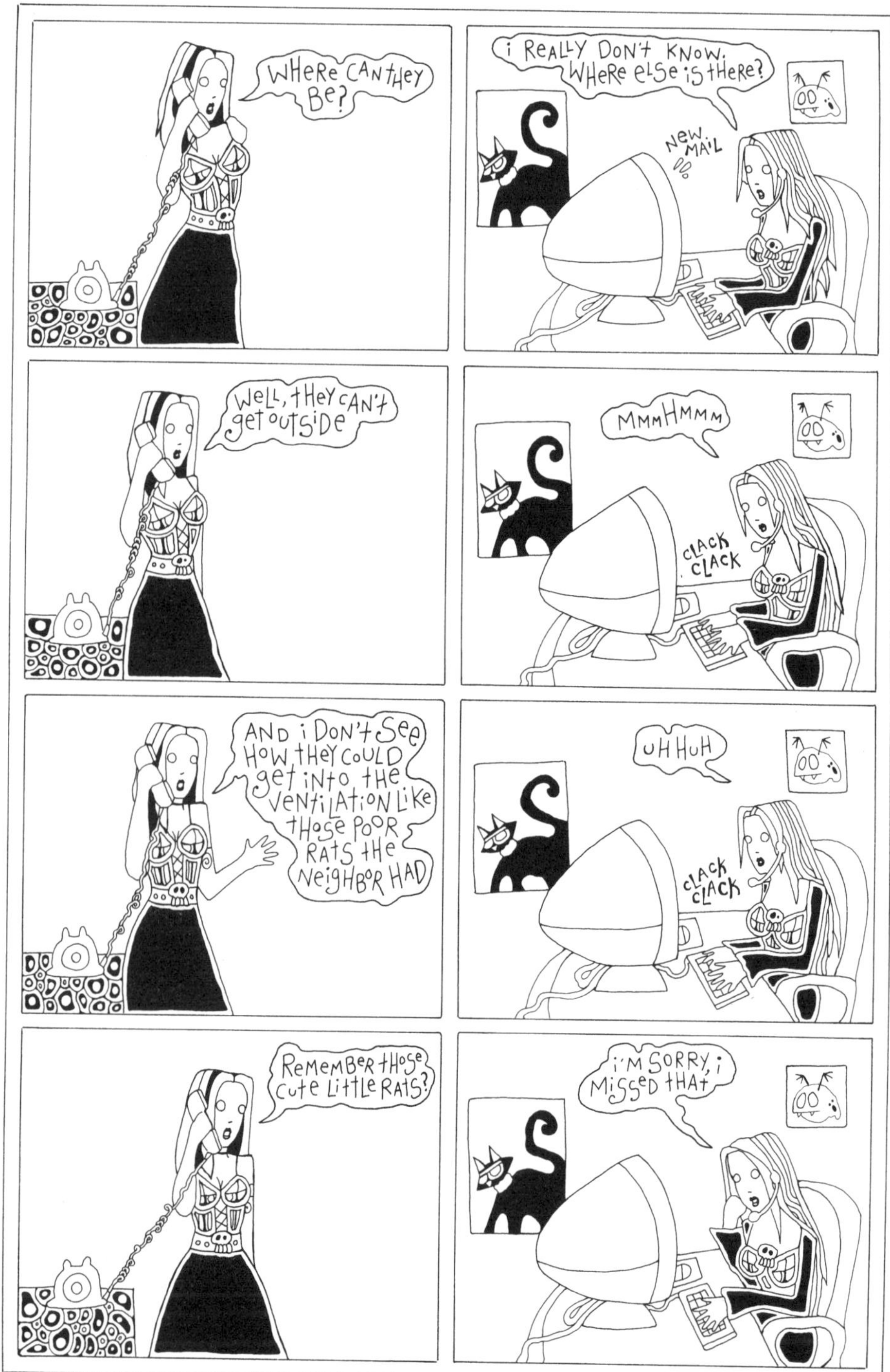
WHERE CAN THEY BE?
i REALLY DON'T KNOW. WHERE ELSE iS THERE?
NEW MAIL
WELL, THEY CAN'T GET OUTSIDE
MMMHMMM
CLACK CLACK
AND i DON'T SEE HOW THEY COULD GET INTO THE VENTILATION LIKE THOSE POOR RATS THE NEIGHBOR HAD
UH HUH
CLACK CLACK
REMEMBER THOSE CUTE LITTLE RATS?
i'M SORRY, i MISSED THAT

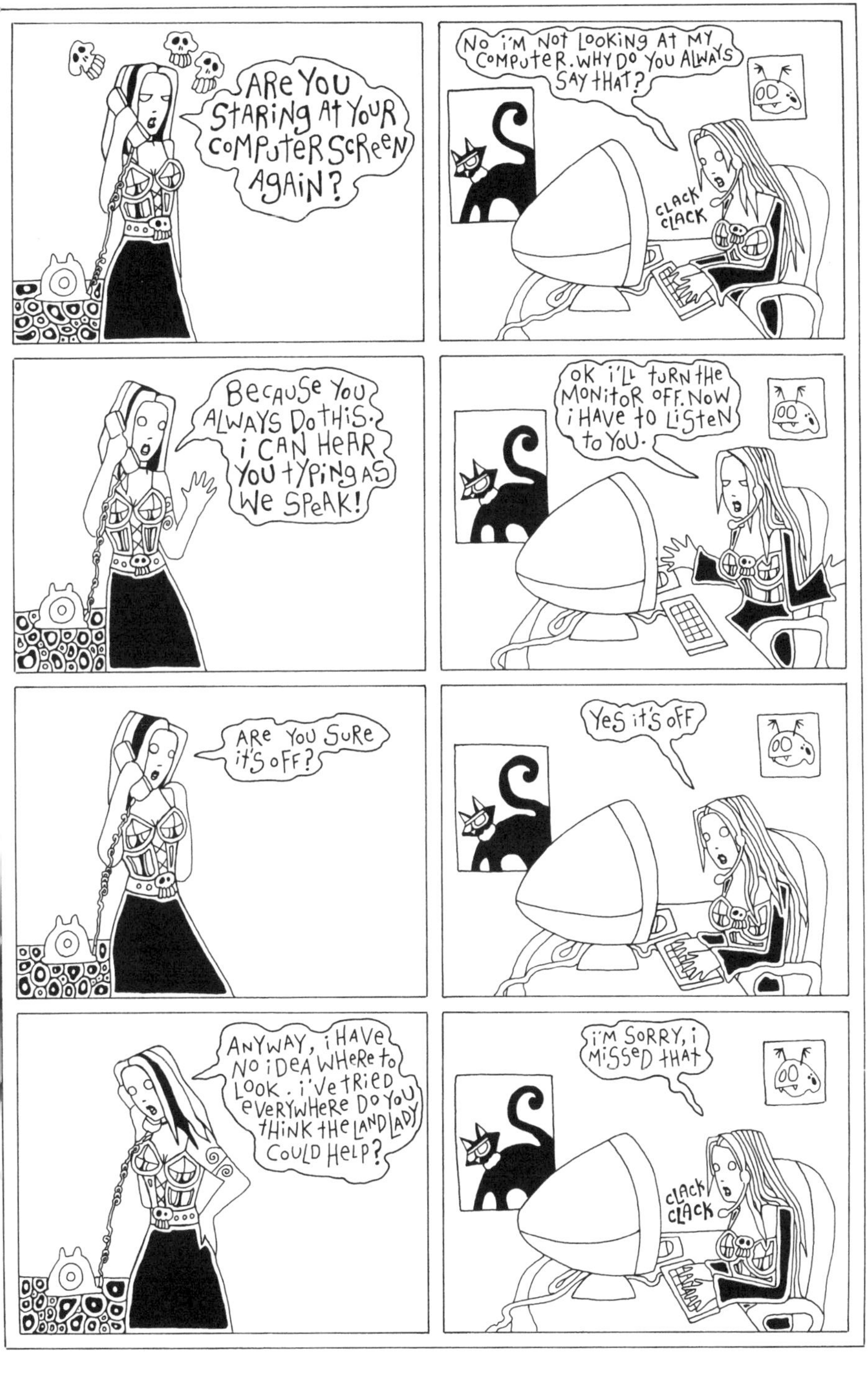
ARE YOU STARING AT YOUR COMPUTER SCREEN AGAIN?
NO I'M NOT LOOKING AT MY COMPUTER. WHY DO YOU ALWAYS SAY THAT?
CLACK CLACK
BECAUSE YOU ALWAYS DO THIS. I CAN HEAR YOU TYPING AS WE SPEAK!
OK I'LL TURN THE MONITOR OFF. NOW I HAVE TO LISTEN TO YOU.
ARE YOU SURE IT'S OFF?
YES IT'S OFF
ANYWAY, I HAVE NO IDEA WHERE TO LOOK. I'VE TRIED EVERYWHERE DO YOU THINK THE LANDLADY COULD HELP?
I'M SORRY, I MISSED THAT
CLACK CLACK

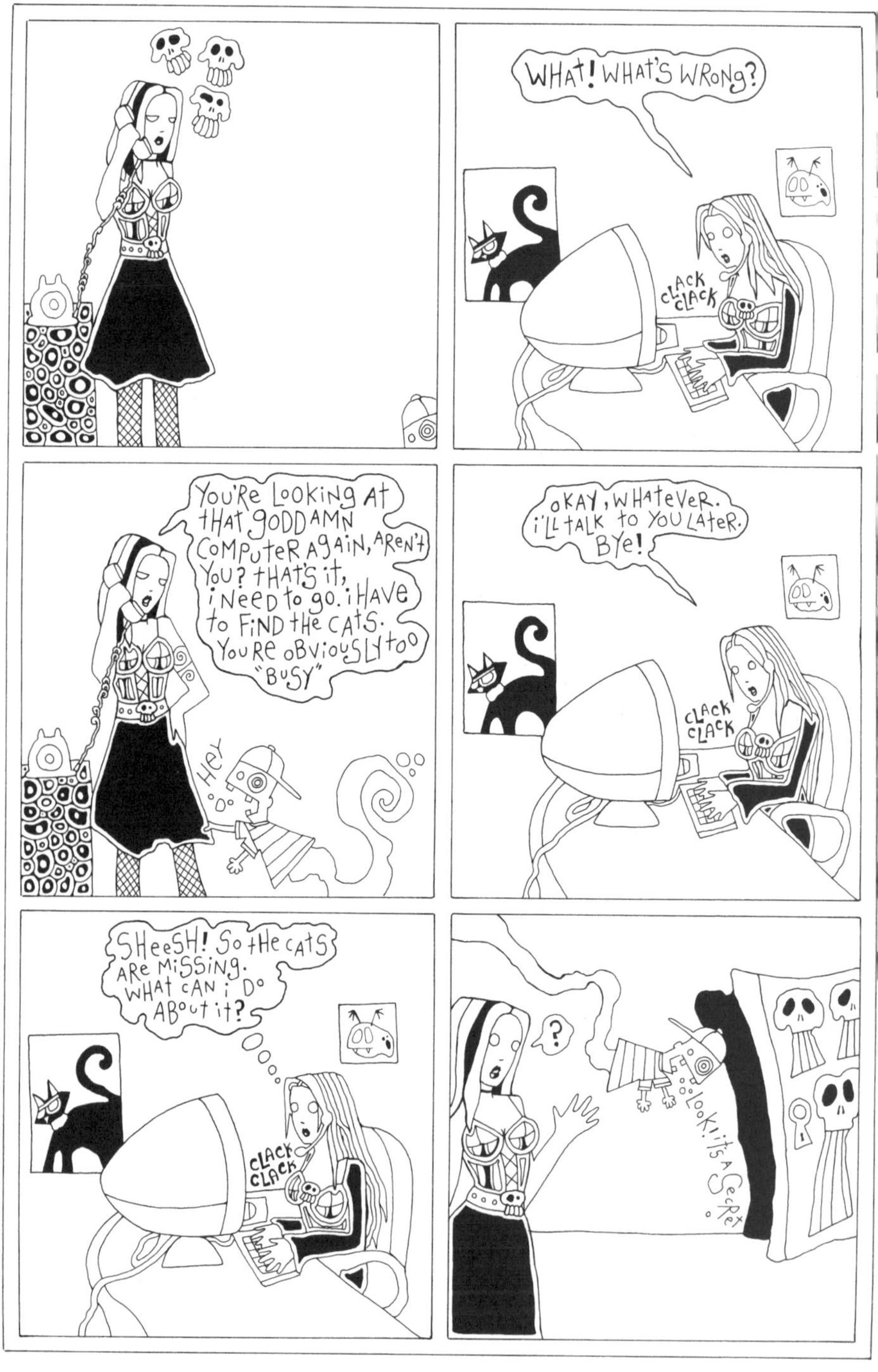

WHAT! WHAT'S WRONG?
CLACK CLACK
YOU'RE LOOKING AT THAT GODDAMN COMPUTER AGAIN, AREN'T YOU? THAT'S IT, I NEED TO GO. I HAVE TO FIND THE CATS. YOU'RE OBVIOUSLY TOO "BUSY"
HEY
OKAY, WHATEVER. I'LL TALK TO YOU LATER. BYE!
CLACK CLACK
SHEESH! SO THE CATS ARE MISSING. WHAT CAN I DO ABOUT IT?
CLACK CLACK
?
LOOK! IT'S A SECRET

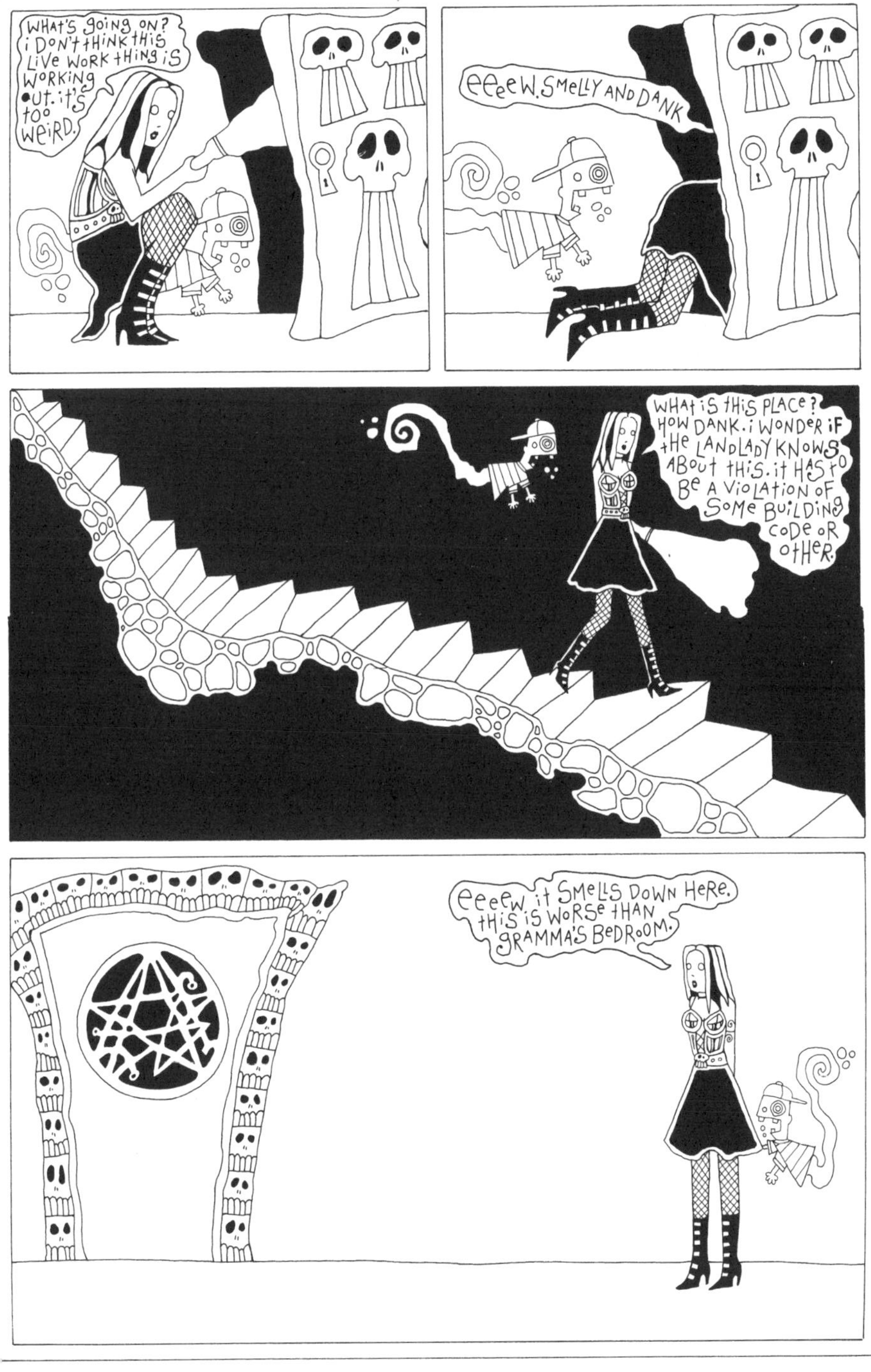
WHAT'S going ON? i DON'T tHiNK tHiS LiVe WORK tHiNg iS WORKiNg Out. it'S tOO WeiRD.
eeeeW. SMeLLY AND DANK
WHAt iS tHiS PLACe? HOW DANK. i WONDeR iF tHe LANDLADY KNOWS ABOut tHiS. it HAS tO Be A ViOLAtiON OF SOMe BuiLDiNg CODe OR OtHeR.
eeeeW it SMeLLS DOWN HeRe. tHiS iS WORSe tHAN gRAMMA'S BeDROOM.

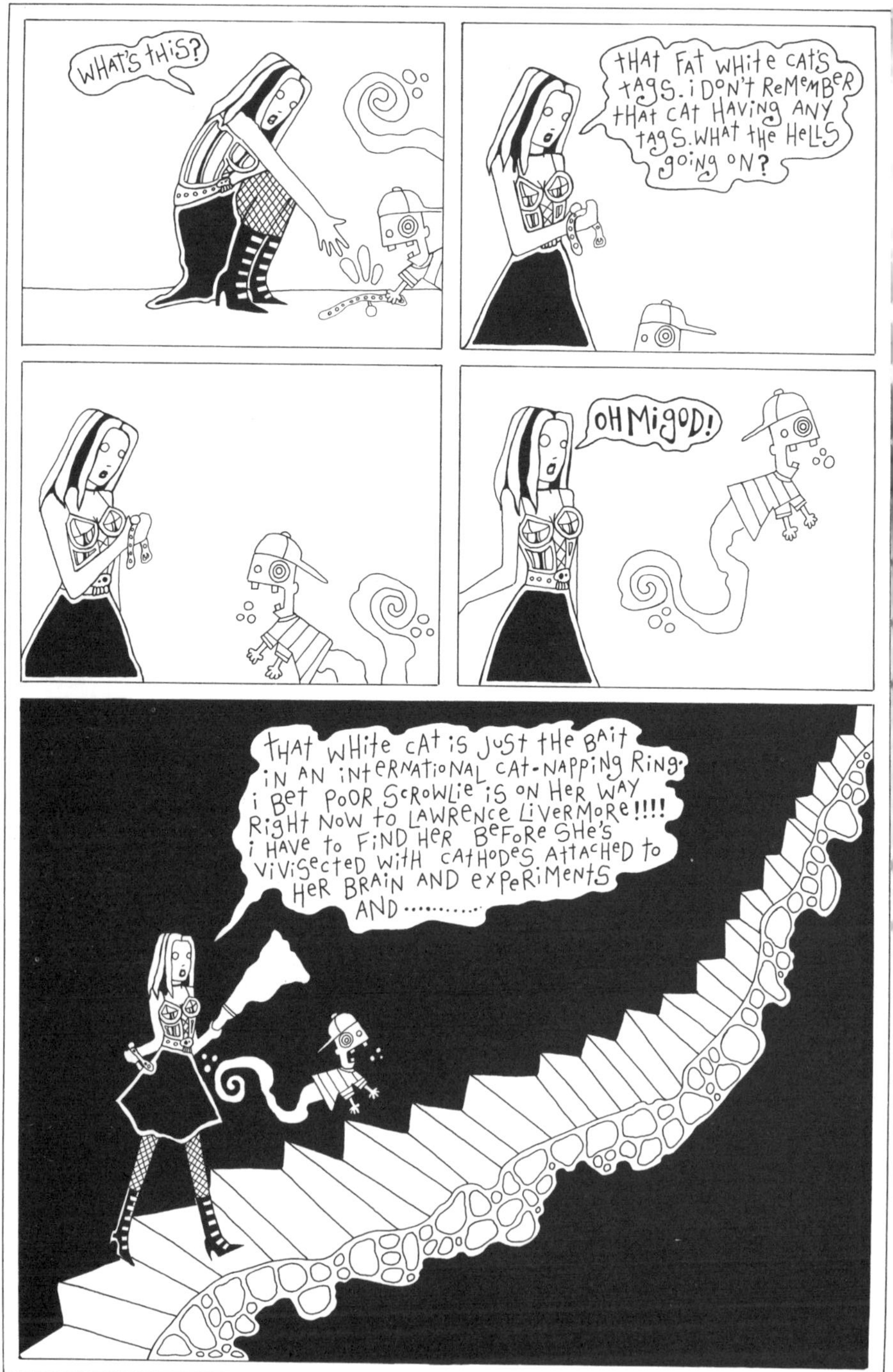
WHAT'S THIS?
THAT FAT WHITE CAT'S TAGS. I DON'T REMEMBER THAT CAT HAVING ANY TAGS. WHAT THE HELLS GOING ON?
OH MIGOD!
THAT WHITE CAT IS JUST THE BAIT IN AN INTERNATIONAL CAT-NAPPING RING. I BET POOR SCROWLIE IS ON HER WAY RIGHT NOW TO LAWRENCE LIVERMORE!!!! I HAVE TO FIND HER BEFORE SHE'S VIVISECTED WITH CATHODES ATTACHED TO HER BRAIN AND EXPERIMENTS AND..........

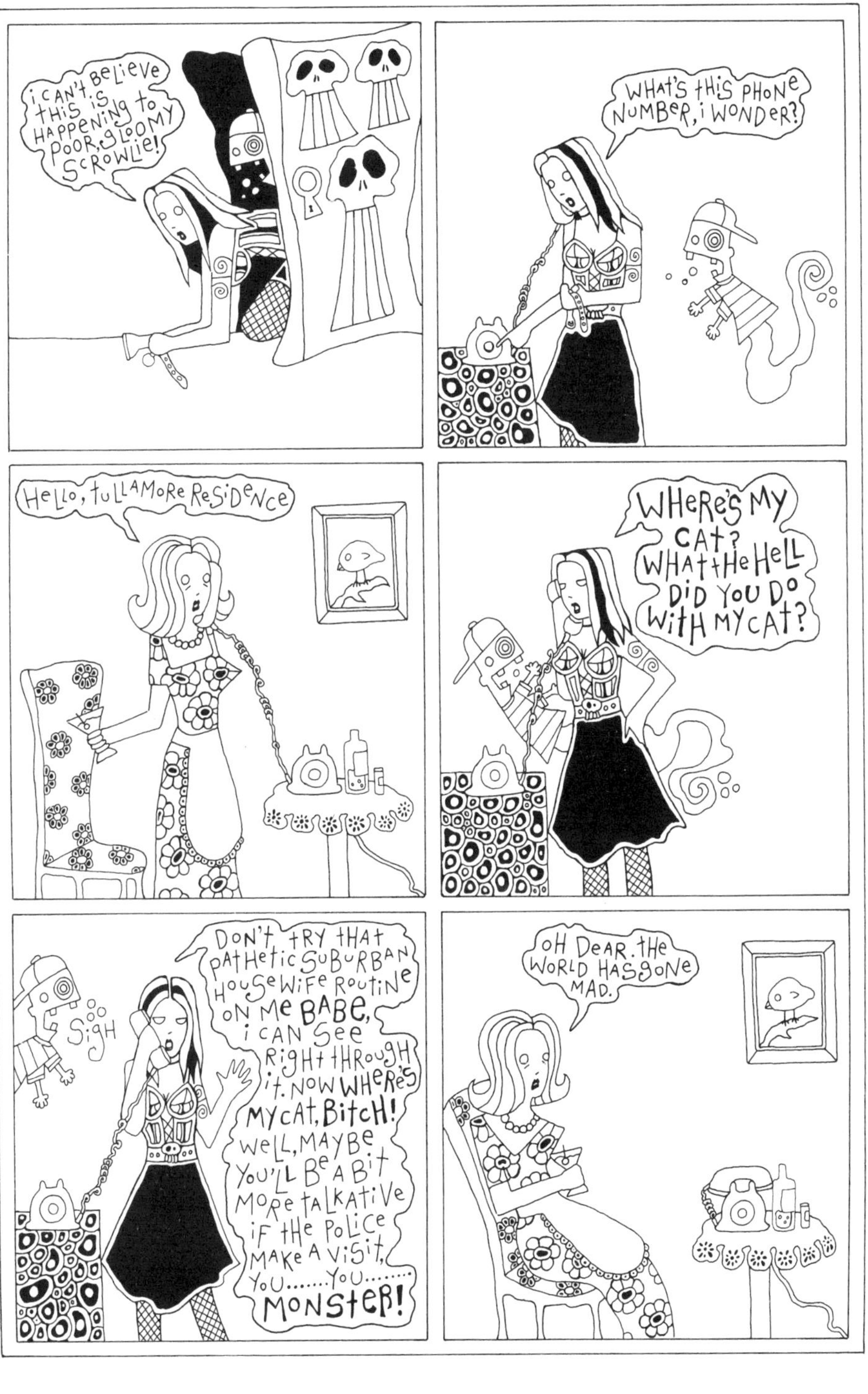
I CAN'T BELIEVE THIS IS HAPPENING TO POOR, GLOOMY SCROWLIE!
WHAT'S THIS PHONE NUMBER, I WONDER?
HELLO, TULLAMORE RESIDENCE
WHERE'S MY CAT? WHAT THE HELL DID YOU DO WITH MY CAT?
SIGH
DON'T TRY THAT PATHETIC SUBURBAN HOUSEWIFE ROUTINE ON ME BABE, I CAN SEE RIGHT THROUGH IT. NOW WHERE'S MY CAT, BITCH! WELL, MAYBE YOU'LL BE A BIT MORE TALKATIVE IF THE POLICE MAKE A VISIT, YOU......YOU........ MONSTER!
OH DEAR. THE WORLD HAS GONE MAD.

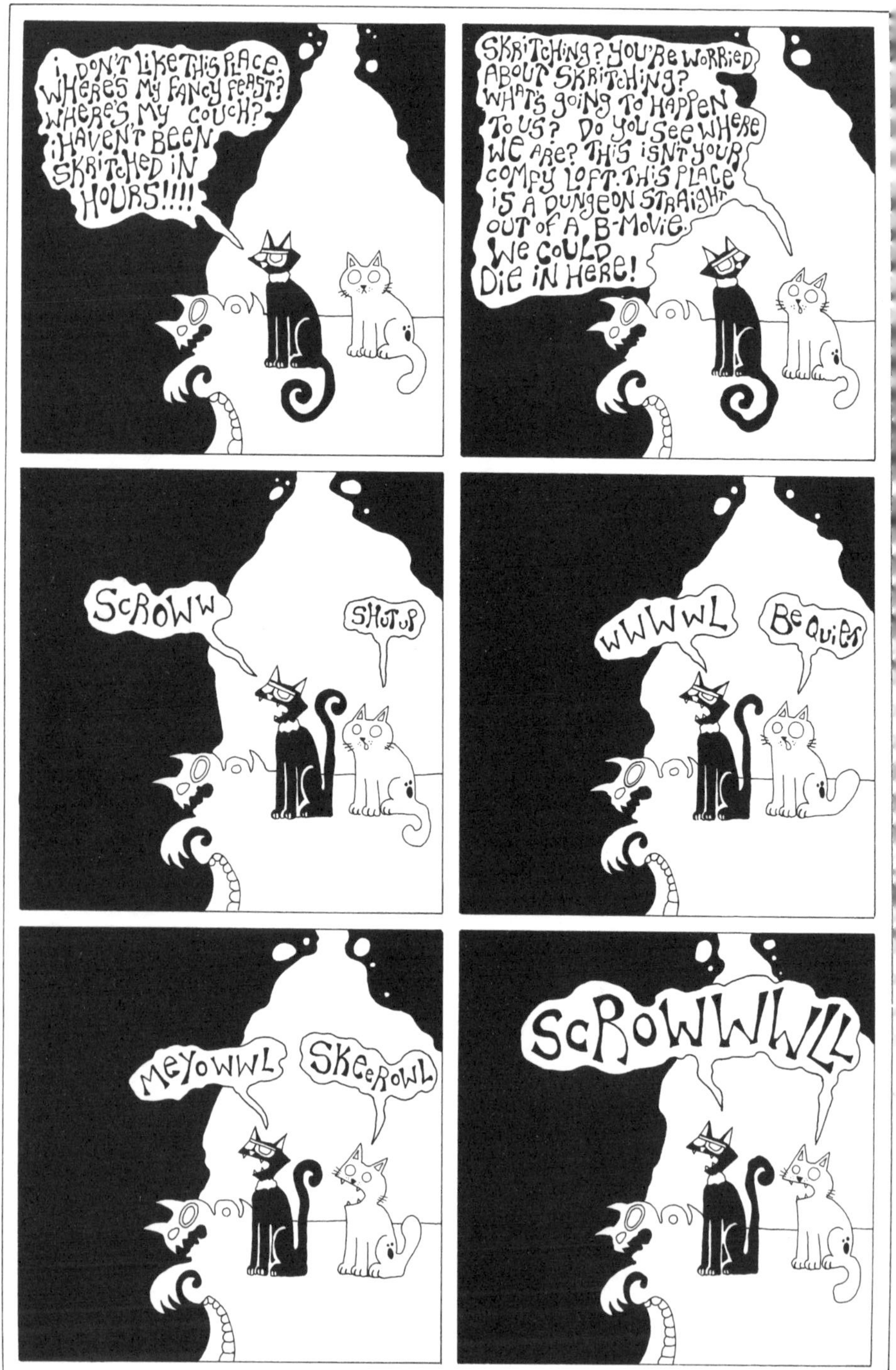
I DON'T LIKE THIS PLACE. WHERE'S MY FANCY FEAST? WHERE'S MY COUCH? I HAVEN'T BEEN SKRITCHED IN HOURS!!!!
SKRITCHING? YOU'RE WORRIED ABOUT SKRITCHING? WHAT'S GOING TO HAPPEN TO US? DO YOU SEE WHERE WE ARE? THIS ISN'T YOUR COMFY LOFT. THIS PLACE IS A DUNGEON STRAIGHT OUT OF A B-MOVIE. WE COULD DIE IN HERE!
SCROWW
SHUT UP
WWWWL
BE QUIET
MEYOWWL
SKEEROWL
SCROWWLL

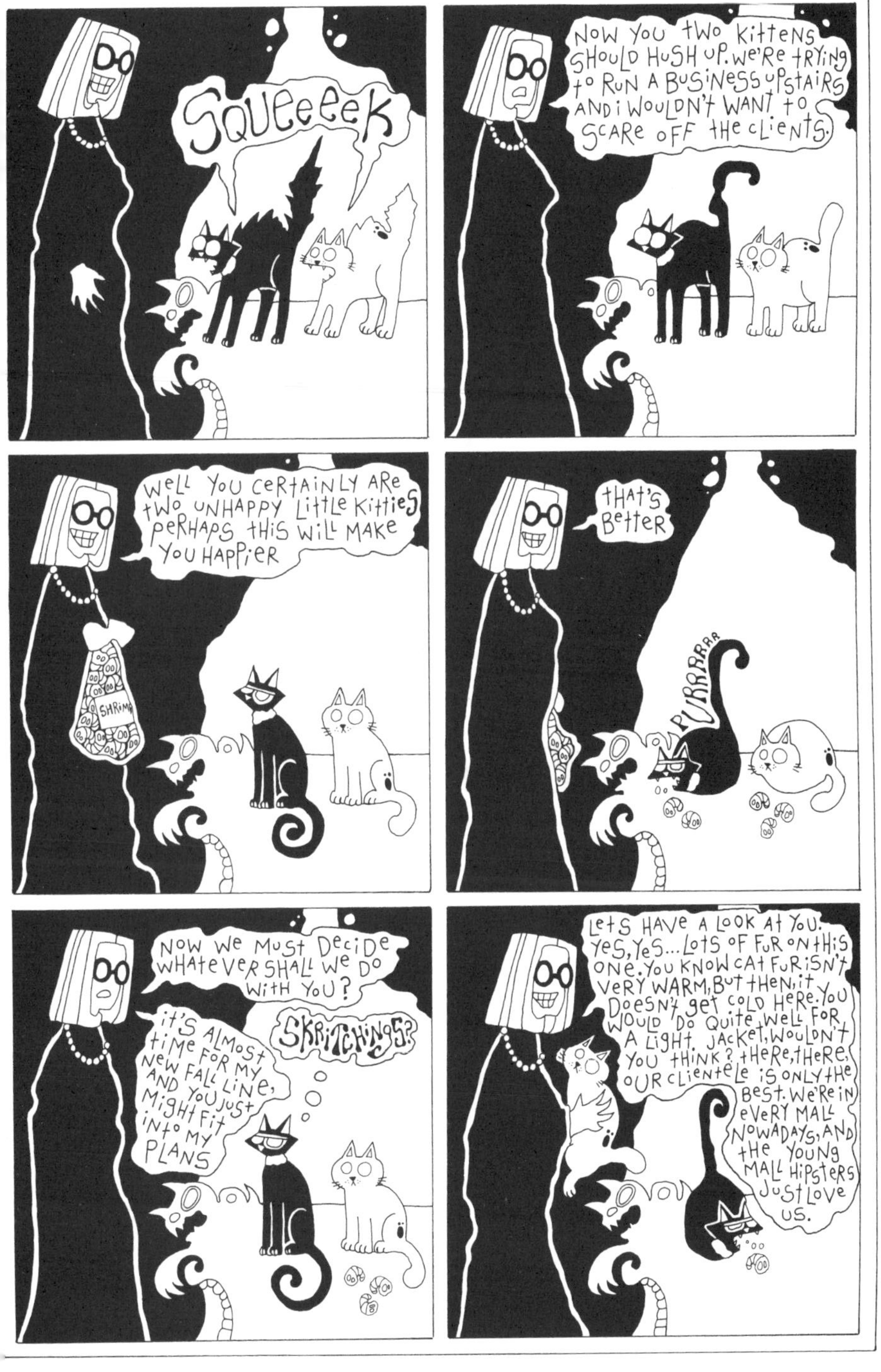
SQUEEEEK
NOW YOU TWO KITTENS SHOULD HUSH UP. WE'RE TRYING TO RUN A BUSINESS UPSTAIRS AND I WOULDN'T WANT TO SCARE OFF THE CLIENTS.
WELL YOU CERTAINLY ARE TWO UNHAPPY LITTLE KITTIES PERHAPS THIS WILL MAKE YOU HAPPIER
SHRIMP
THAT'S BETTER
PURRRRRR
NOW WE MUST DECIDE WHATEVER SHALL WE DO WITH YOU?
IT'S ALMOST TIME FOR MY NEW FALL LINE, AND YOU JUST MIGHT FIT INTO MY PLANS
SKRITCHINGS?
LETS HAVE A LOOK AT YOU. YES, YES... LOTS OF FUR ON THIS ONE. YOU KNOW CAT FUR ISN'T VERY WARM, BUT THEN, IT DOESN'T GET COLD HERE. YOU WOULD DO QUITE WELL FOR A LIGHT JACKET, WOULDN'T YOU THINK? THERE, THERE, OUR CLIENTELE IS ONLY THE BEST. WE'RE IN EVERY MALL NOWADAYS, AND THE YOUNG MALL HIPSTERS JUST LOVE US.

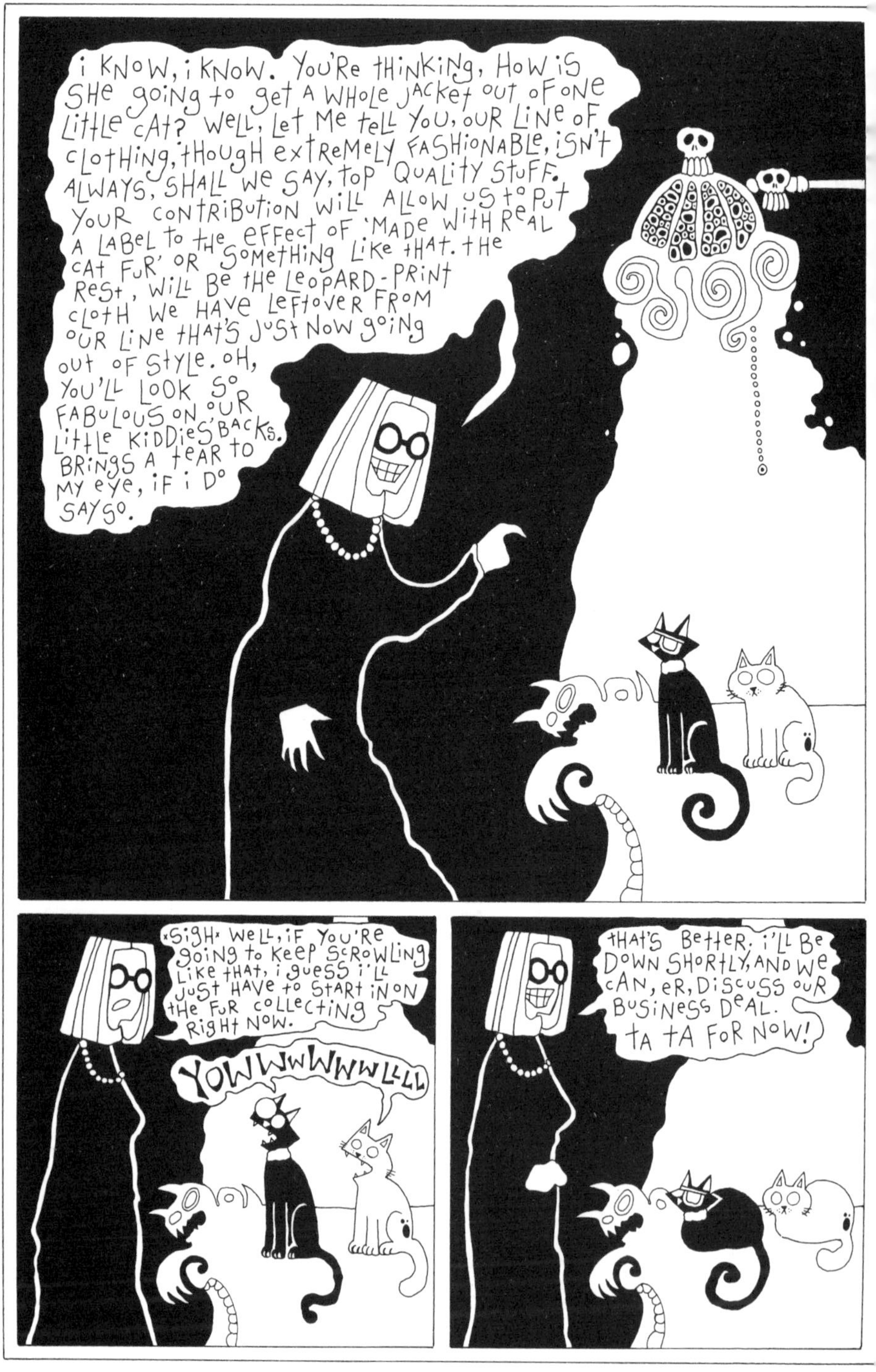
i KNOW, i KNOW. YOU'RE THINKING, HOW IS SHE GOING TO GET A WHOLE JACKET OUT OF ONE LITTLE CAT? WELL, LET ME TELL YOU, OUR LINE OF CLOTHING, THOUGH EXTREMELY FASHIONABLE, ISN'T ALWAYS, SHALL WE SAY, TOP QUALITY STUFF. YOUR CONTRIBUTION WILL ALLOW US TO PUT A LABEL TO THE EFFECT OF 'MADE WITH REAL CAT FUR' OR SOMETHING LIKE THAT. THE REST, WILL BE THE LEOPARD-PRINT CLOTH WE HAVE LEFTOVER FROM OUR LINE THAT'S JUST NOW GOING OUT OF STYLE. OH, YOU'LL LOOK SO FABULOUS ON OUR LITTLE KIDDIES' BACKS. BRINGS A TEAR TO MY EYE, IF I DO SAY SO.
SIGH WELL, IF YOU'RE GOING TO KEEP SCROWLING LIKE THAT, I GUESS I'LL JUST HAVE TO START IN ON THE FUR COLLECTING RIGHT NOW.
YOWWWWWWWLLLL
THAT'S BETTER. I'LL BE DOWN SHORTLY, AND WE CAN, ER, DISCUSS OUR BUSINESS DEAL. TA TA FOR NOW!

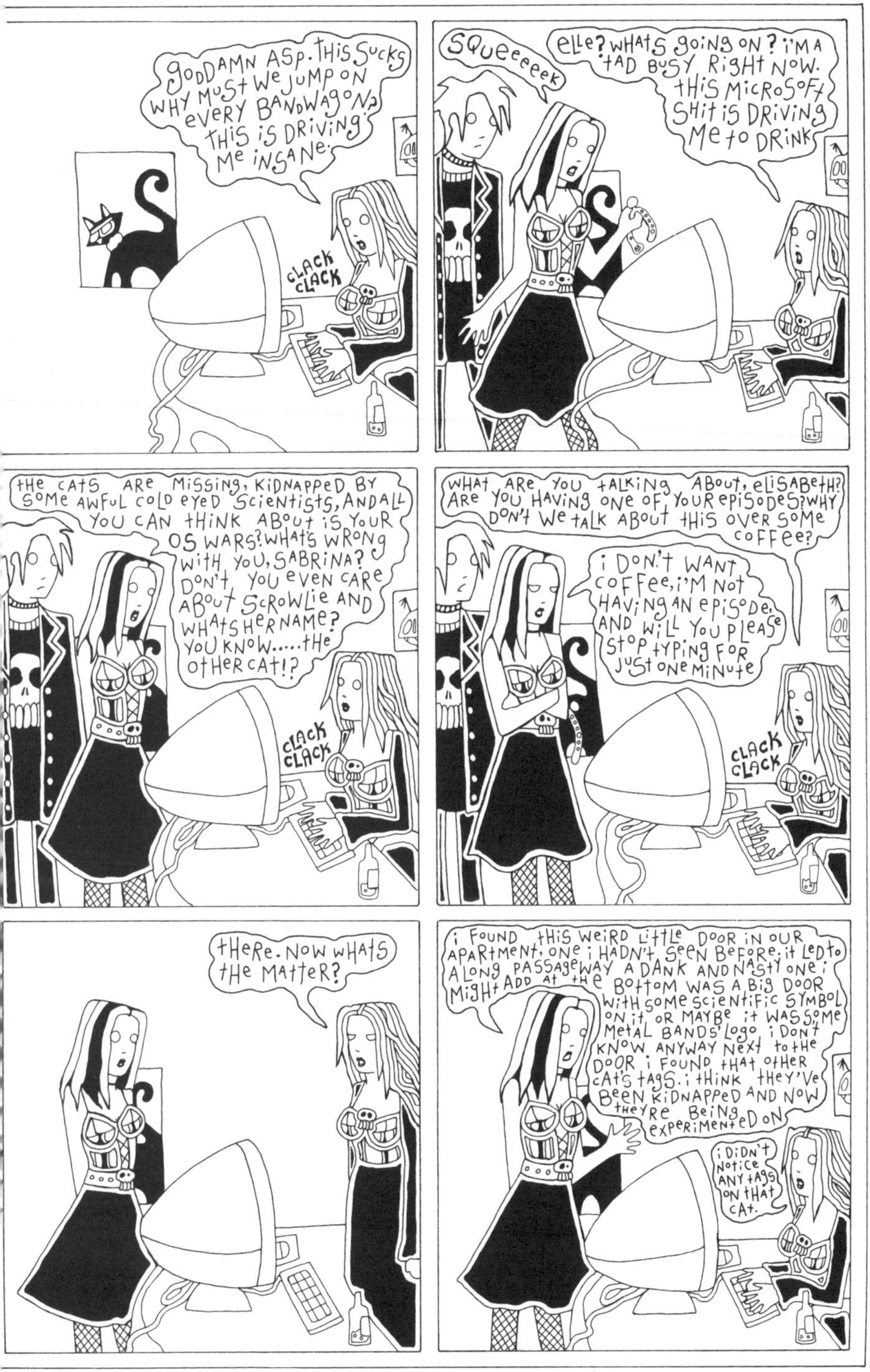
GODDAMN ASP. THIS SUCKS WHY MUST WE JUMP ON EVERY BANDWAGON? THIS IS DRIVING ME INSANE.
CLACK CLACK
SQUEeeeeek
ELLE? WHATS GOING ON? I'M A TAD BUSY RIGHT NOW. THIS MICROSOFT SHIT IS DRIVING ME TO DRINK
THE CATS ARE MISSING, KIDNAPPED BY SOME AWFUL COLD EYED SCIENTISTS, AND ALL YOU CAN THINK ABOUT IS YOUR OS WARS? WHAT'S WRONG WITH YOU, SABRINA? DON'T YOU EVEN CARE ABOUT SCROWLIE AND WHATSHERNAME? YOU KNOW.....THE OTHER CAT!?
CLACK CLACK
WHAT ARE YOU TALKING ABOUT, ELISABETH? ARE YOU HAVING ONE OF YOUR EPISODES? WHY DON'T WE TALK ABOUT THIS OVER SOME COFFEE?
I DON'T WANT COFFEE, I'M NOT HAVING AN EPISODE. AND WILL YOU PLEASE STOP TYPING FOR JUST ONE MINUTE
CLACK CLACK
THERE. NOW WHATS THE MATTER?
I FOUND THIS WEIRD LITTLE DOOR IN OUR APARTMENT, ONE I HADN'T SEEN BEFORE. IT LED TO A LONG PASSAGEWAY A DANK AND NASTY ONE I MIGHT ADD AT THE BOTTOM WAS A BIG DOOR WITH SOME SCIENTIFIC SYMBOL ON IT OR MAYBE IT WAS SOME METAL BANDS' LOGO I DON'T KNOW ANYWAY NEXT TO THE DOOR I FOUND THAT OTHER CAT'S TAGS. I THINK THEY'VE BEEN KIDNAPPED AND NOW THEY'RE BEING EXPERIMENTED ON
I DIDN'T NOTICE ANY TAGS ON THAT CAT.

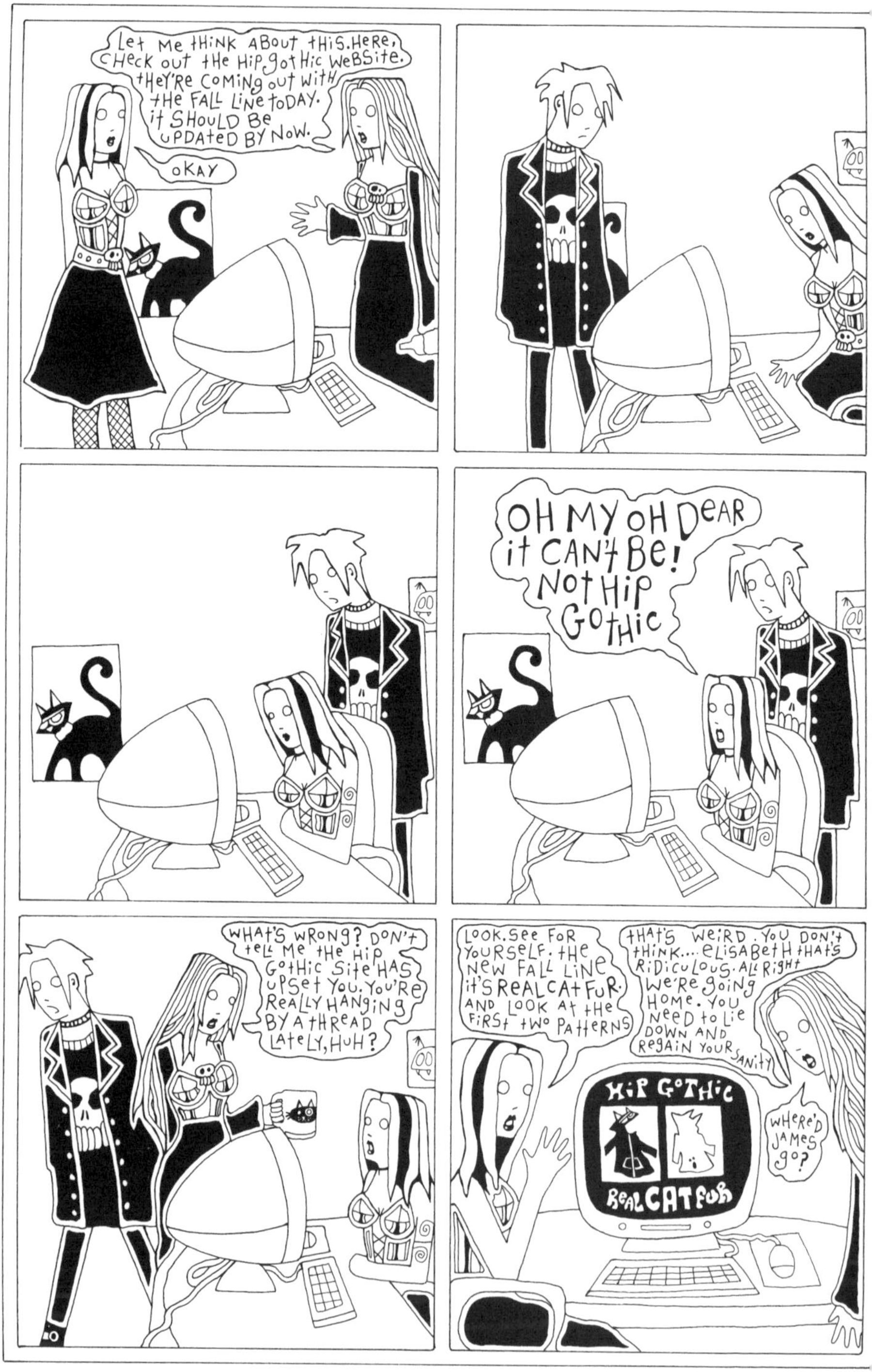
LET ME THINK ABOUT THIS. HERE, CHECK OUT THE HIP GOTHIC WEBSITE. THEY'RE COMING OUT WITH THE FALL LINE TODAY. IT SHOULD BE UPDATED BY NOW.
OKAY
OH MY OH DEAR IT CAN'T BE! NOT HIP GOTHIC
WHAT'S WRONG? DON'T TELL ME THE HIP GOTHIC SITE HAS UPSET YOU. YOU'RE REALLY HANGING BY A THREAD LATELY, HUH?
LOOK. SEE FOR YOURSELF. THE NEW FALL LINE IT'S REAL CAT FUR. AND LOOK AT THE FIRST TWO PATTERNS
THAT'S WEIRD. YOU DON'T THINK.... ELISABETH THAT'S RIDICULOUS. ALL RIGHT WE'RE GOING HOME. YOU NEED TO LIE DOWN AND REGAIN YOUR SANITY
HIP GOTHIC
REAL CAT FUR
WHERE'D JAMES GO?

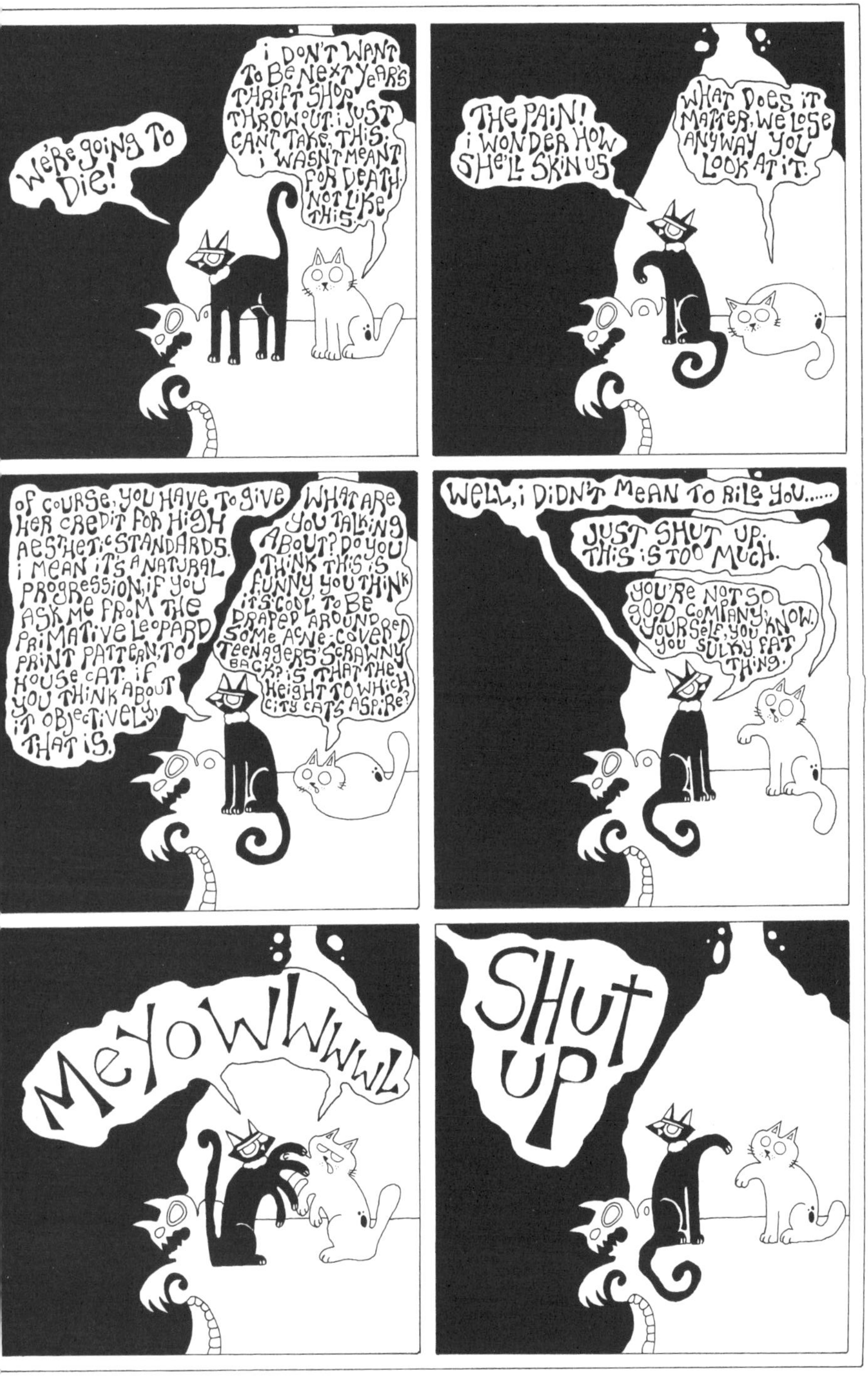
We're going to Die!
i DON'T WANT To Be NEXT YeAR'S THRIFT SHOP THROWOUT. i JUST CAN'T TAKE THIS. i WASN'T MEANT FOR DEATH. NOT LIKE THIS.
THE PAIN! i WONDER HOW SHE'LL SKIN US
WHAT DOES IT MATTER. WE LOSE ANYWAY YOU LOOK AT IT.
of course, you have to give her credit for high aesthetic standards. i mean it's a natural progression, if you ask me from the primative leopard print pattern, to house cat. if you think about it objectively, that is.
What are you talking about? Do you think this is funny you think it's 'cool' to be draped around some acne-covered teenagers' scrawny back? is that the height to which city cats aspire?
WELL, i DIDN'T MEAN TO RILE YOU......
JUST SHUT UP. THIS IS TOO MUCH.
YOU'RE NOT SO GOOD COMPANY, YOURSELF, YOU KNOW. YOU SULKY FAT THING.
MeYOWWWWL
SHUT UP

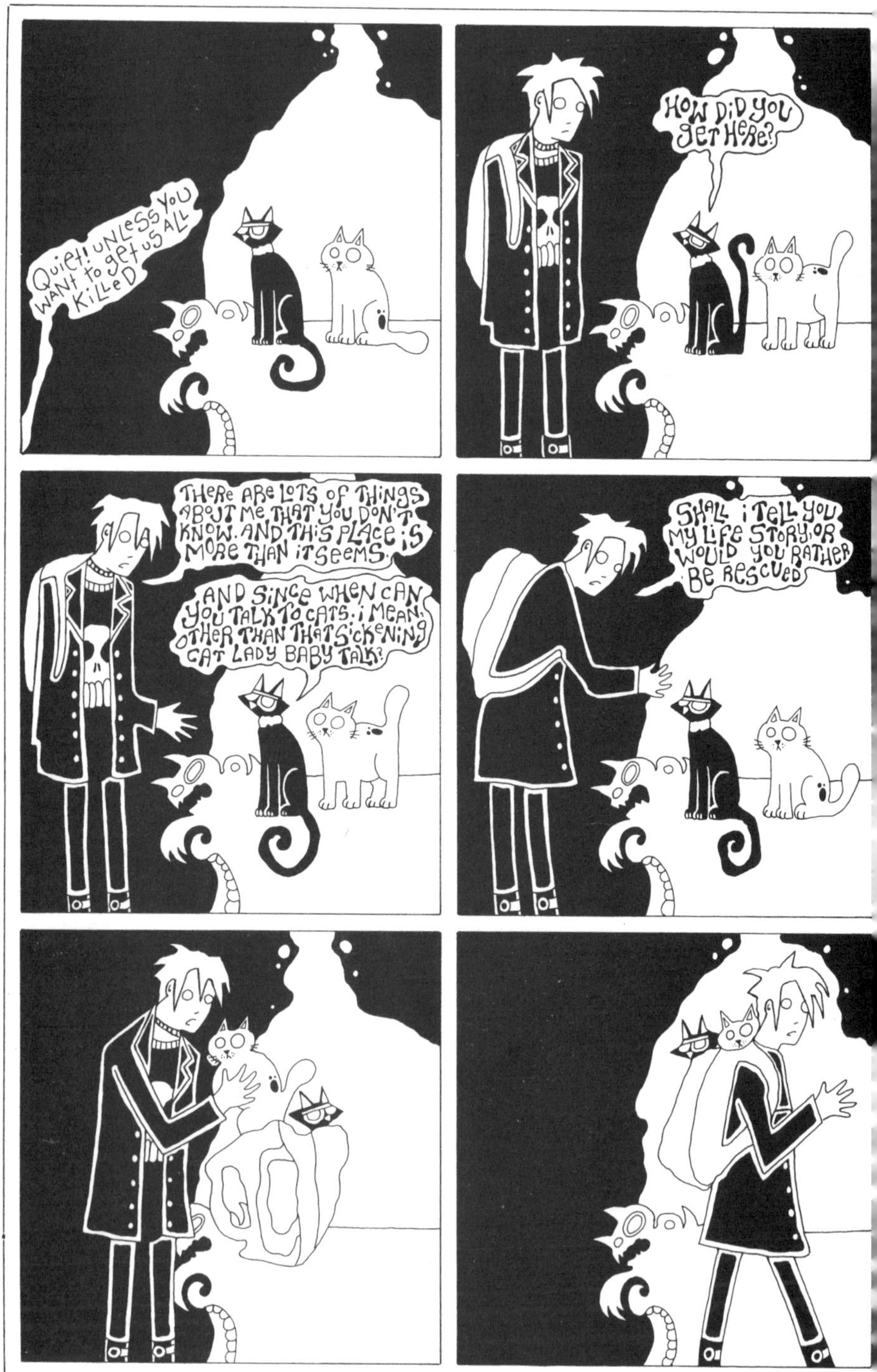
Quiet! unless you want to get us all killed
How did you get here?
There are lots of things about me that you don't know. And this place is more than it seems.
And since when can you talk to cats. I mean, other than that sickening cat lady baby talk?
Shall I tell you my life story, or would you rather be rescued

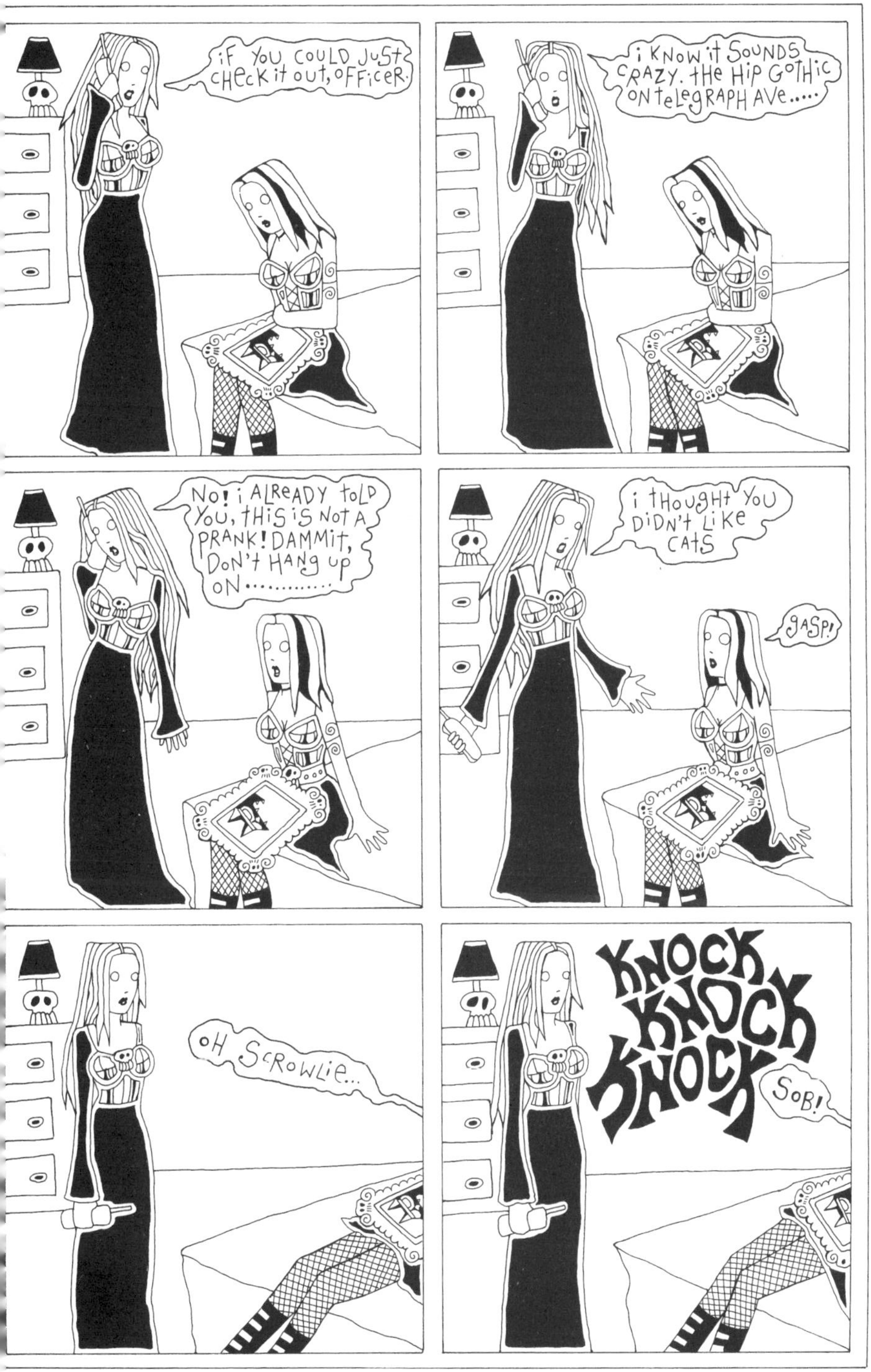
if you could just check it out, officer.
i know it sounds crazy. the hip gothic on telegraph ave.....
No! i already told you, this is not a prank! dammit, don't hang up on...........
i thought you didn't like cats
gasp!
oh scrowlie...
KNOCK KNOCK KNOCK
SOB!

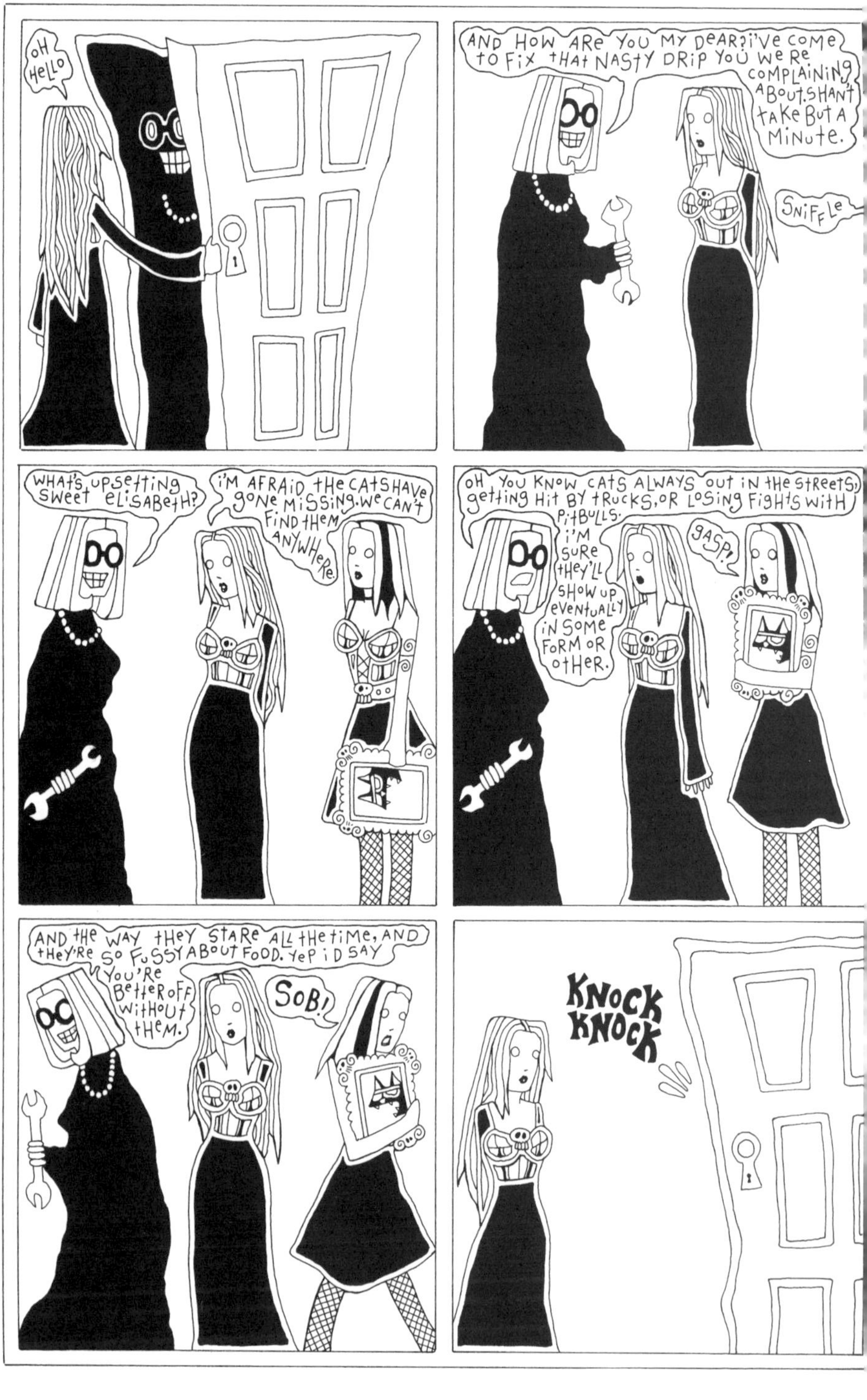
OH HELLO
AND HOW ARE YOU MY DEAR? I'VE COME TO FIX THAT NASTY DRIP YOU WERE COMPLAINING ABOUT. SHAN'T TAKE BUT A MINUTE.
SNIFFLE
WHAT'S UPSETTING SWEET ELISABETH?
I'M AFRAID THE CATS HAVE GONE MISSING. WE CAN'T FIND THEM ANYWHERE.
OH YOU KNOW CATS ALWAYS OUT IN THE STREETS, GETTING HIT BY TRUCKS, OR LOSING FIGHTS WITH PITBULLS.
I'M SURE THEY'LL SHOW UP EVENTUALLY IN SOME FORM OR OTHER.
GASP!
AND THE WAY THEY STARE ALL THE TIME, AND THEY'RE SO FUSSY ABOUT FOOD. YEP I D SAY YOU'RE BETTER OFF WITHOUT THEM.
SOB!
KNOCK KNOCK

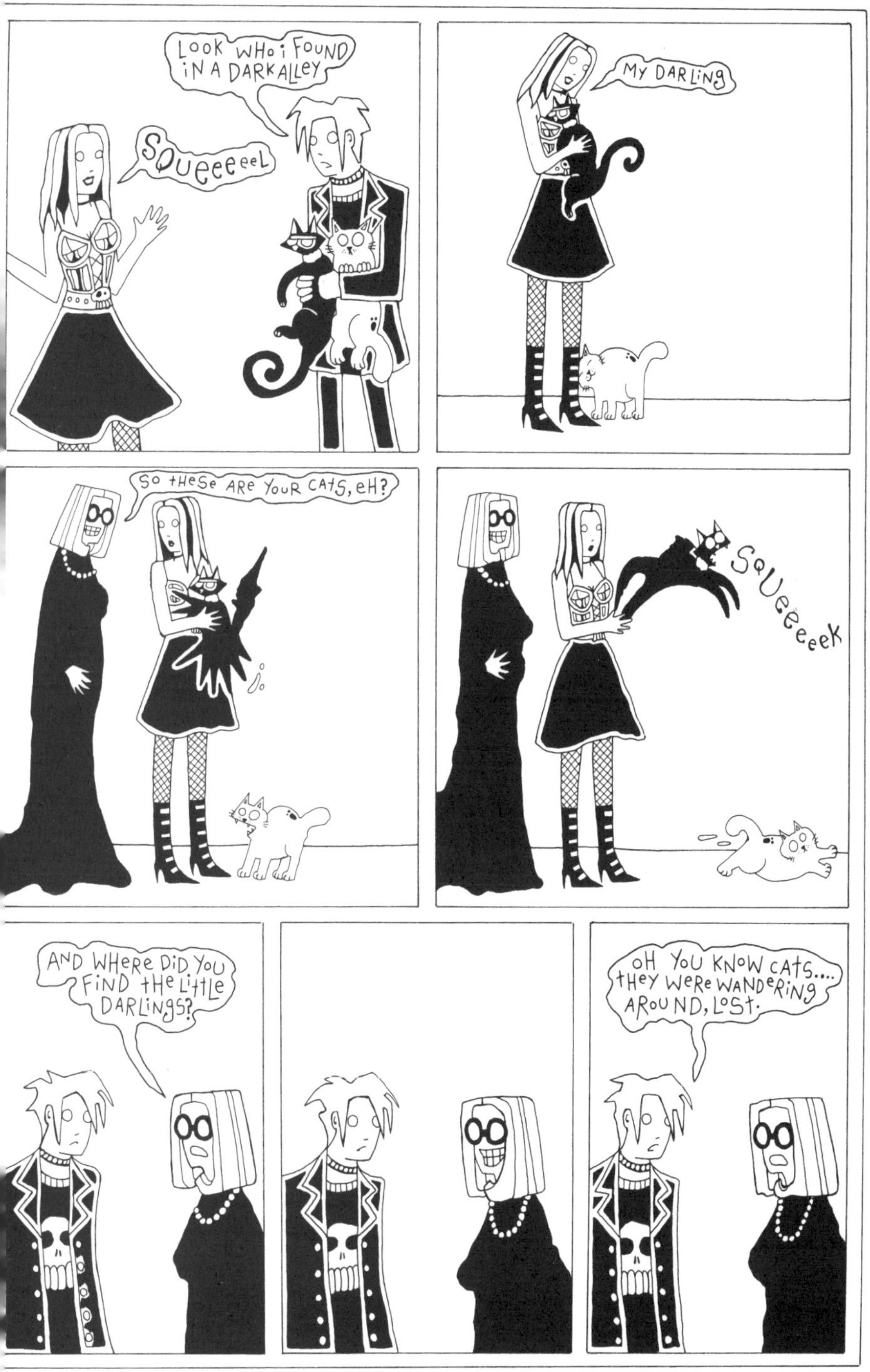
LOOK WHO i FOUND iN A DARK ALLEY
SQUEEEEEL
MY DARLING
SO THESE ARE YOUR CATS, EH?
SQUEEEEEEK
AND WHERE DID YOU FIND THE LITTLE DARLINGS?
OH YOU KNOW CATS.... THEY WERE WANDERING AROUND, LOST.

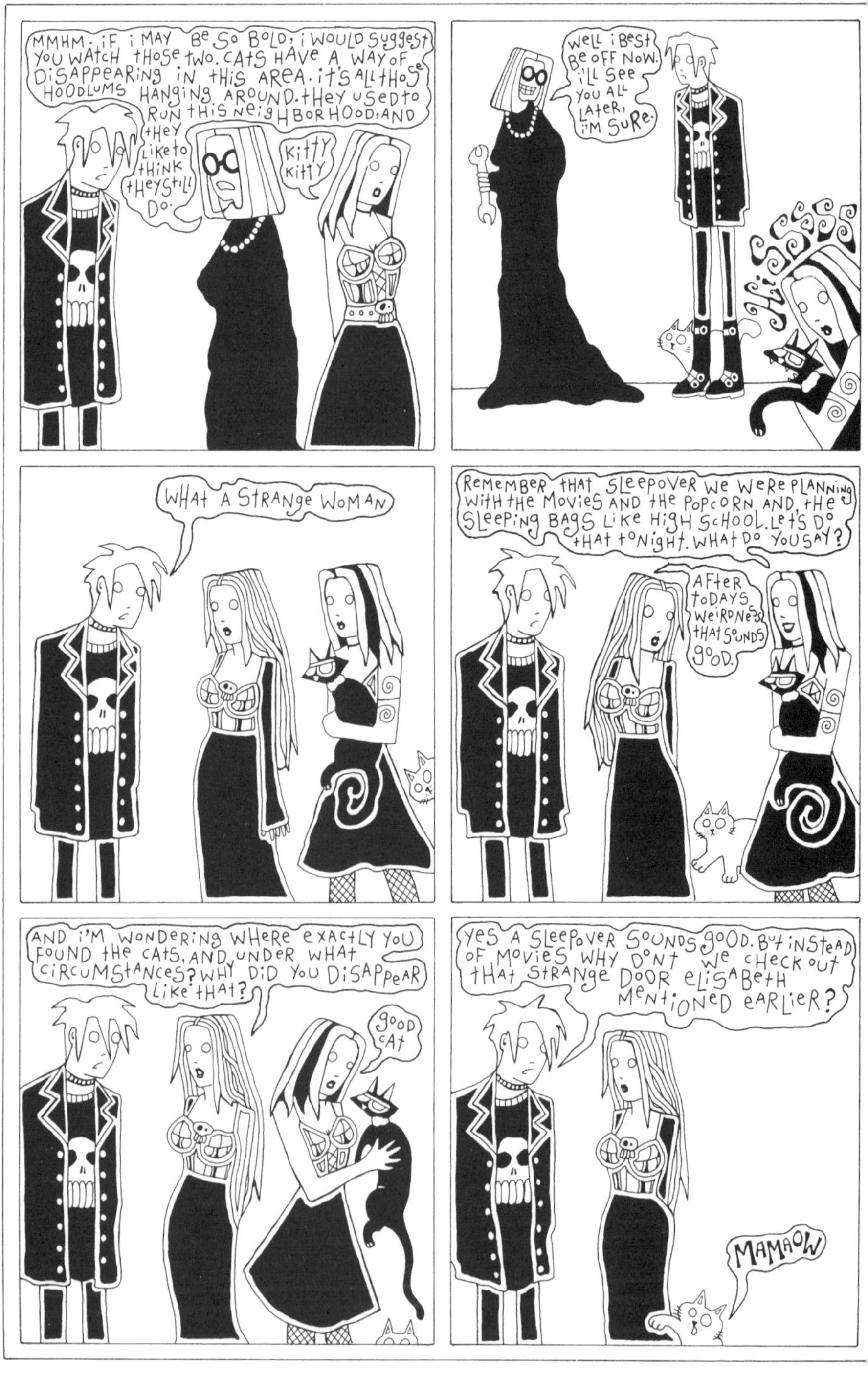
MMHM. IF I MAY BE SO BOLD, I WOULD SUGGEST YOU WATCH THOSE TWO. CATS HAVE A WAY OF DISAPPEARING IN THIS AREA. IT'S ALL THOSE HOODLUMS HANGING AROUND. THEY USED TO RUN THIS NEIGHBORHOOD, AND THEY LIKE TO THINK THEY STILL DO.
KITTY KITTY
WELL I BEST BE OFF NOW. I'LL SEE YOU ALL LATER, I'M SURE.
HISSSSSS
WHAT A STRANGE WOMAN
REMEMBER THAT SLEEPOVER WE WERE PLANNING WITH THE MOVIES AND THE POPCORN AND THE SLEEPING BAGS LIKE HIGH SCHOOL. LET'S DO THAT TONIGHT. WHAT DO YOU SAY?
AFTER TODAYS WEIRDNESS THAT SOUNDS GOOD.
AND I'M WONDERING WHERE EXACTLY YOU FOUND THE CATS, AND UNDER WHAT CIRCUMSTANCES? WHY DID YOU DISAPPEAR LIKE THAT?
GOOD CAT
YES A SLEEPOVER SOUNDS GOOD. BUT INSTEAD OF MOVIES WHY DON'T WE CHECK OUT THAT STRANGE DOOR ELISABETH MENTIONED EARLIER?
MAMAOW

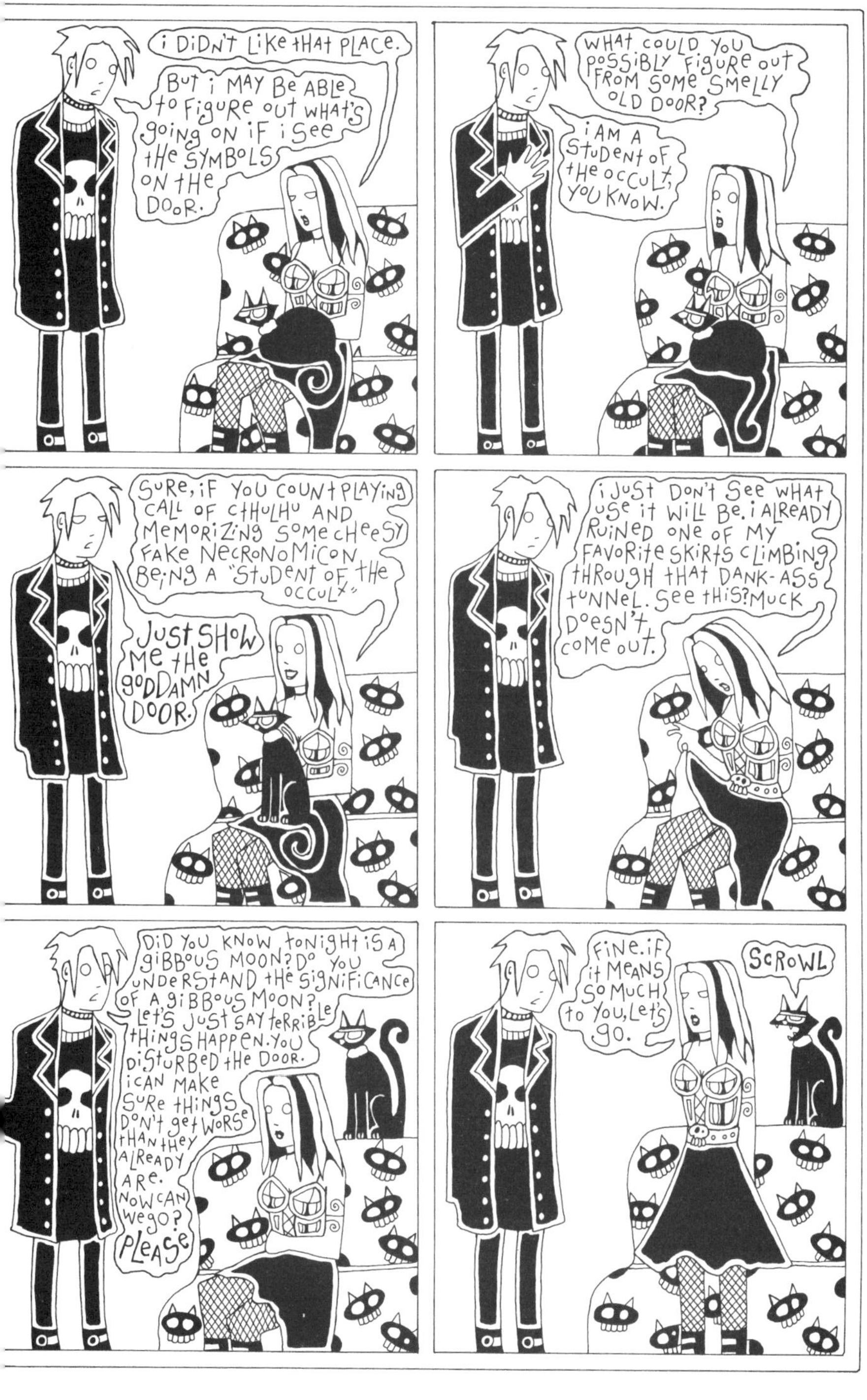
i DIDN'T LIKE THAT PLACE.
BUT i MAY BE ABLE TO FIGURE OUT WHAT'S GOING ON IF i SEE THE SYMBOLS ON THE DOOR.
WHAT COULD YOU POSSIBLY FIGURE OUT FROM SOME SMELLY OLD DOOR?
i AM A STUDENT OF THE OCCULT, YOU KNOW.
SURE, iF YOU COUNT PLAYING CALL OF CTHULHU AND MEMORIZING SOME CHEESY FAKE NECRONOMICON BEING A "STUDENT OF THE OCCULT"
JUST SHOW ME THE GODDAMN DOOR.
i JUST DON'T SEE WHAT USE iT WILL BE. i ALREADY RUINED ONE OF MY FAVORITE SKIRTS CLIMBING THROUGH THAT DANK-ASS TUNNEL. SEE THIS? MUCK DOESN'T COME OUT.
DID YOU KNOW TONIGHT IS A GIBBOUS MOON? DO YOU UNDERSTAND THE SIGNIFICANCE OF A GIBBOUS MOON? LET'S JUST SAY TERRIBLE THINGS HAPPEN. YOU DISTURBED THE DOOR. i CAN MAKE SURE THINGS DON'T GET WORSE THAN THEY ALREADY ARE. NOW CAN WE GO? PLEASE
FINE. iF iT MEANS SO MUCH TO YOU, LET'S GO.
SCROWL

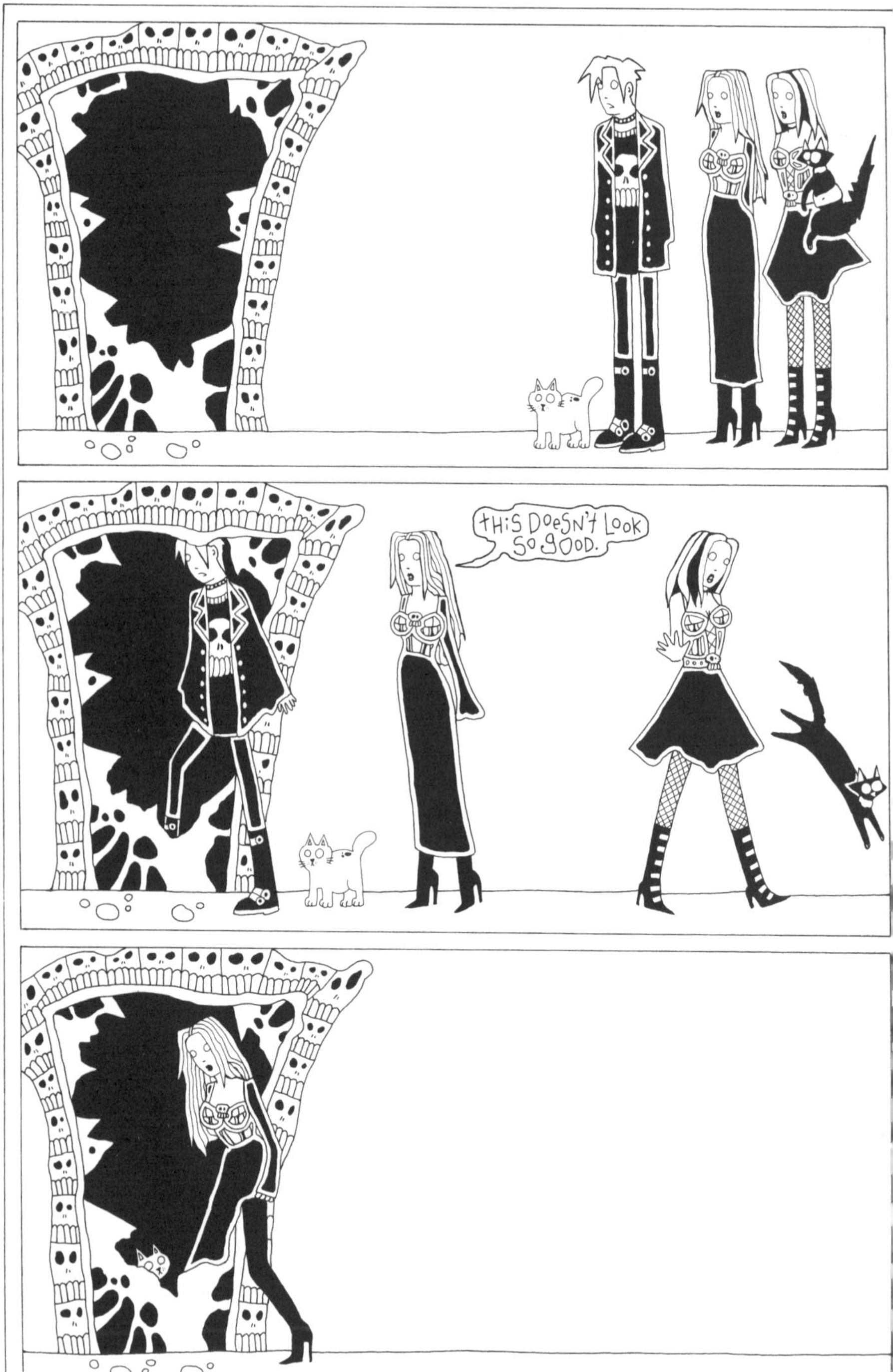
THIS DOESN'T LOOK SO GOOD.

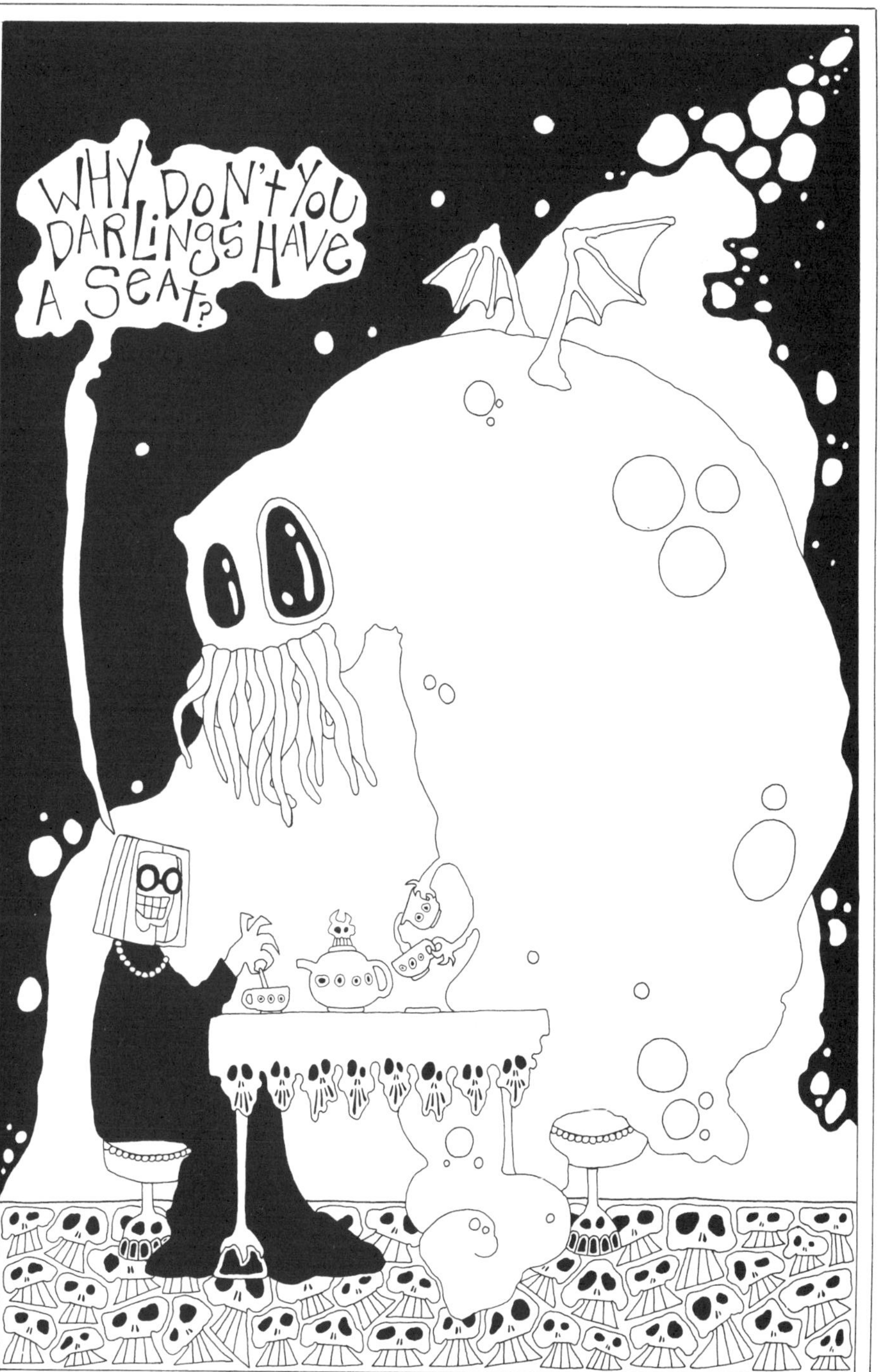
WHY DON'T YOU DARLINGS HAVE A SEAT?

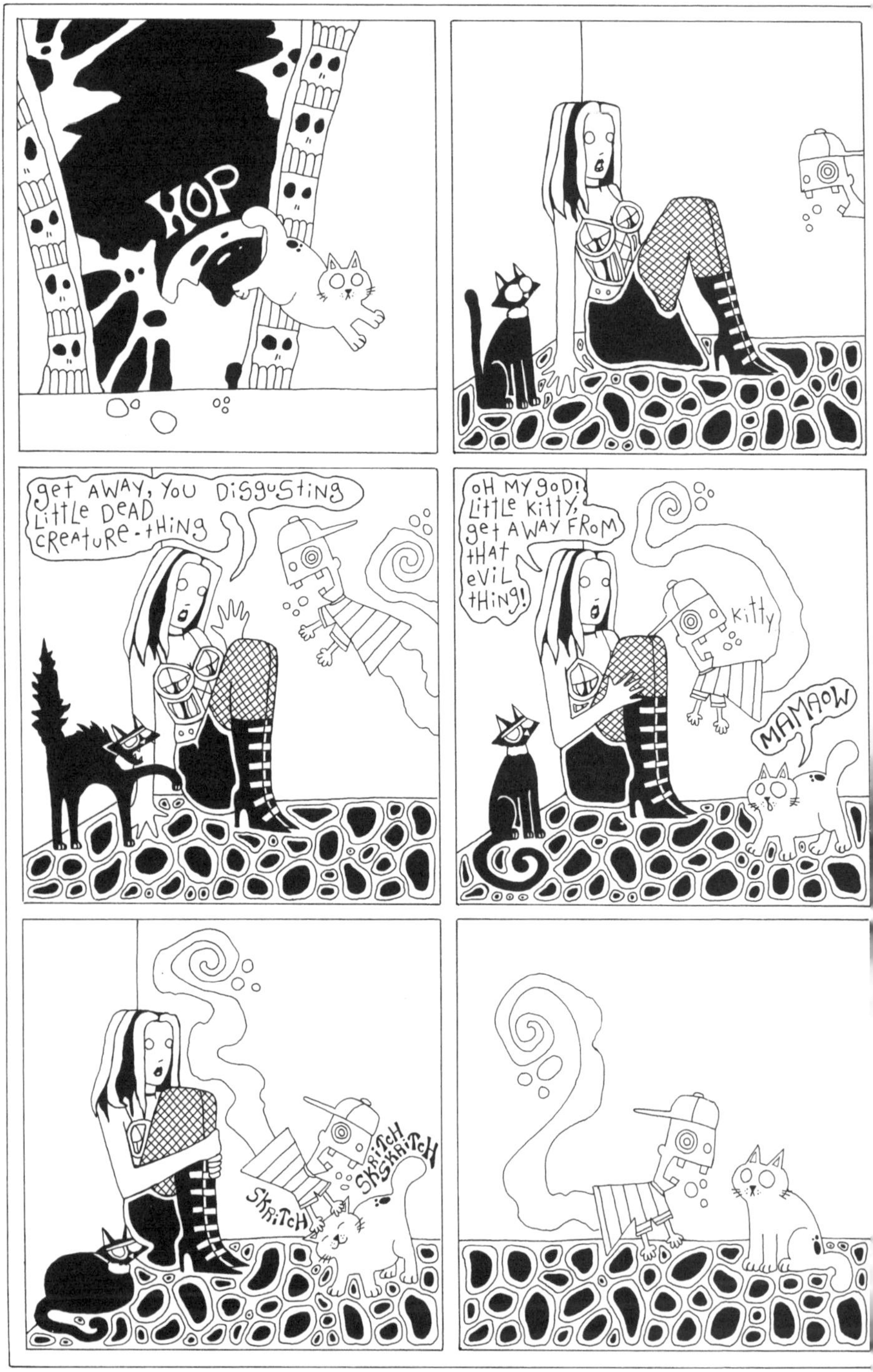
HOP
get AWAY, YOU DISGUSTING LITTLE DEAD CREATURE-THING
OH MY GOD! LITTLE KITTY, get AWAY FROM THAT EVIL THING!
kitty
MAMAOW
SKRITCH
SKRITCH SKRITCH

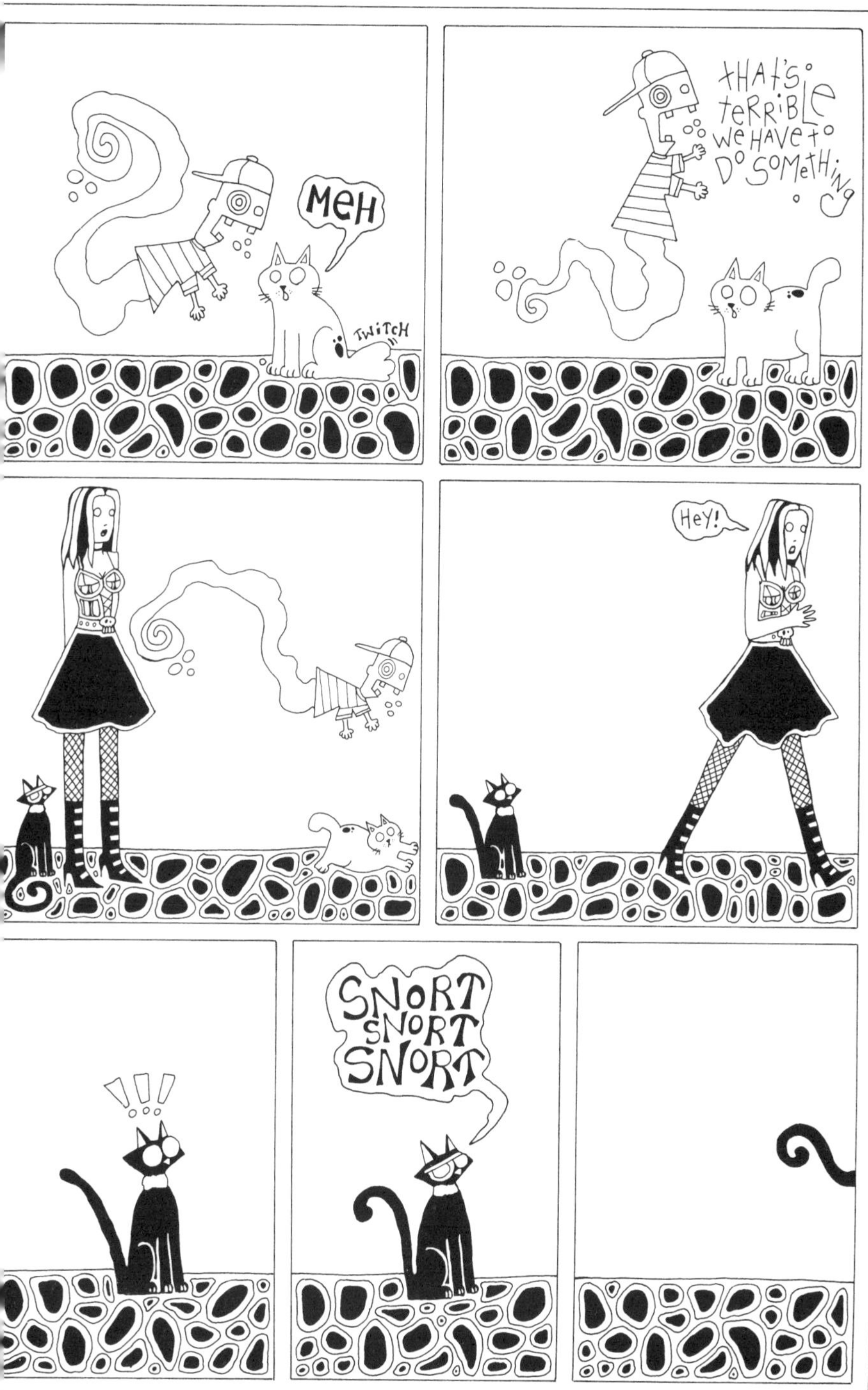
MEH
TWITCH
that's terrible we have to do something
Hey!
SNORT SNORT SNORT

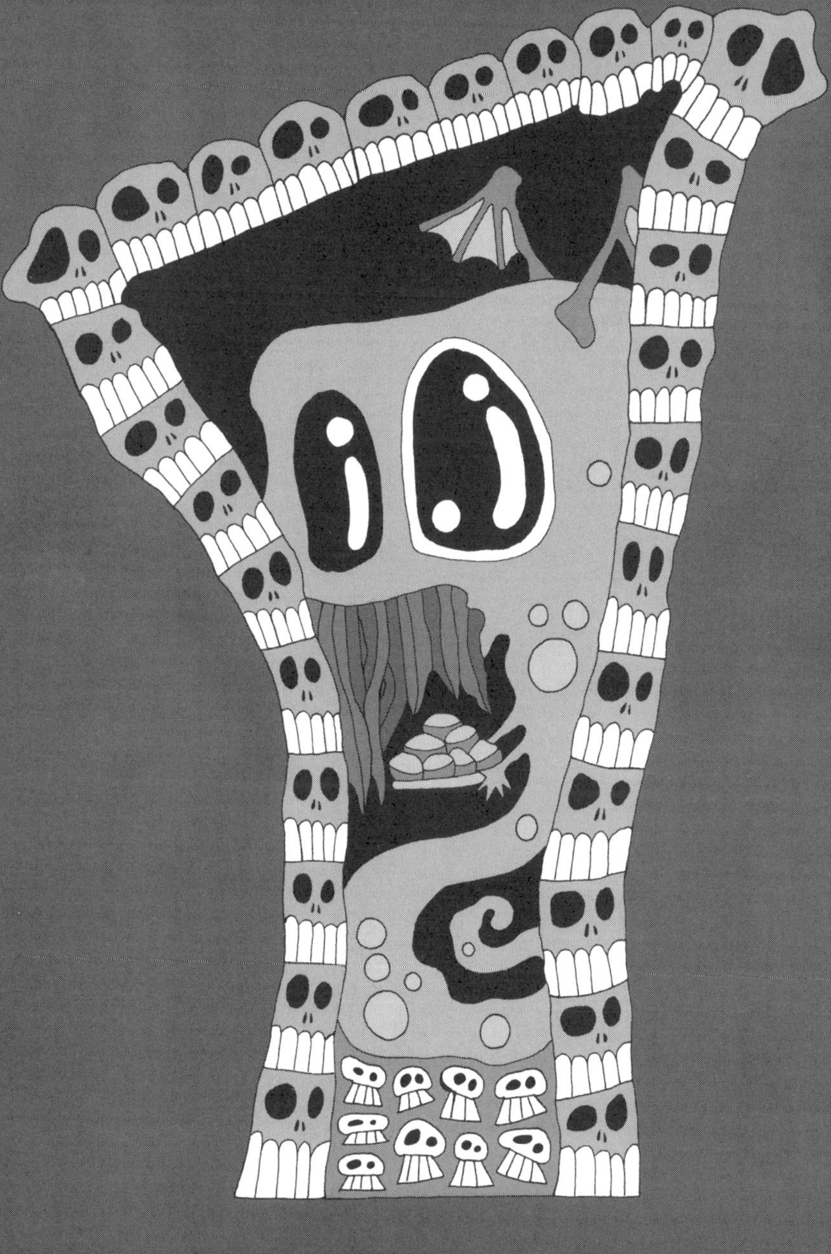

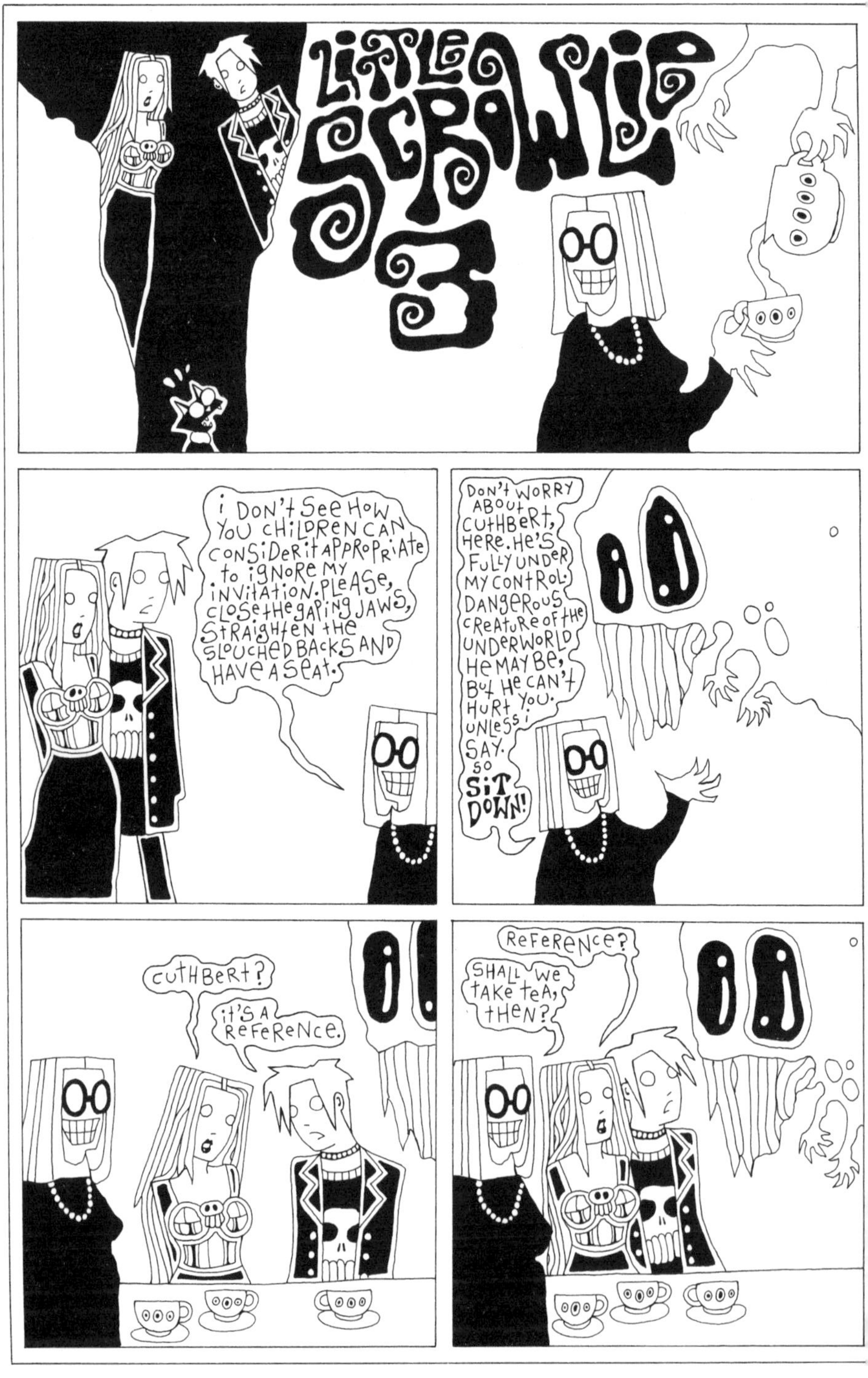
LITTLE SCROWLIE 3
i DON'T SEE HOW YOU CHILDREN CAN CONSIDER IT APPROPRIATE to iGNORE MY iNVITATION. PLEASE, CLOSE THE GAPING JAWS, STRAIGHTEN THE SLOUCHED BACKS AND HAVE A SEAT.
DON'T WORRY ABOUT CUTHBERT, HERE. HE'S FULLY UNDER MY CONTROL. DANGEROUS CREATURE OF THE UNDERWORLD HE MAY BE, BUT HE CAN'T HURT YOU. UNLESS i SAY. SO SIT DOWN!
CUTHBERT?
iT'S A REFERENCE.
REFERENCE?
SHALL WE TAKE TEA, THEN?

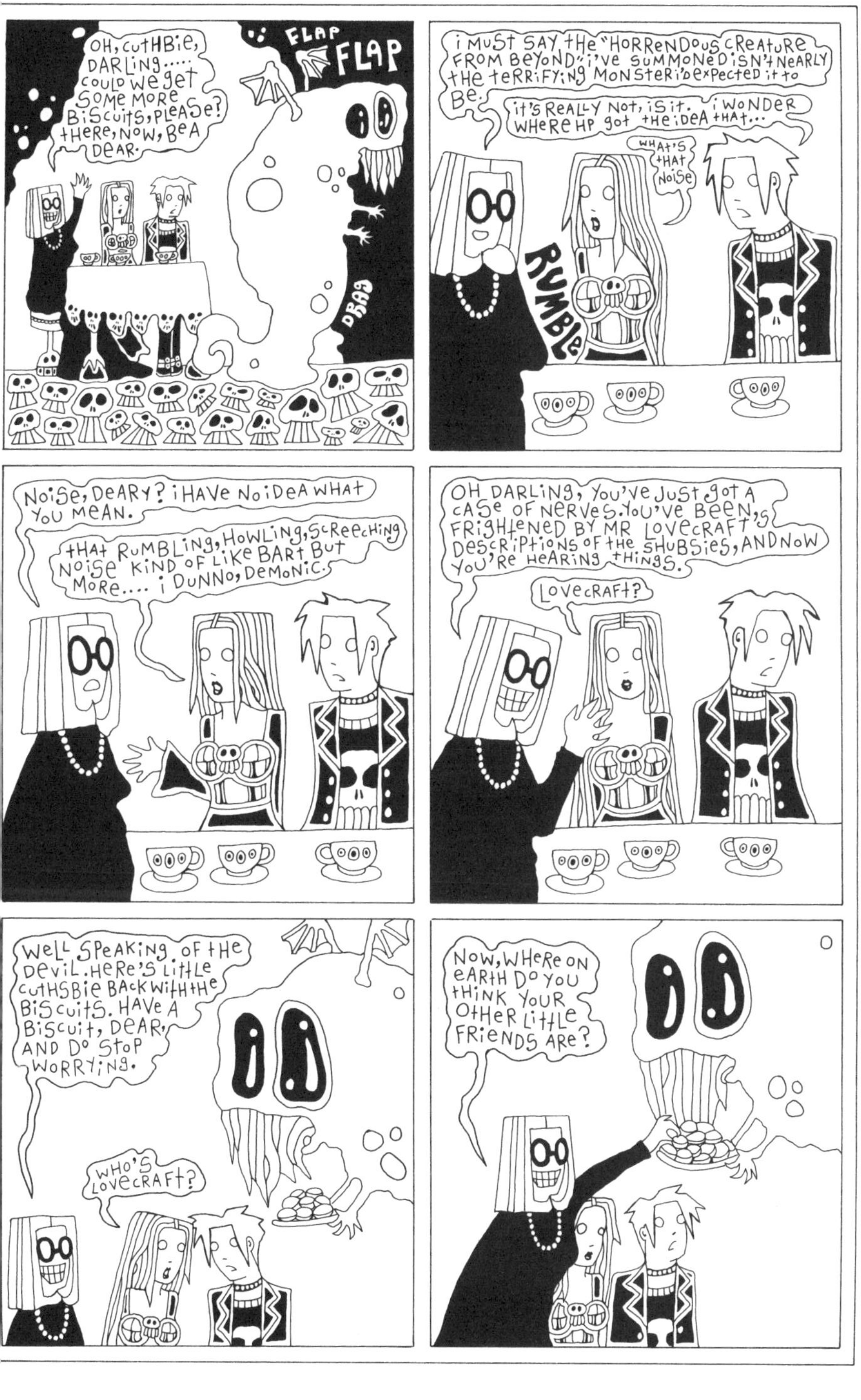
OH, CUTHBIE, DARLING..... COULD WE GET SOME MORE BISCUITS, PLEASE? THERE, NOW, BE A DEAR.
FLAP
FLAP
DRAG
I MUST SAY THE "HORRENDOUS CREATURE FROM BEYOND" I'VE SUMMONED ISN'T NEARLY THE TERRIFYING MONSTER I'D EXPECTED IT TO BE.
IT'S REALLY NOT, IS IT. I WONDER WHERE HP GOT THE IDEA THAT...
WHAT'S THAT NOISE
RUMBLE
NOISE, DEARY? I HAVE NO IDEA WHAT YOU MEAN.
THAT RUMBLING, HOWLING, SCREECHING NOISE KIND OF LIKE BART BUT MORE.... I DUNNO, DEMONIC.
OH DARLING, YOU'VE JUST GOT A CASE OF NERVES. YOU'VE BEEN FRIGHTENED BY MR LOVECRAFT'S DESCRIPTIONS OF THE SHUBSIES, AND NOW YOU'RE HEARING THINGS.
LOVECRAFT?
WELL SPEAKING OF THE DEVIL. HERE'S LITTLE CUTHSBIE BACK WITH THE BISCUITS. HAVE A BISCUIT, DEAR, AND DO STOP WORRYING.
WHO'S LOVECRAFT?
NOW, WHERE ON EARTH DO YOU THINK YOUR OTHER LITTLE FRIENDS ARE?

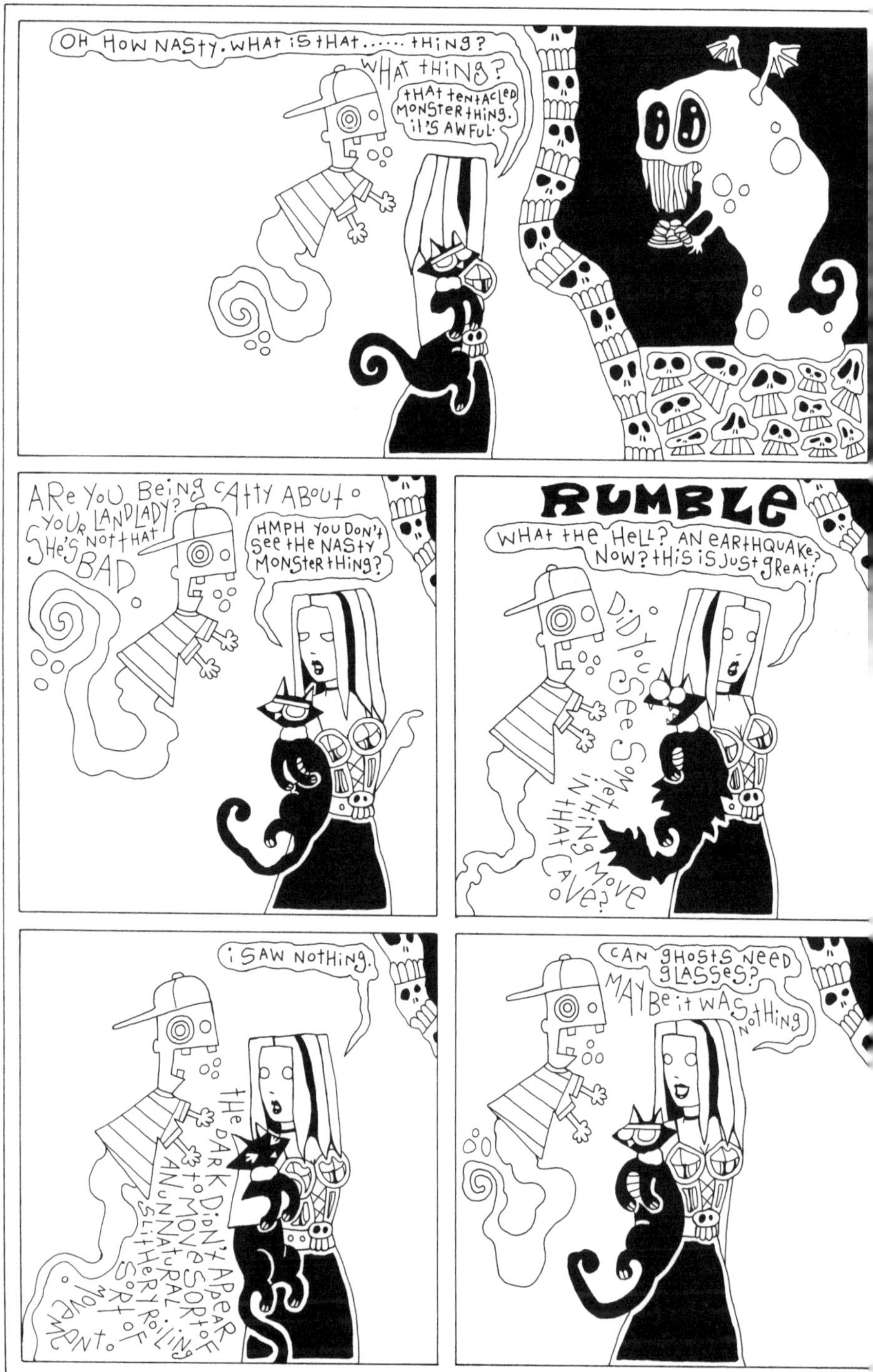
OH HOW NASTY. WHAT IS THAT...... THING?
WHAT THING?
THAT TENTACLED MONSTER THING. IT'S AWFUL.
ARE YOU BEING CATTY ABOUT YOUR LANDLADY? SHE'S NOT THAT BAD
HMPH YOU DON'T SEE THE NASTY MONSTER THING?
RUMBLE
WHAT THE HELL? AN EARTHQUAKE? NOW? THIS IS JUST GREAT!
DID YOU SEE SOMETHING MOVE IN THAT CAVE?
I SAW NOTHING.
THE DARK DIDN'T APPEAR TO MOVE SORT OF AN UNNATURAL SLITHERY ROLLING SORT OF MOVEMENT.
CAN GHOSTS NEED GLASSES?
MAYBE IT WAS NOTHING

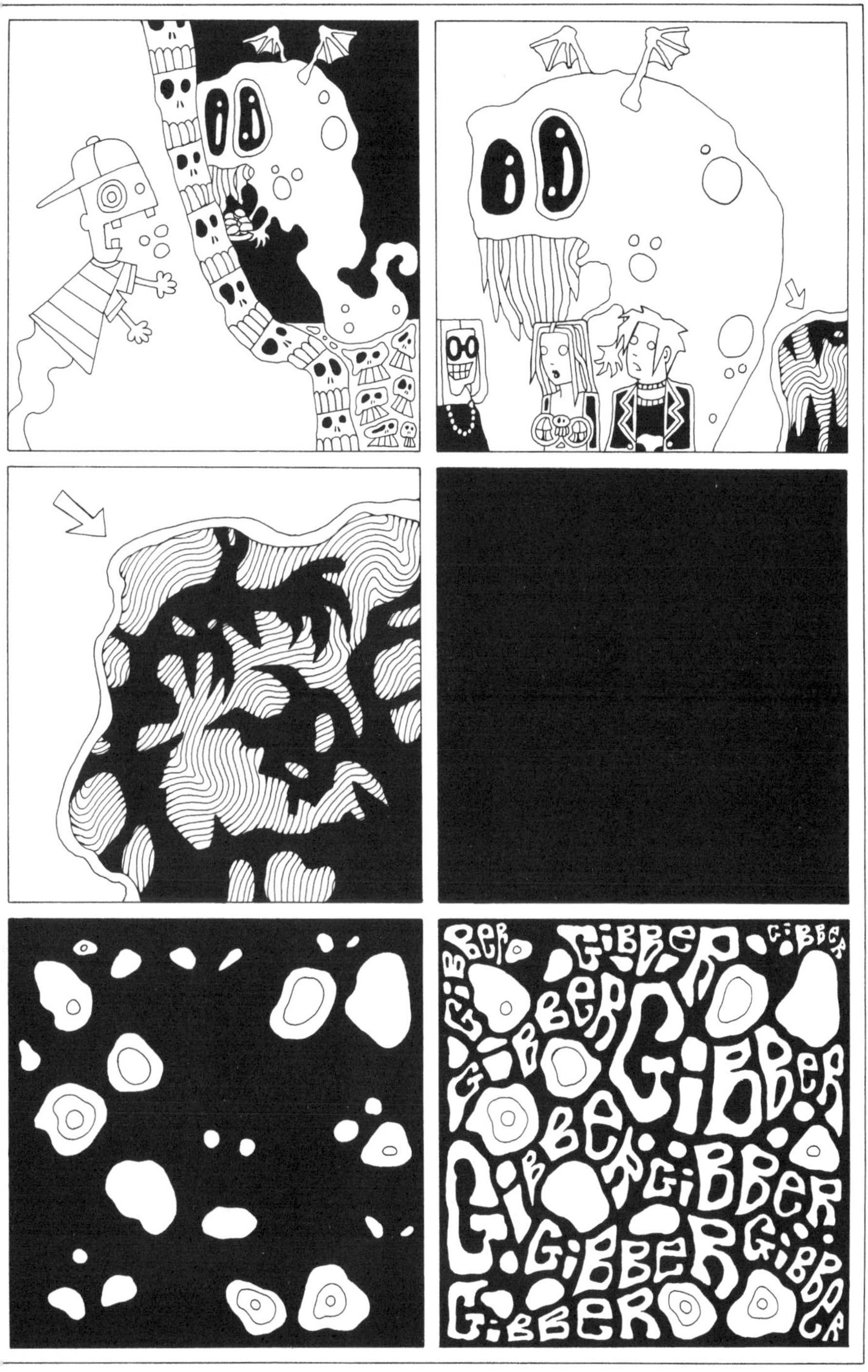
GIBBER
GIBBER
GIBBER
GIBBER
GIBBER
GIBBER
GIBBER
GIBBER
GIBBER

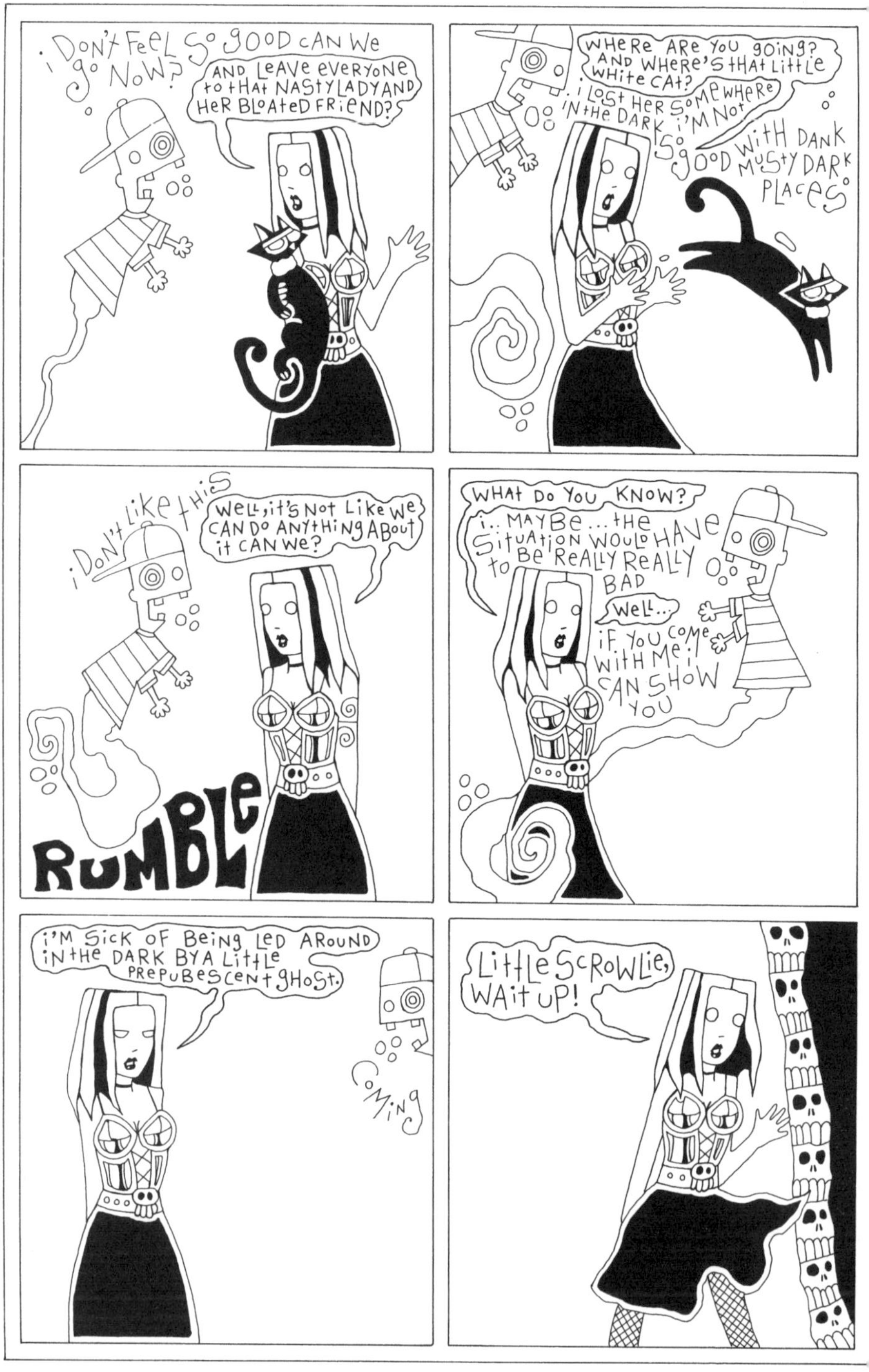
i Don't Feel So good can we go Now?
AND Leave everyone to that NASTY LADY AND HeR BLOATED FRIEND?
Where are you going? And where's that little white cat?
i Lost her somewhere in the DARK, i'M Not so good with dank musty dark places
i Don't Like this
Well, it's not like we can do anything about it can we?
RUMBLE
What do you know?
i.. maybe ... the situation would have to be really really bad
Well...
if you come with me i can show you
i'm sick of being led around in the dark by a little prepubescent ghost.
Coming
Little Scrowlie, wait up!

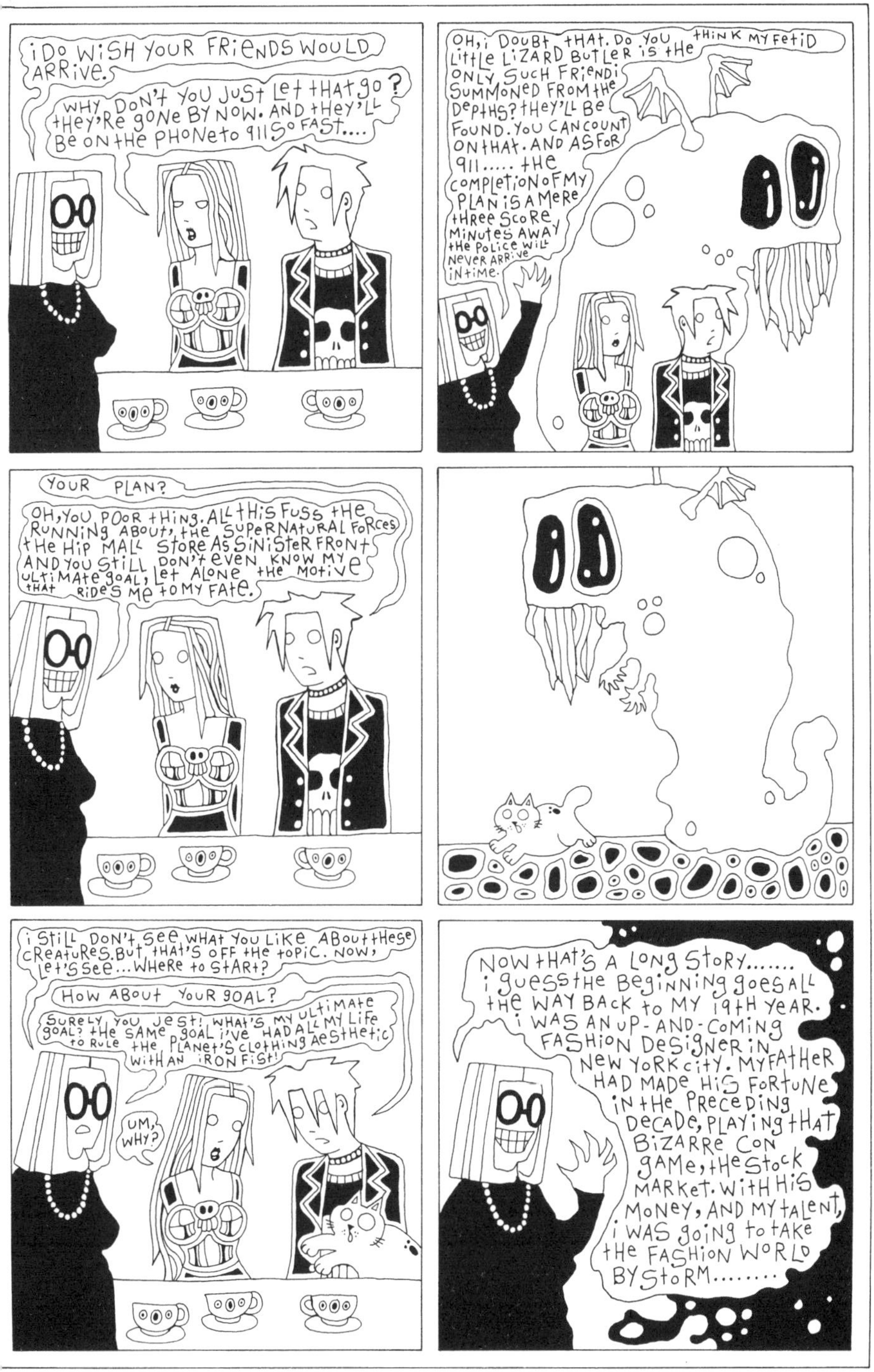
i Do WiSH YOUR FRiENDS WOULD ARRive.
WHY DON'T YOU JUST Let tHAt go? tHey're gONe BY NOW. AND tHey'LL Be ON tHe PHONE to 911 So FASt....
OH, i DOUBt tHAt. Do YOU tHiNK MY FetiD LittLe LiZARD BUtLeR iS tHe ONLY SUCH FRieND i SUMMONED FROM tHe DePtHS? tHeY'LL Be FOUND. YOU CAN COUNt ON tHAt. AND AS FoR 911..... tHe COMPLetiON OF MY PLAN iS A MeRe tHRee SCoRe MiNUteS AWAY tHe POLiCe WiLL NeveR ARRive iN time.
YOUR PLAN?
OH, YOU POOR tHiNg. ALL tHiS FUSS tHe RUNNiNg ABOUt, tHe SUPeRNAtURAL FoRces tHe HiP MALL StoRe AS SiNiSteR FRONt AND YOU StiLL DON't eveN KNOW MY ULtiMAte goAL, Let ALoNe tHe MOtive tHAt RiDeS Me to MY FAte.
i StiLL DON't See WHAt YOU LiKe ABOUt tHeSe CReAtUReS. BUt tHAt'S OFF tHe toPiC. NOW, Let'S See... WHeRe to StARt?
HOW ABOUt YOUR goAL?
UM, WHY?
SUReLY YOU JeSt! WHAt'S MY ULtiMAte goAL? tHe SAMe goAL i've HAD ALL MY LiFe to RULe tHe PLANet'S CLotHiNg AeStHetic WitH AN iRON FiSt!
NOW tHAt'S A LoNg StoRY....... i gueSS tHe BegiNNiNg goeS ALL tHe WAY BACK to MY 19tH YeAR. i WAS AN UP-AND-COMiNg FASHiON DeSigNeR iN NeW YORK city. MY FAtHeR HAD MADe HiS FoRtUNe iN tHe PReceDiNg DecADe, PLAYiNg tHAt BiZARRe CON gAMe, tHe StocK MARKet. WitH HiS MONeY, AND MY tALeNt, i WAS goiNg to tAKe tHe FASHiON WORLD BY StoRM........

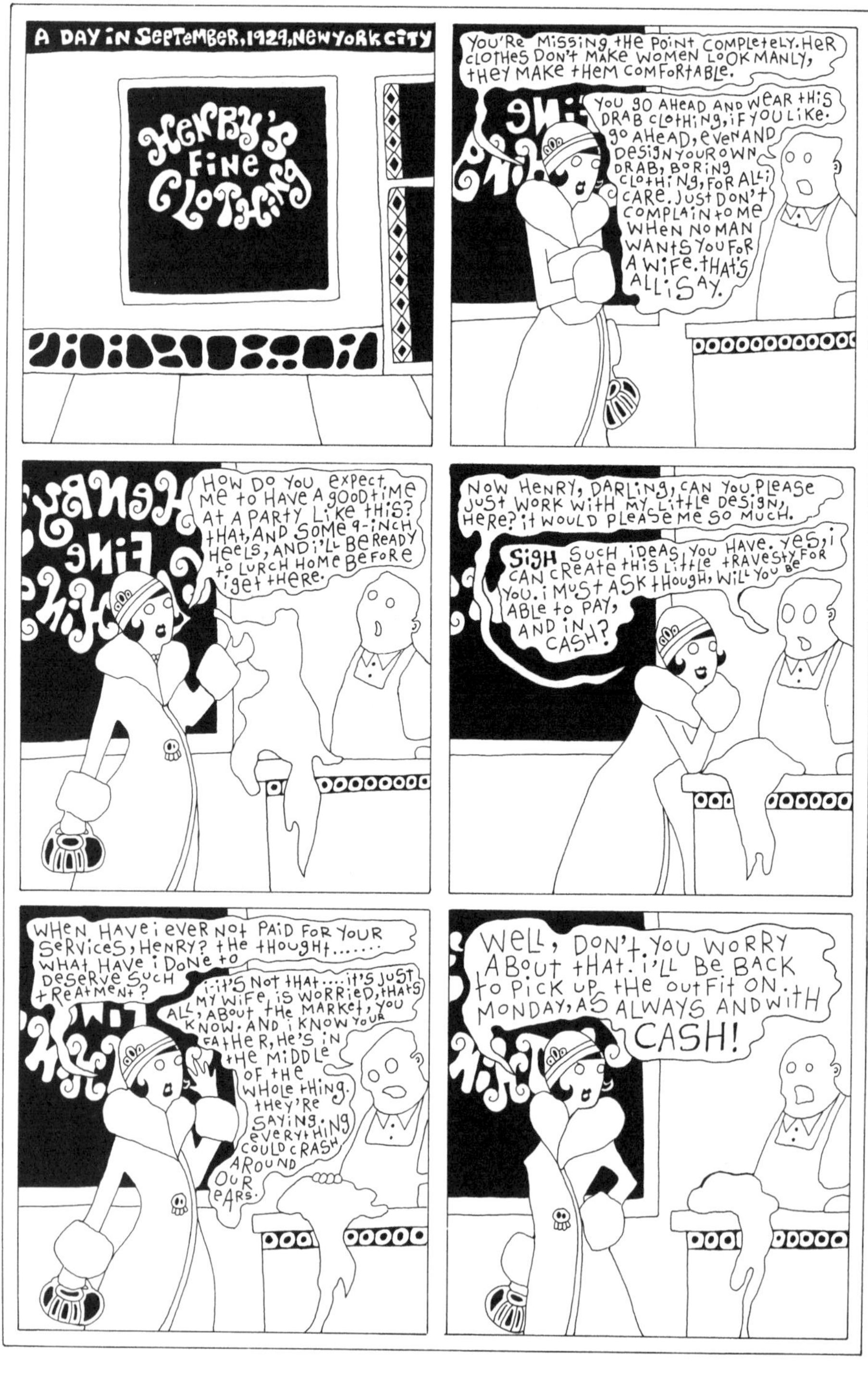

A DAY IN SEPTEMBER, 1929, NEW YORK CITY
HENRY'S FINE CLOTHING
YOU'RE MISSING THE POINT COMPLETELY. HER CLOTHES DON'T MAKE WOMEN LOOK MANLY, THEY MAKE THEM COMFORTABLE.
YOU GO AHEAD AND WEAR THIS DRAB CLOTHING, IF YOU LIKE. GO AHEAD, EVEN AND DESIGN YOUR OWN DRAB, BORING CLOTHING, FOR ALL I CARE. JUST DON'T COMPLAIN TO ME WHEN NO MAN WANTS YOU FOR A WIFE. THAT'S ALL I SAY.
HOW DO YOU EXPECT ME TO HAVE A GOOD TIME AT A PARTY LIKE THIS? THAT, AND SOME 9-INCH HEELS, AND I'LL BE READY TO LURCH HOME BEFORE I GET THERE.
NOW HENRY, DARLING, CAN YOU PLEASE JUST WORK WITH MY LITTLE DESIGN, HERE? IT WOULD PLEASE ME SO MUCH.
SIGH SUCH IDEAS YOU HAVE. YES, I CAN CREATE THIS LITTLE TRAVESTY FOR YOU. I MUST ASK THOUGH, WILL YOU BE ABLE TO PAY, AND IN CASH?
WHEN HAVE I EVER NOT PAID FOR YOUR SERVICES, HENRY? THE THOUGHT....... WHAT HAVE I DONE TO DESERVE SUCH TREATMENT?
I-IT'S NOT THAT.... IT'S JUST MY WIFE IS WORRIED, THAT'S ALL, ABOUT THE MARKET, YOU KNOW. AND I KNOW YOUR FATHER, HE'S IN THE MIDDLE OF THE WHOLE THING. THEY'RE SAYING EVERYTHING COULD CRASH AROUND OUR EARS.
WELL, DON'T YOU WORRY ABOUT THAT. I'LL BE BACK TO PICK UP THE OUTFIT ON MONDAY, AS ALWAYS AND WITH CASH!

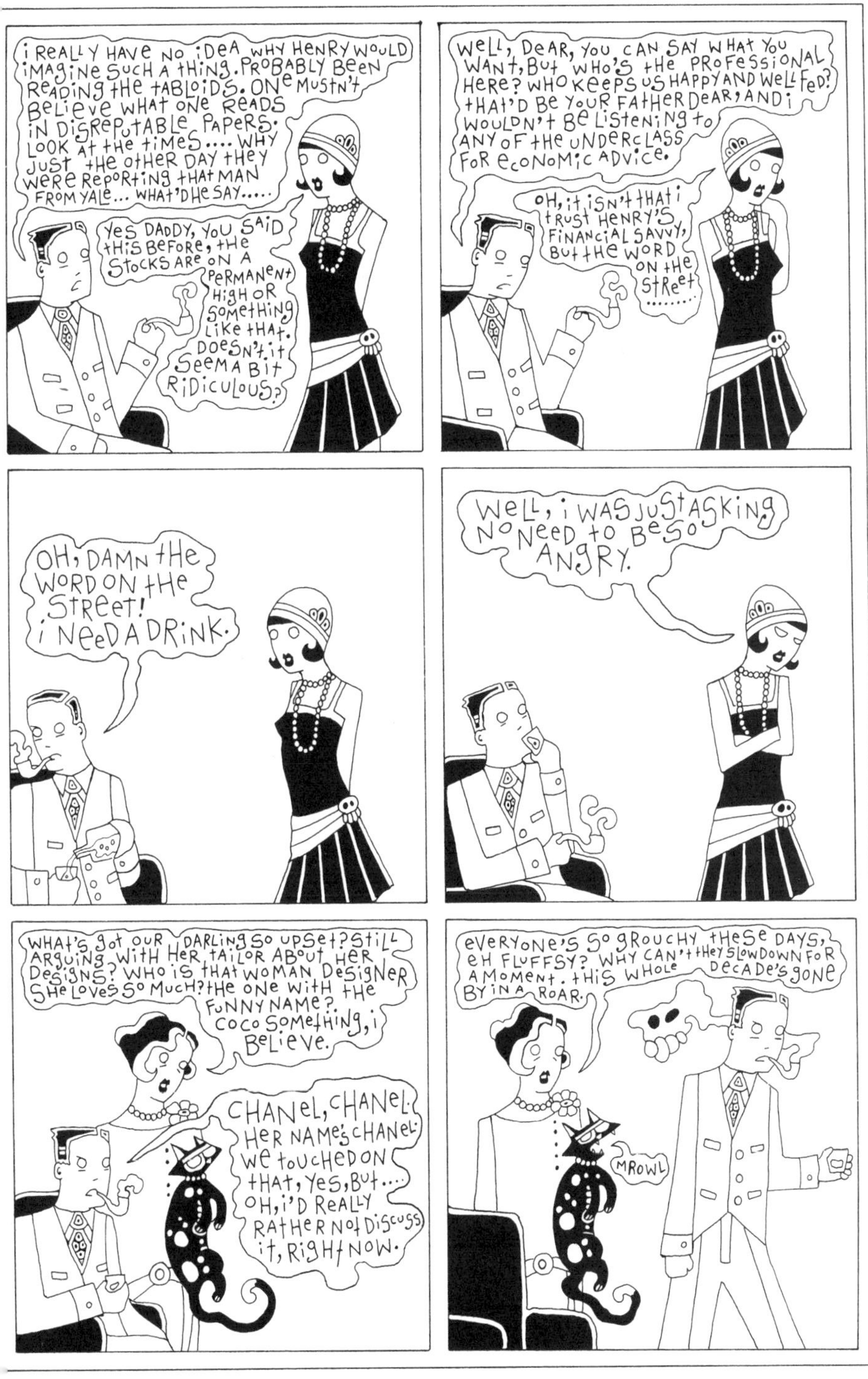
I REALLY HAVE NO IDEA WHY HENRY WOULD IMAGINE SUCH A THING. PROBABLY BEEN READING THE TABLOIDS. ONE MUSTN'T BELIEVE WHAT ONE READS IN DISREPUTABLE PAPERS. LOOK AT THE TIMES.... WHY JUST THE OTHER DAY THEY WERE REPORTING THAT MAN FROM YALE... WHAT'D HE SAY.....
YES DADDY, YOU SAID THIS BEFORE, THE STOCKS ARE ON A PERMANENT HIGH OR SOMETHING LIKE THAT. DOESN'T IT SEEM A BIT RIDICULOUS?
WELL, DEAR, YOU CAN SAY WHAT YOU WANT, BUT WHO'S THE PROFESSIONAL HERE? WHO KEEPS US HAPPY AND WELL FED? THAT'D BE YOUR FATHER DEAR, AND I WOULDN'T BE LISTENING TO ANY OF THE UNDERCLASS FOR ECONOMIC ADVICE.
OH, IT ISN'T THAT I TRUST HENRY'S FINANCIAL SAVVY, BUT THE WORD ON THE STREET........
OH, DAMN THE WORD ON THE STREET! I NEED A DRINK.
WELL, I WAS JUST ASKING. NO NEED TO BE SO ANGRY.
WHAT'S GOT OUR DARLING SO UPSET? STILL ARGUING WITH HER TAILOR ABOUT HER DESIGNS? WHO IS THAT WOMAN DESIGNER SHE LOVES SO MUCH? THE ONE WITH THE FUNNY NAME? COCO SOMETHING, I BELIEVE.
CHANEL, CHANEL. HER NAME'S CHANEL. WE TOUCHED ON THAT, YES, BUT.... OH, I'D REALLY RATHER NOT DISCUSS IT, RIGHT NOW.
EVERYONE'S SO GROUCHY THESE DAYS, EH FLUFFSY? WHY CAN'T THEY SLOW DOWN FOR A MOMENT. THIS WHOLE DECADE'S GONE BY IN A ROAR.
MROWL

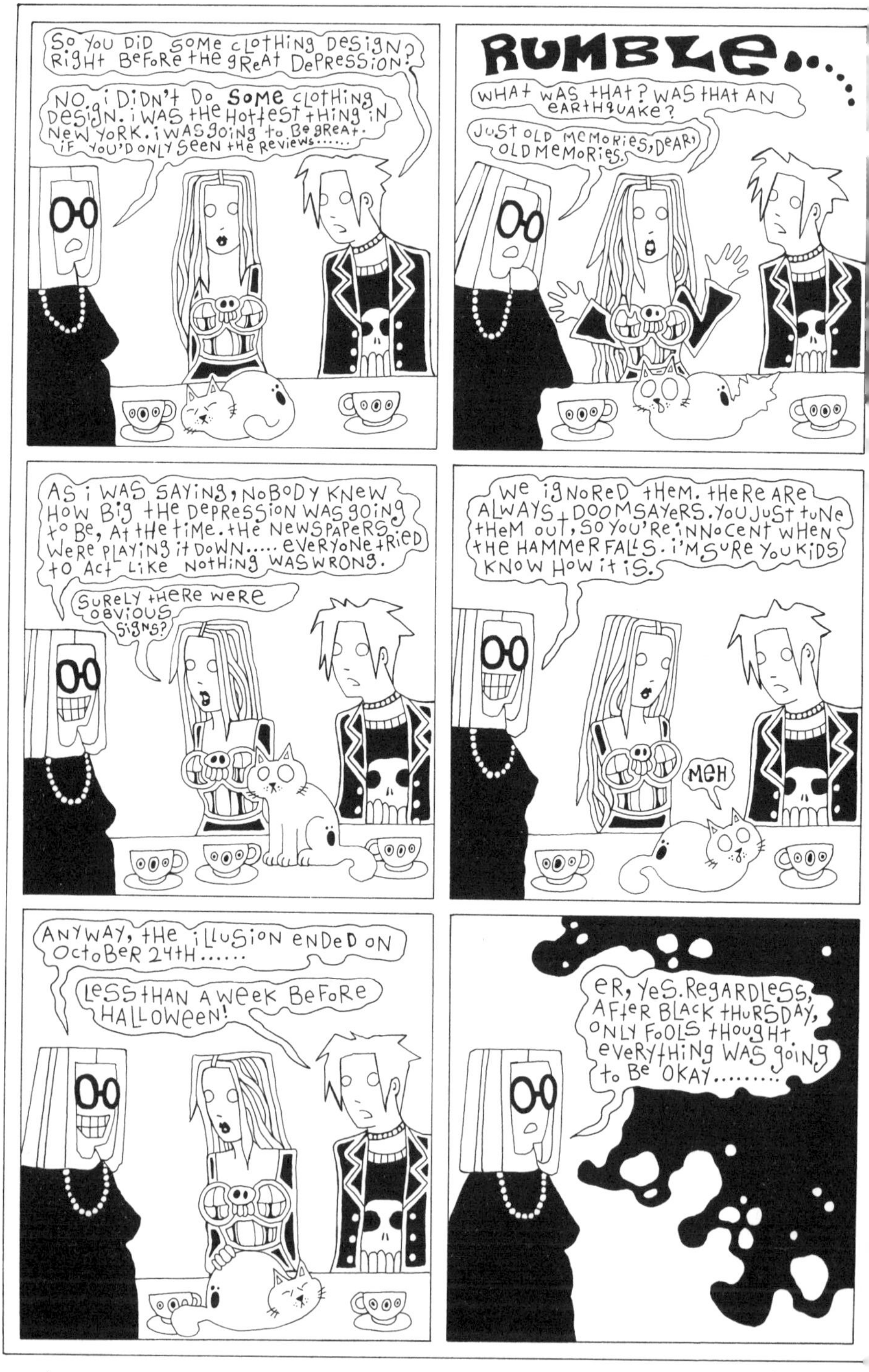
So you did some clothing design? Right before the great depression?
No, i didn't do some clothing design. i was the hottest thing in New York. i was going to be great. if you'd only seen the reviews......
RUMBLE......
What was that? Was that an earthquake?
Just old memories, dear, old memories.
As i was saying, nobody knew how big the depression was going to be, at the time. The newspapers were playing it down..... everyone tried to act like nothing was wrong.
Surely there were obvious signs?
We ignored them. There are always doomsayers. You just tune them out, so you're innocent when the hammer falls. i'm sure you kids know how it is.
MEH
Anyway, the illusion ended on October 24th......
Less than a week before Halloween!
Er, yes. Regardless, after Black Thursday, only fools thought everything was going to be okay........

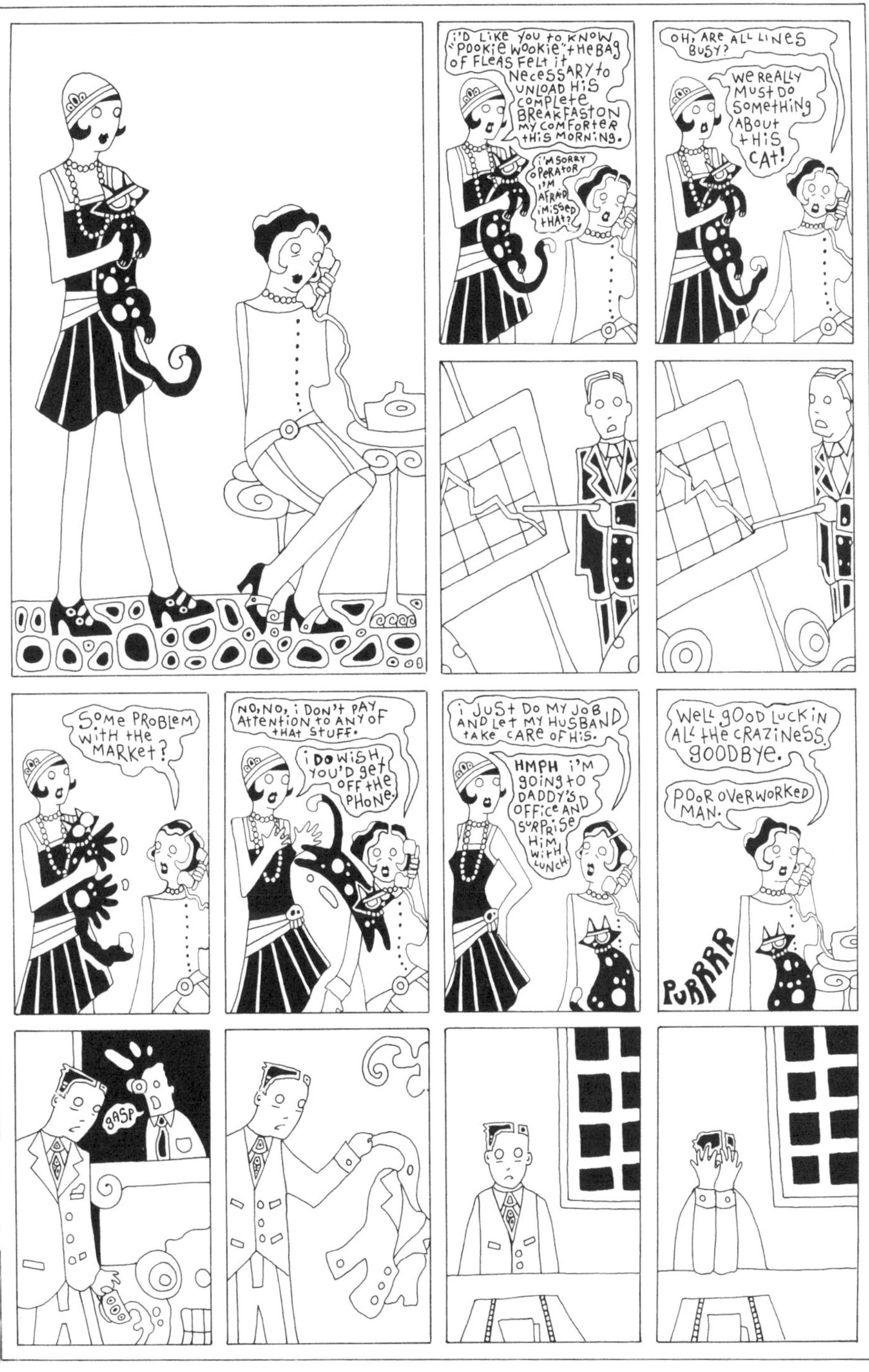
i'D LIKE YOU TO KNOW "POOKIE WOOKIE" THE BAG OF FLEAS FELT IT NECESSARY TO UNLOAD HIS COMPLETE BREAKFAST ON MY COMFORTER THIS MORNING.
i'M SORRY OPERATOR i'M AFRAID i MISSED THAT?
OH, ARE ALL LINES BUSY?
WE REALLY MUST DO SOMETHING ABOUT THIS CAT!
SOME PROBLEM WITH THE MARKET?
NO, NO, i DON'T PAY ATTENTION TO ANY OF THAT STUFF.
i DO WISH YOU'D GET OFF THE PHONE.
i JUST DO MY JOB AND LET MY HUSBAND TAKE CARE OF HIS.
HMPH i'M GOING TO DADDY'S OFFICE AND SURPRISE HIM WITH LUNCH.
WELL GOOD LUCK IN ALL THE CRAZINESS. GOODBYE.
POOR OVERWORKED MAN.
PURRRR
GASP

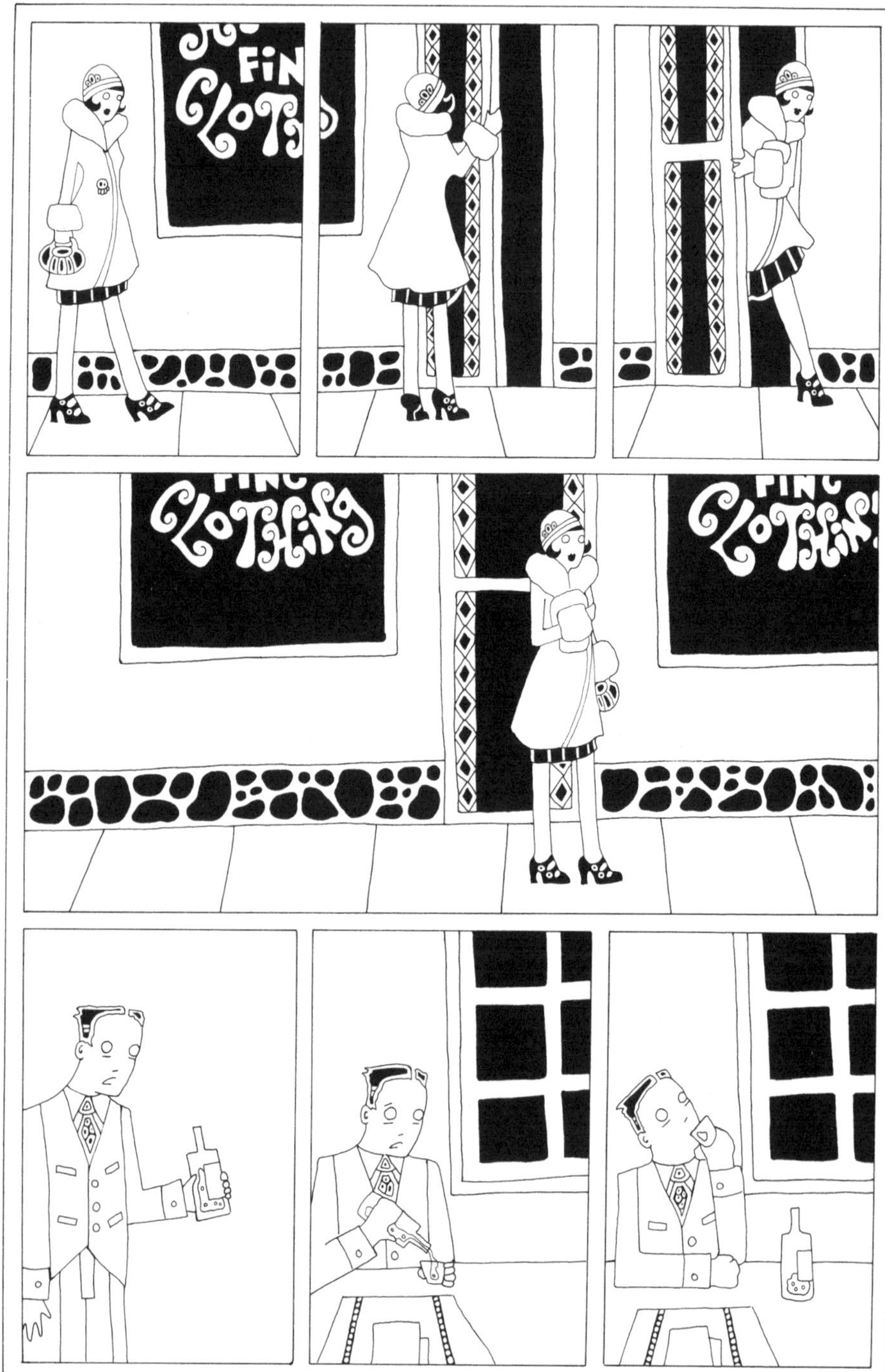
CLOTHING

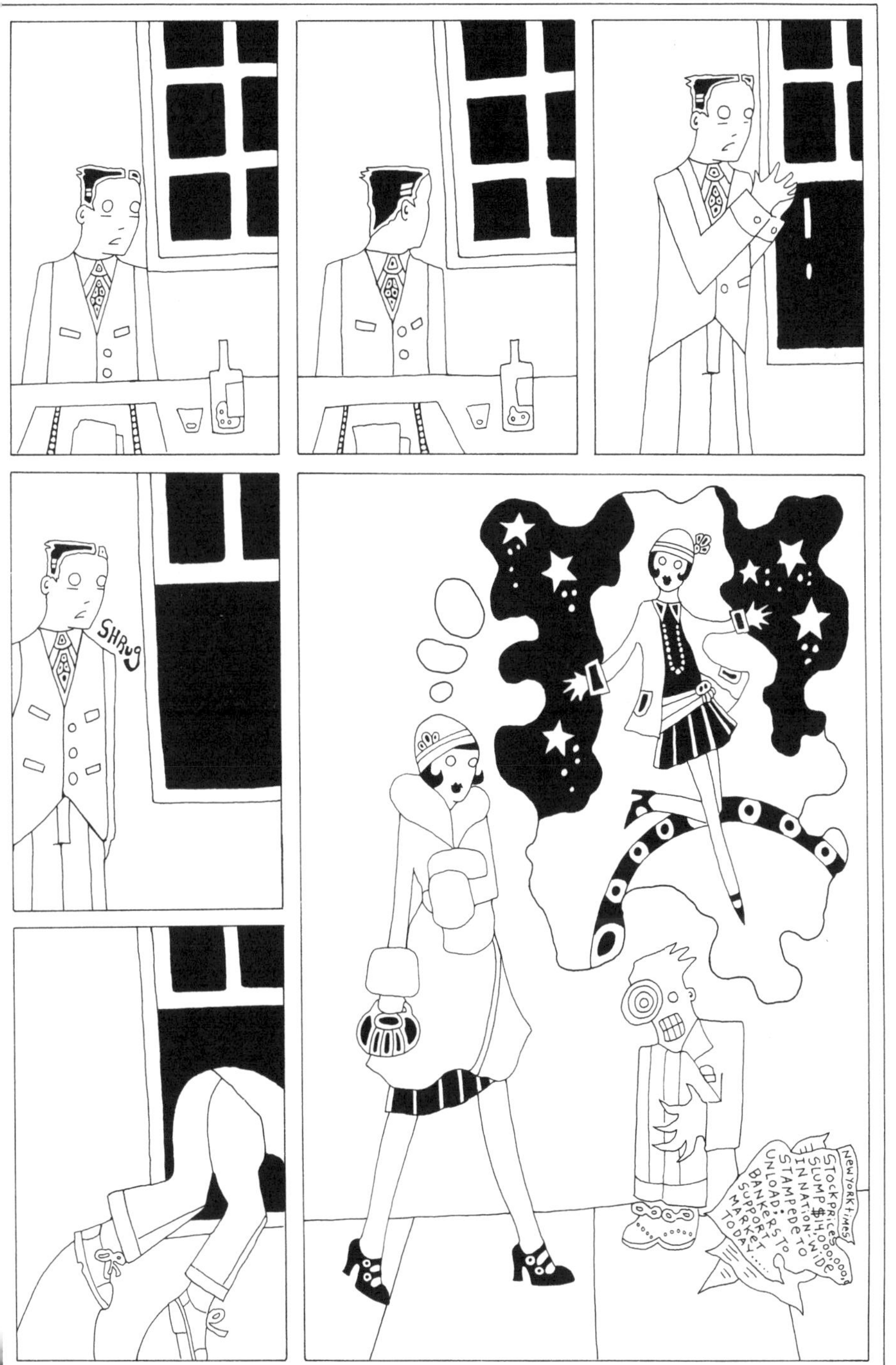
SHRUG
NEW YORK times
STOCK PRICES SLUMP $14,000,000,000 IN NATION-WIDE STAMPEDE TO UNLOAD; BANKERS TO SUPPORT MARKET TODAY.....

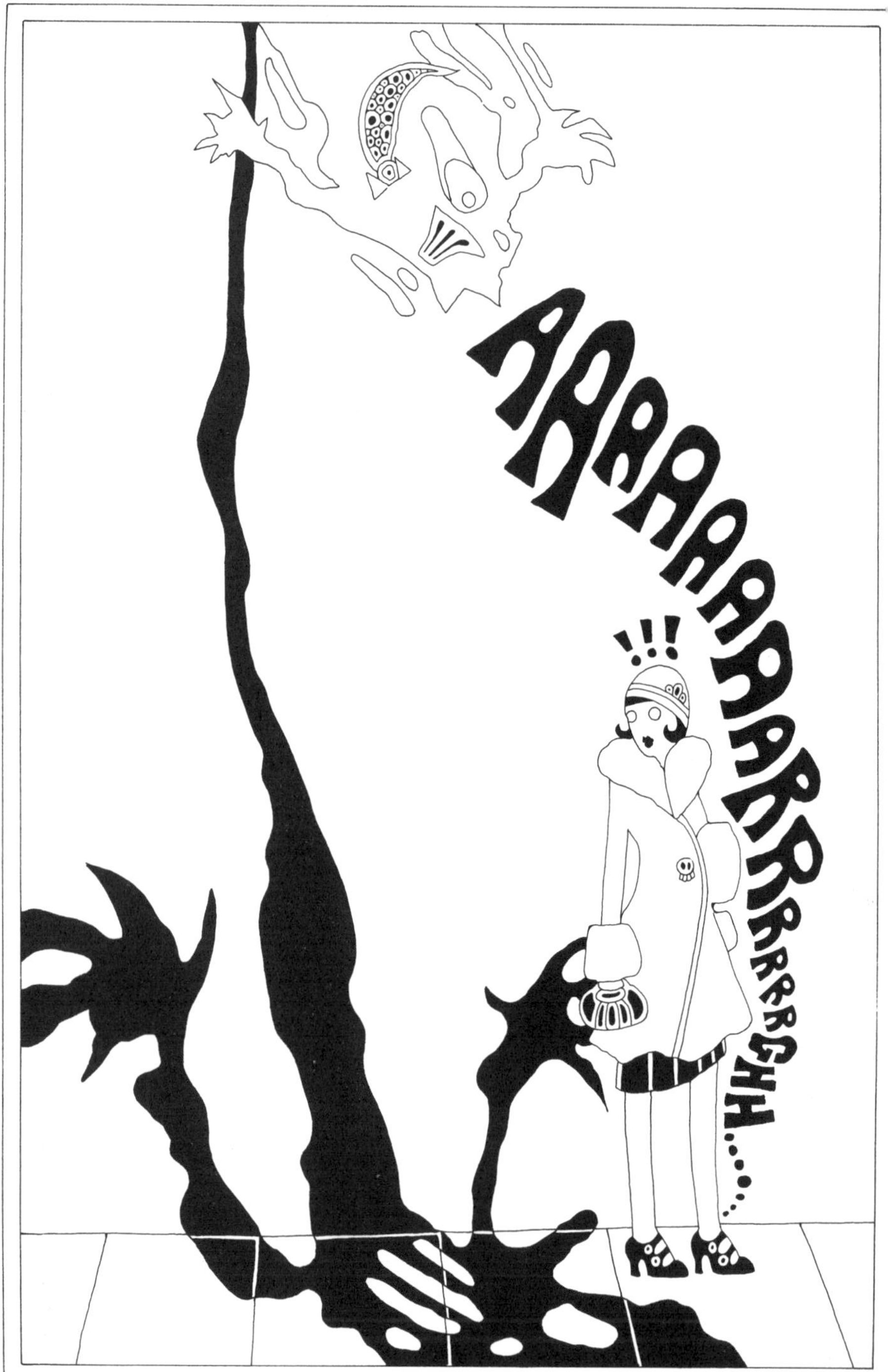
AAAAAAAAAARRRRRRGHH...
!!!

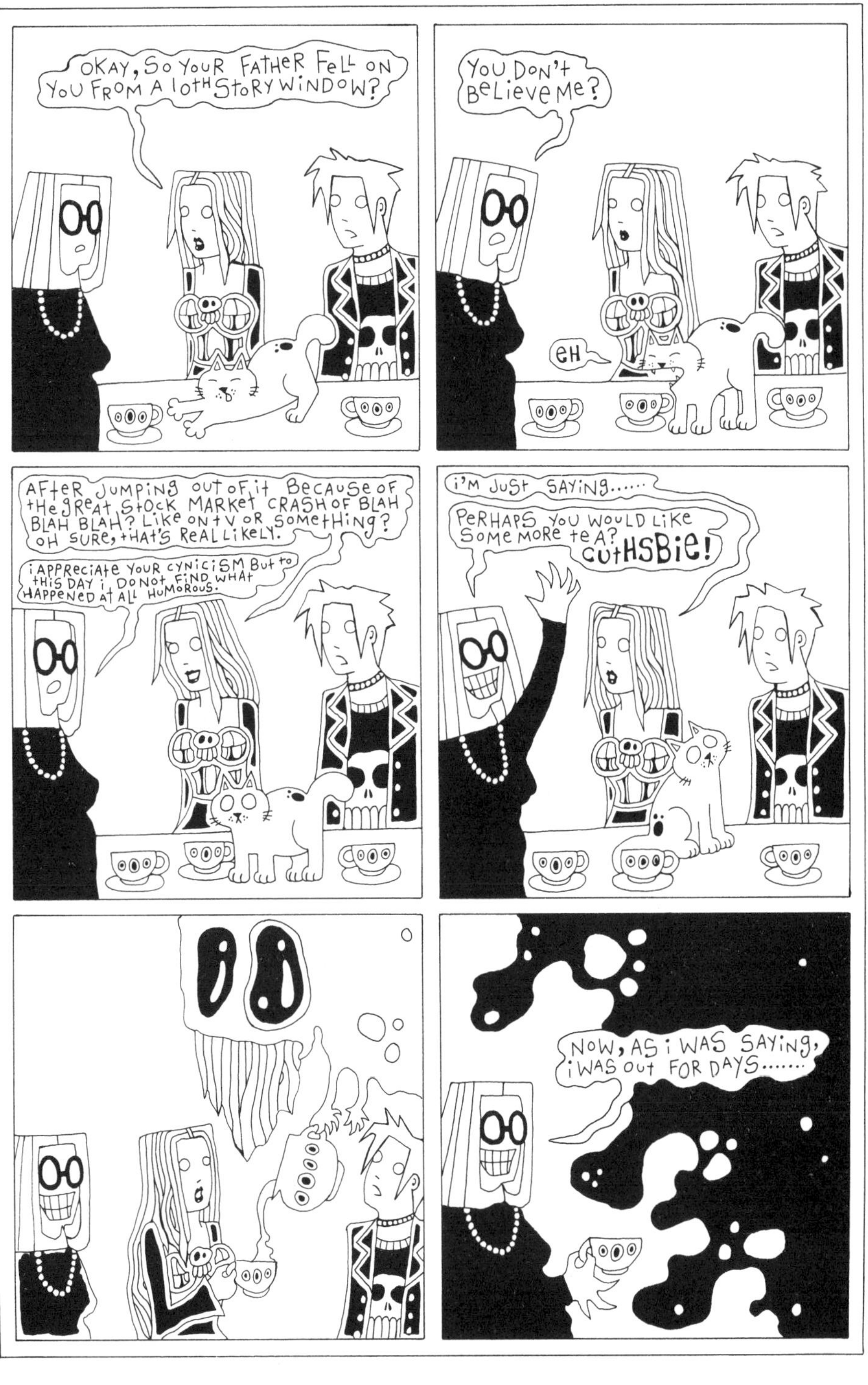
OKAY, SO YOUR FATHER FELL ON YOU FROM A 10th STORY WINDOW?
YOU DON'T BELIEVE ME?
EH
AFTER JUMPING OUT OF IT BECAUSE OF THE GREAT STOCK MARKET CRASH OF BLAH BLAH BLAH? LIKE ON TV OR SOMETHING? OH SURE, THAT'S REAL LIKELY.
I APPRECIATE YOUR CYNICISM BUT TO THIS DAY I DO NOT FIND WHAT HAPPENED AT ALL HUMOROUS.
I'M JUST SAYING......
PERHAPS YOU WOULD LIKE SOME MORE TEA? CUTHSBIE!
NOW, AS I WAS SAYING, I WAS OUT FOR DAYS.......

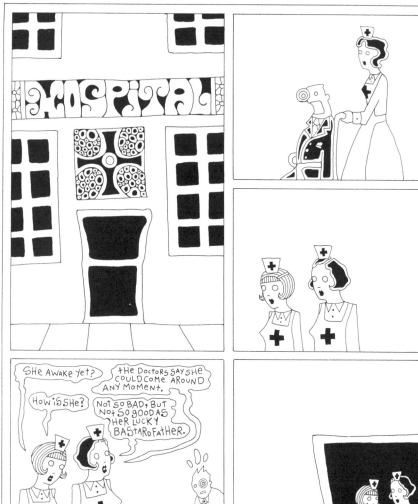

SHE AWAKE YET? tHE DOCTORS SAY SHE COULD COME AROUND ANY MOMENT.

How iS SHE? NOt SO BAD, BUt NOt SO GOOD AS HER LUCKY BASTARD FATHER.

AND HER EYES? OH HER ViSiON iS GONE, ALONG WiTH HER LOOKS.

BLiND, iS SHE? DAMN CLOSE.

Hope SHE tAKES it WELL.

13

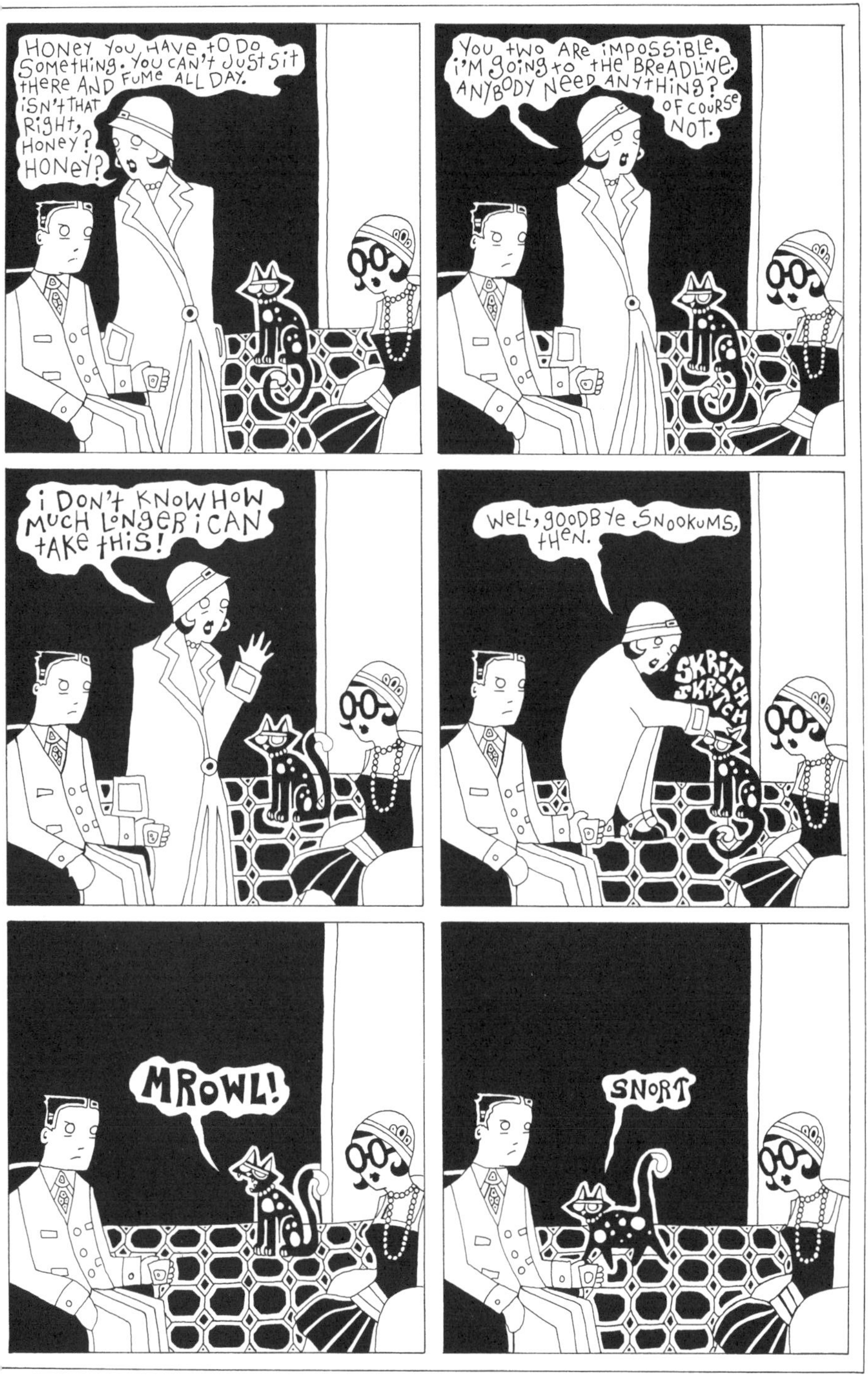
HONEY YOU HAVE TO DO SOMETHING. YOU CAN'T JUST SIT THERE AND FUME ALL DAY.
ISN'T THAT RIGHT, HONEY? HONEY?
YOU TWO ARE IMPOSSIBLE. I'M GOING TO THE BREADLINE. ANYBODY NEED ANYTHING?
OF COURSE NOT.
I DON'T KNOW HOW MUCH LONGER I CAN TAKE THIS!
WELL, GOODBYE SNOOKUMS, THEN.
SKRITCH SKRITCH
MROWL!
SNORT

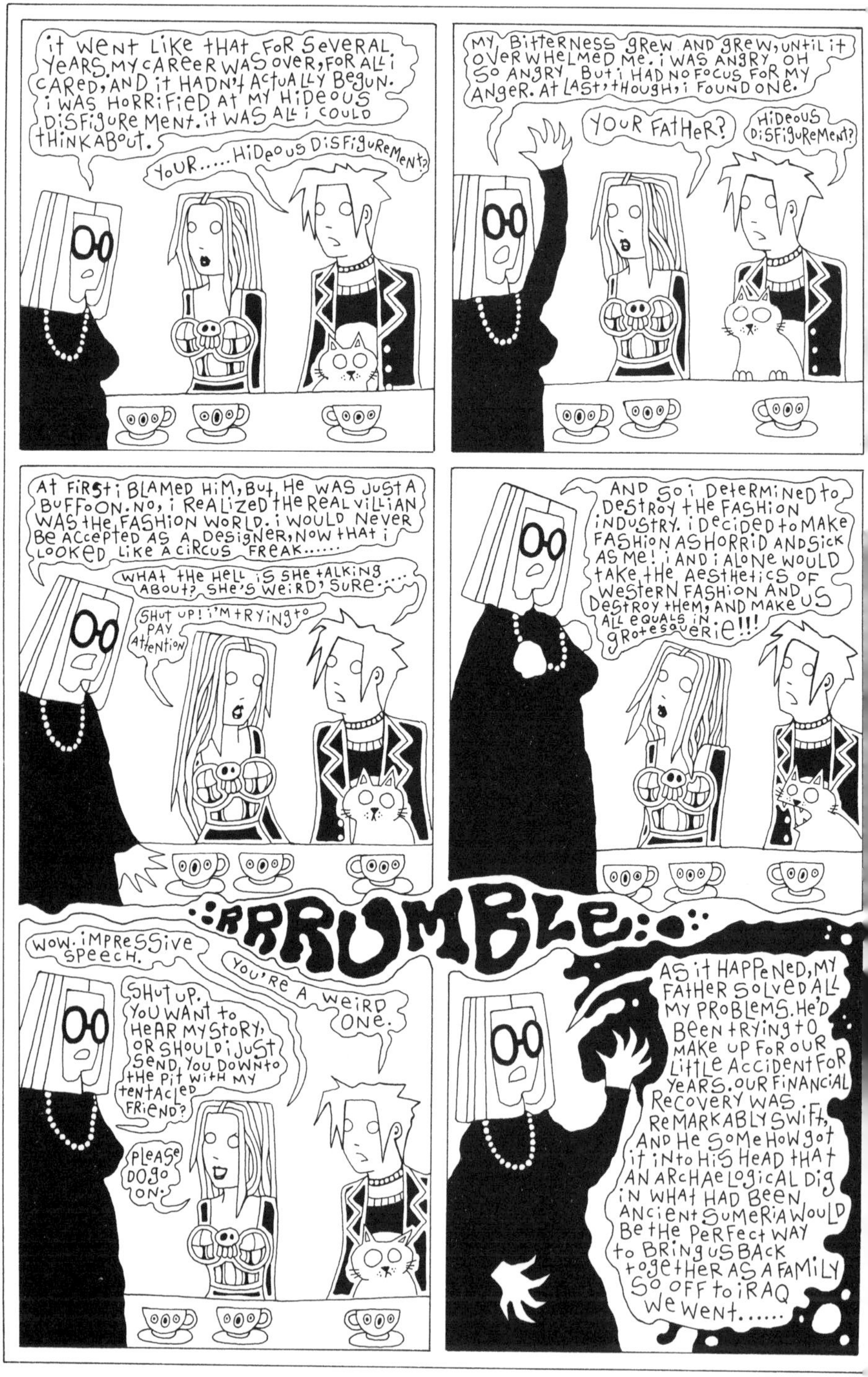
it went like that for several years. my career was over, for all i cared, and it hadn't actually begun. i was horrified at my hideous disfigurement. it was all i could think about.
Your..... hideous disfigurement?
My bitterness grew and grew, until it overwhelmed me. i was angry, oh so angry. But i had no focus for my anger. At last, though, i found one.
Your father?
Hideous disfigurement?
At first i blamed him, but he was just a buffoon. No, i realized the real villian was the fashion world. i would never be accepted as a designer, now that i looked like a circus freak......
What the hell is she talking about? She's weird, sure.....
Shut up! i'm trying to pay attention
And so i determined to destroy the fashion industry. i decided to make fashion as horrid and sick as me! i and i alone would take the aesthetics of western fashion and destroy them, and make us all equals in grotesquerie!!!
RRRUMBLE
Wow. impressive speech.
You're a weird one.
Shut up. You want to hear my story, or should i just send you down to the pit with my tentacled friend?
Please do go on.
As it happened, my father solved all my problems. He'd been trying to make up for our little accident for years. Our financial recovery was remarkably swift, and he somehow got it into his head that an archaelogical dig in what had been ancient Sumeria would be the perfect way to bring us back together as a family. So off to iraq we went.....

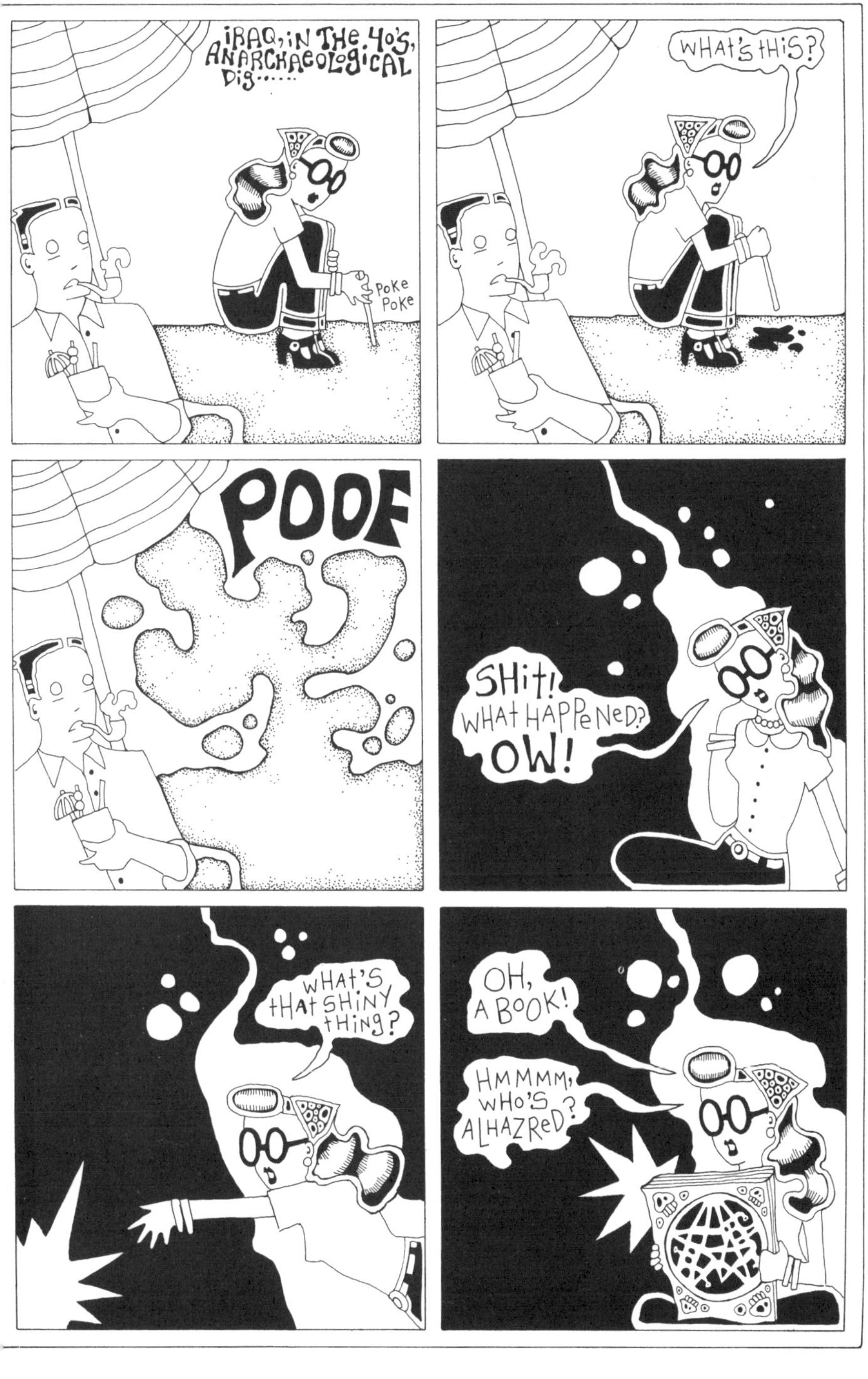
IRAQ, IN THE 40'S, AN ARCHAEOLOGICAL DIG......
POKE POKE
WHAT'S THIS?
POOF
SHIT! WHAT HAPPENED? OW!
WHAT'S THAT SHINY THING?
OH, A BOOK!
HMMMM, WHO'S ALHAZRED?

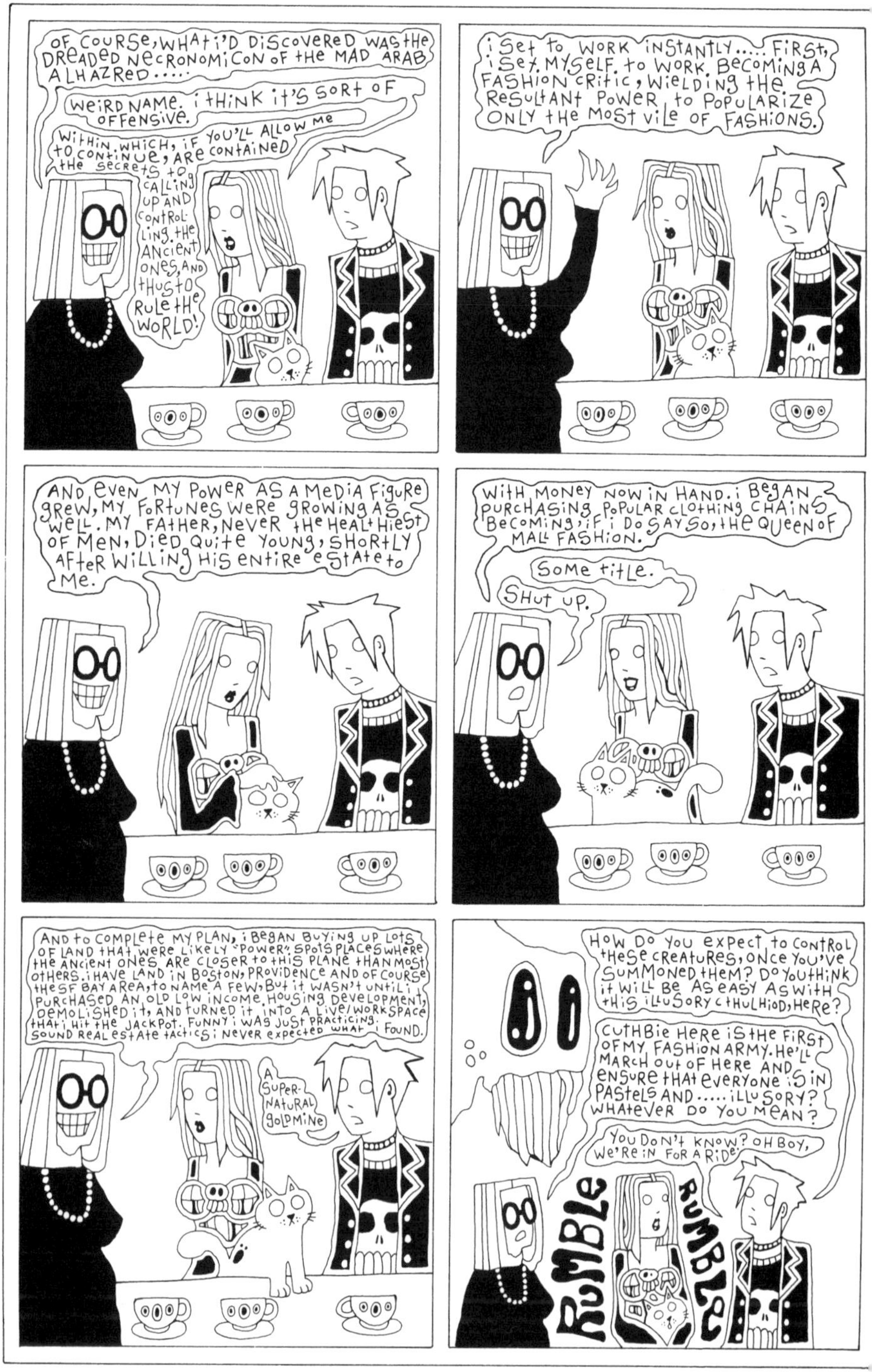
OF COURSE, WHAT I'D DISCOVERED WAS THE DREADED NECRONOMICON OF THE MAD ARAB ALHAZRED.....
WEIRD NAME. I THINK IT'S SORT OF OFFENSIVE.
WITHIN WHICH, IF YOU'LL ALLOW ME TO CONTINUE, ARE CONTAINED THE SECRETS TO CALLING UP AND CONTROLLING THE ANCIENT ONES, AND THUS TO RULE THE WORLD!
I SET TO WORK INSTANTLY..... FIRST, I SET MYSELF TO WORK BECOMING A FASHION CRITIC, WIELDING THE RESULTANT POWER TO POPULARIZE ONLY THE MOST VILE OF FASHIONS.
AND EVEN MY POWER AS A MEDIA FIGURE GREW, MY FORTUNES WERE GROWING AS WELL. MY FATHER, NEVER THE HEALTHIEST OF MEN, DIED QUITE YOUNG, SHORTLY AFTER WILLING HIS ENTIRE ESTATE TO ME.
WITH MONEY NOW IN HAND, I BEGAN PURCHASING POPULAR CLOTHING CHAINS BECOMING, IF I DO SAY SO, THE QUEEN OF MALL FASHION.
SOME TITLE.
SHUT UP.
AND TO COMPLETE MY PLAN, I BEGAN BUYING UP LOTS OF LAND THAT WERE LIKELY "POWER" SPOTS PLACES WHERE THE ANCIENT ONES ARE CLOSER TO THIS PLANE THAN MOST OTHERS. I HAVE LAND IN BOSTON, PROVIDENCE AND OF COURSE THE SF BAY AREA, TO NAME A FEW, BUT IT WASN'T UNTIL I PURCHASED AN OLD LOW INCOME HOUSING DEVELOPMENT, DEMOLISHED IT, AND TURNED IT INTO A LIVE/WORKSPACE THAT I HIT THE JACKPOT. FUNNY I WAS JUST PRACTICING SOUND REAL ESTATE TACTICS; I NEVER EXPECTED WHAT I FOUND.
A SUPER-NATURAL GOLDMINE
HOW DO YOU EXPECT TO CONTROL THESE CREATURES, ONCE YOU'VE SUMMONED THEM? DO YOU THINK IT WILL BE AS EASY AS WITH THIS ILLUSORY CTHULHIOD, HERE?
CUTHBIE HERE IS THE FIRST OF MY FASHION ARMY. HE'LL MARCH OUT OF HERE AND ENSURE THAT EVERYONE IS IN PASTELS AND..... ILLUSORY? WHATEVER DO YOU MEAN?
YOU DON'T KNOW? OH BOY, WE'RE IN FOR A RIDE.
RUMBLE
RUMBLE

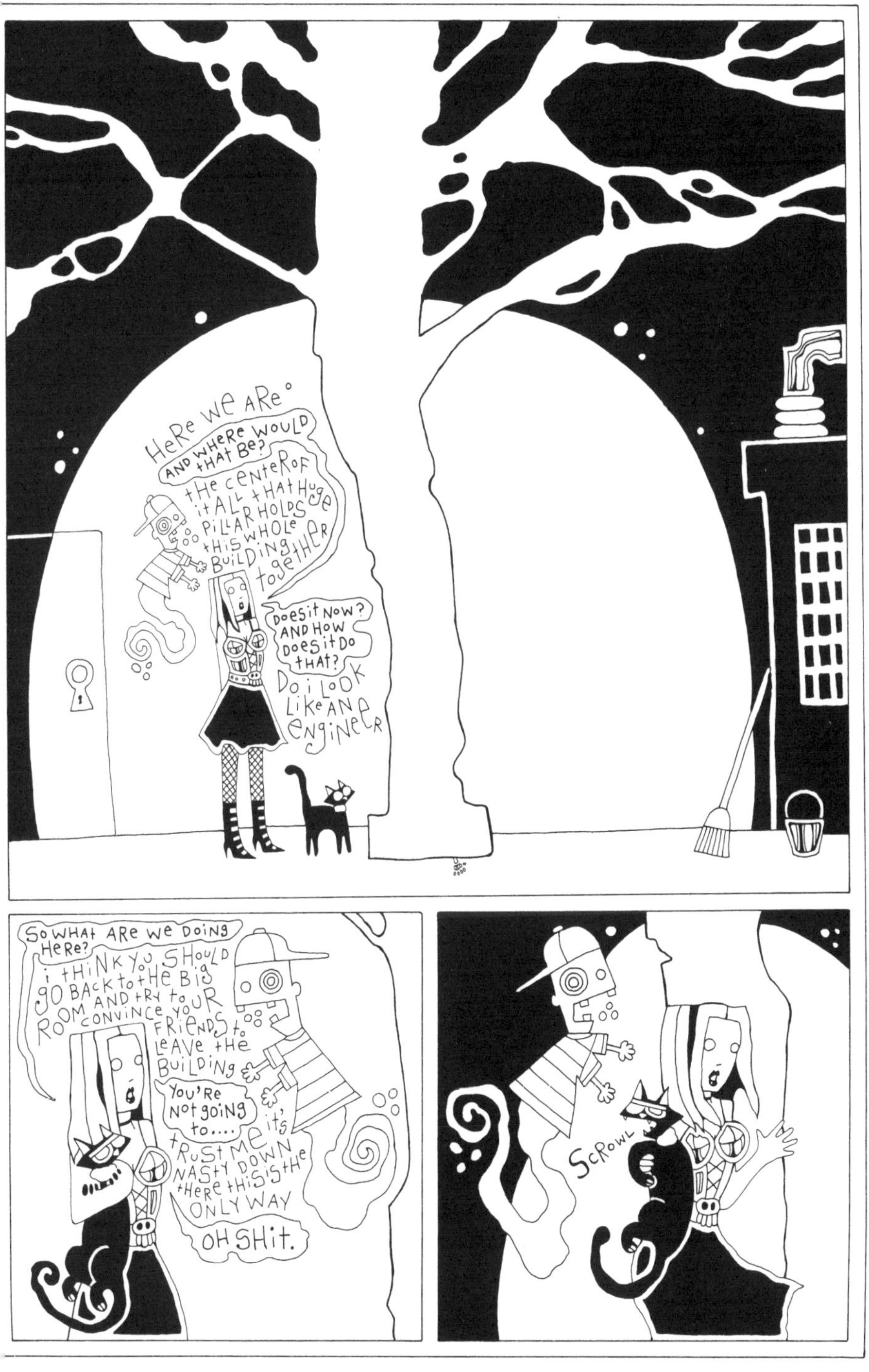
HeRe WE ARe.
AND WHERE WOULD tHAt Be?
tHe centeR of it ALL tHAt Huge PiLLAR HOLDS tHis WHOLe BuiLDing togetHeR
Does it Now? AND HOW Does it Do tHAt?
Do i Look Like AN engineeR
So WHAt ARe We DoiNg Here?
i tHiNK you SHouLD go BAck to tHe Big Room AND tRy to convince youR FRiENDS to LeAVe tHe BuiLDiNg
you'Re Not goiNg to....
tRust Me it's NASty DOWN tHere tHis is tHe ONLY WAY
OH SHit.
SCROWL

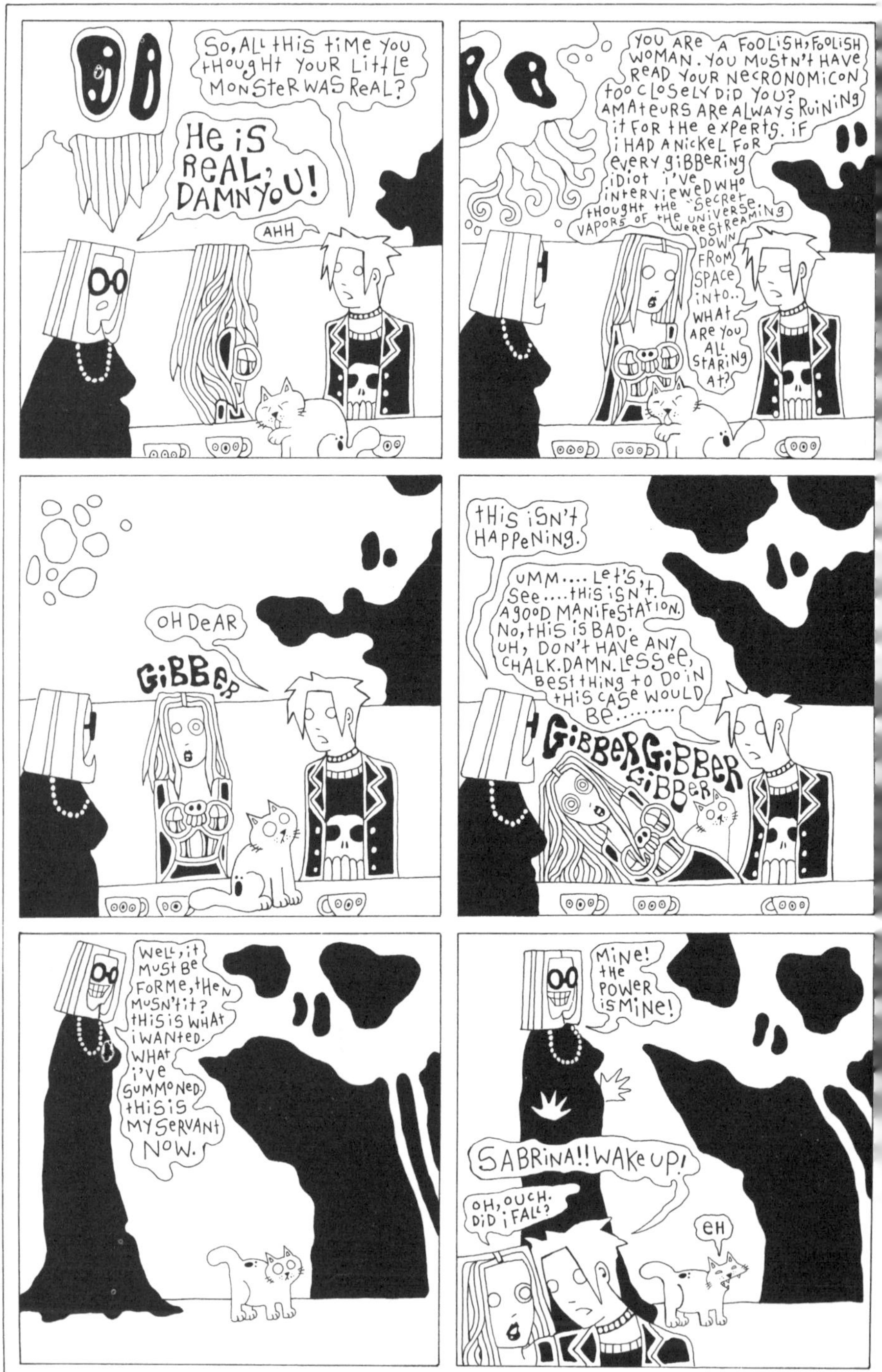
So, All this time you thought your Little Monster was Real?
He is Real, DAMN YoU!
AHH
You are a foolish, foolish woman. You mustn't have read your Necronomicon too closely did you? Amateurs are always ruining it for the experts. If i had a nickel for every gibbering idiot i've interviewed who thought the secret vapors of the universe were streaming down from space into.. what are you all staring at?
OH DeAR
GiBBeR
tHis iSn't HAPPeNiNg.
UMM.... Let's see.... this isn't. A good manifestation. No, this is bad. Uh, don't have any chalk. Damn. Lessee, best thing to do in this case would be.........
GiBBeR GiBBeR GiBBeR
Well, it must be for me, then mustn't it? This is what i wanted. What i've summoned. This is my servant now.
Mine! the power is mine!
SABRiNA!! WAKe UP!
OH, OUCH. DiD i FALL?
eH

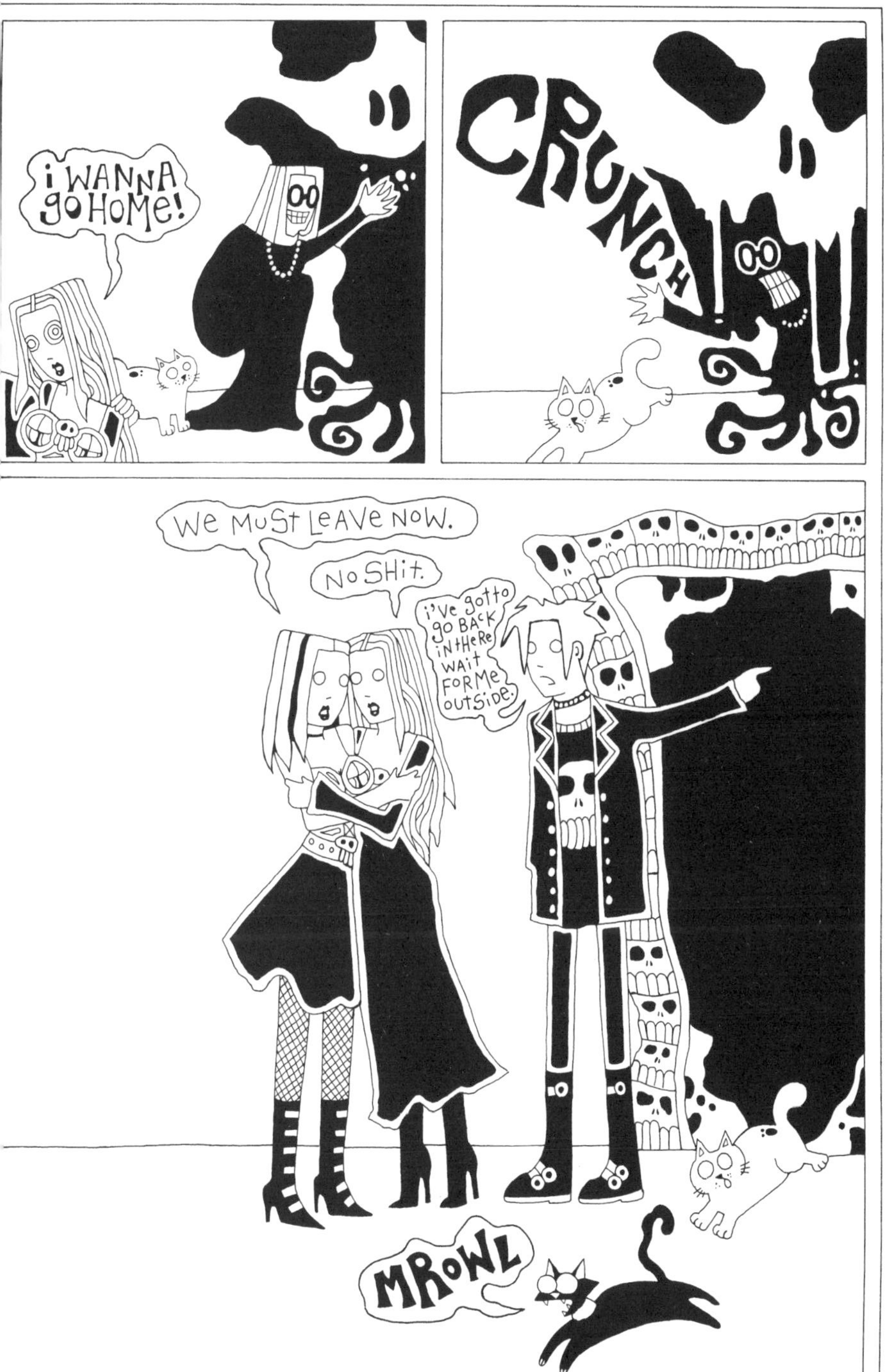
i WANNA go HoMe!
CRUNCH
We MuST LeAVe NOW.
No SHit.
i've gotto go BACK in tHeRe wait FoR Me outSiDe.
MRoWL

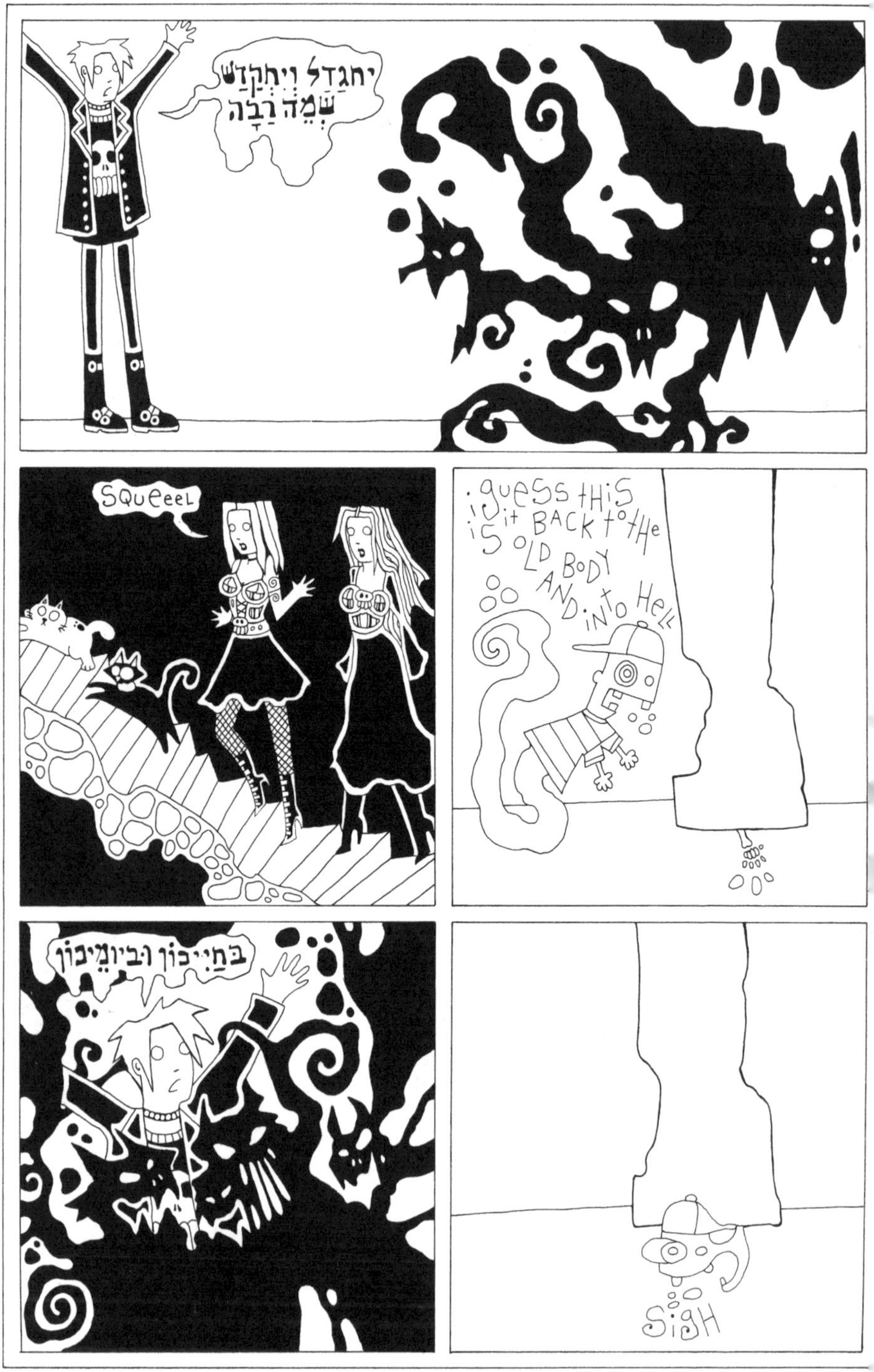
יתגדל ויתקדש שמה רבה
SQUeeeL
guess this is it BACK to the OLD BODY AND into Hell
בחייכון וביומיכון
SigH

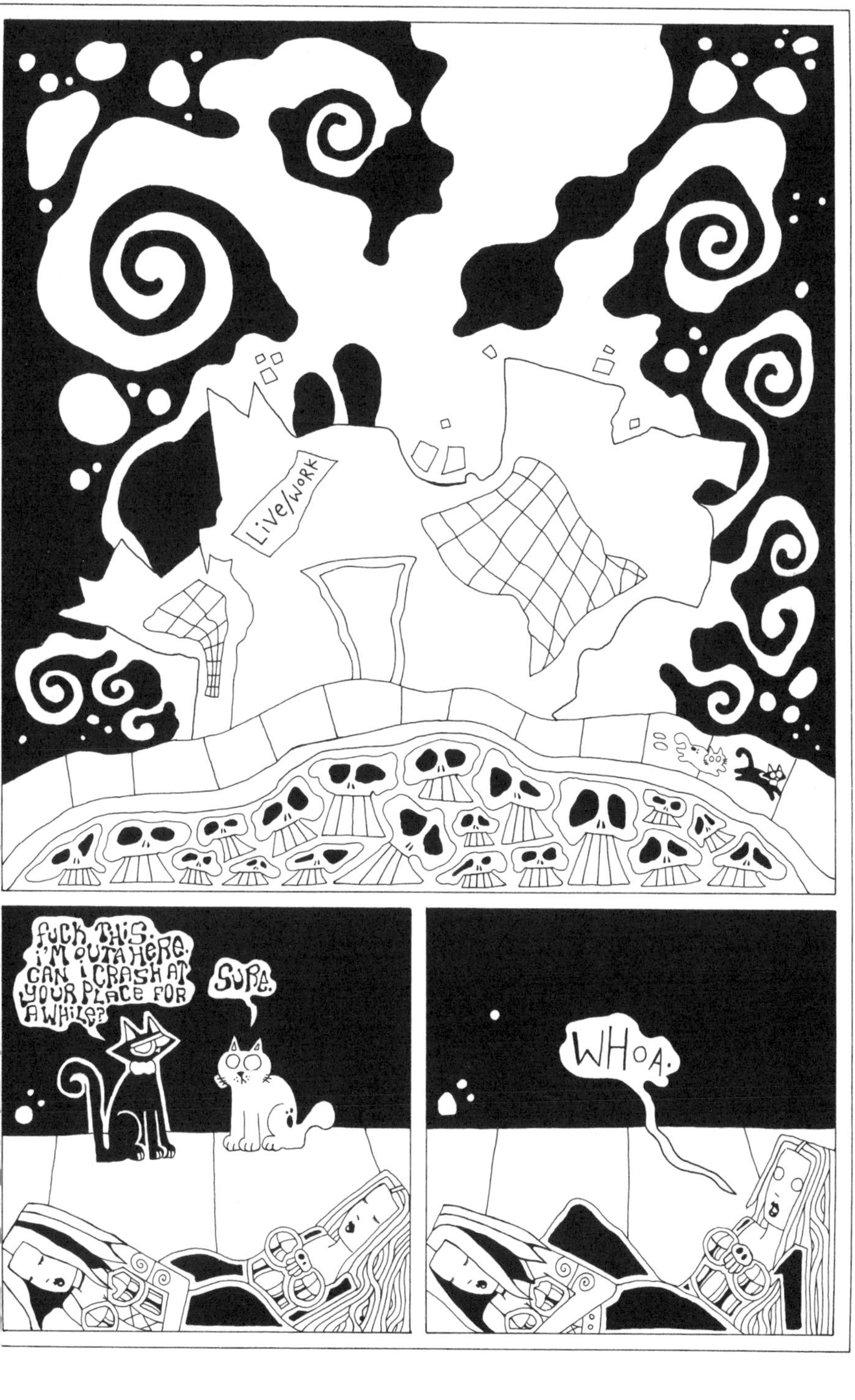
Live/WORK
FUCK THIS. I'M OUTA HERE. CAN I CRASH AT YOUR PLACE FOR A WHILE?
SURE.
WHOA.

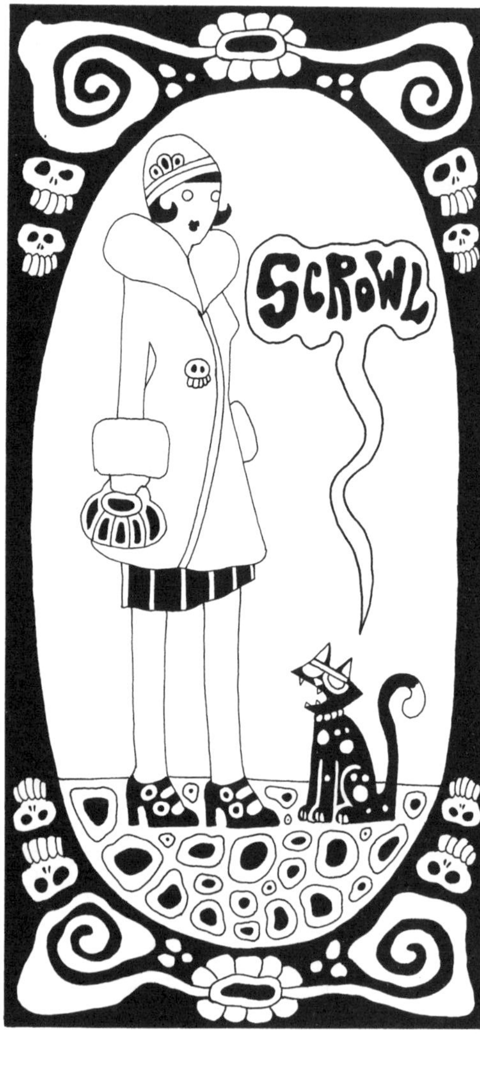
SCROWL

4

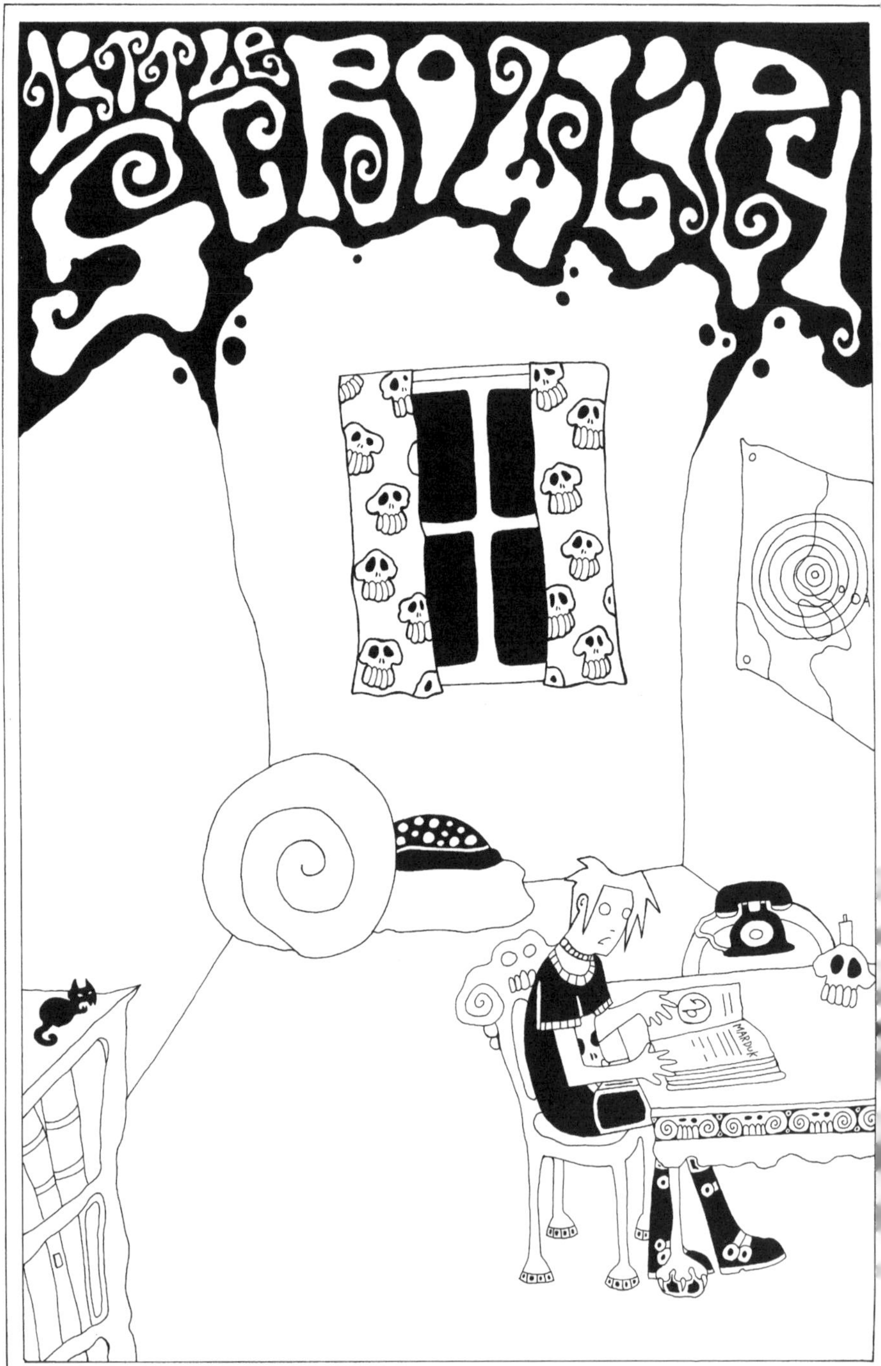
LITTLE
MARDUK

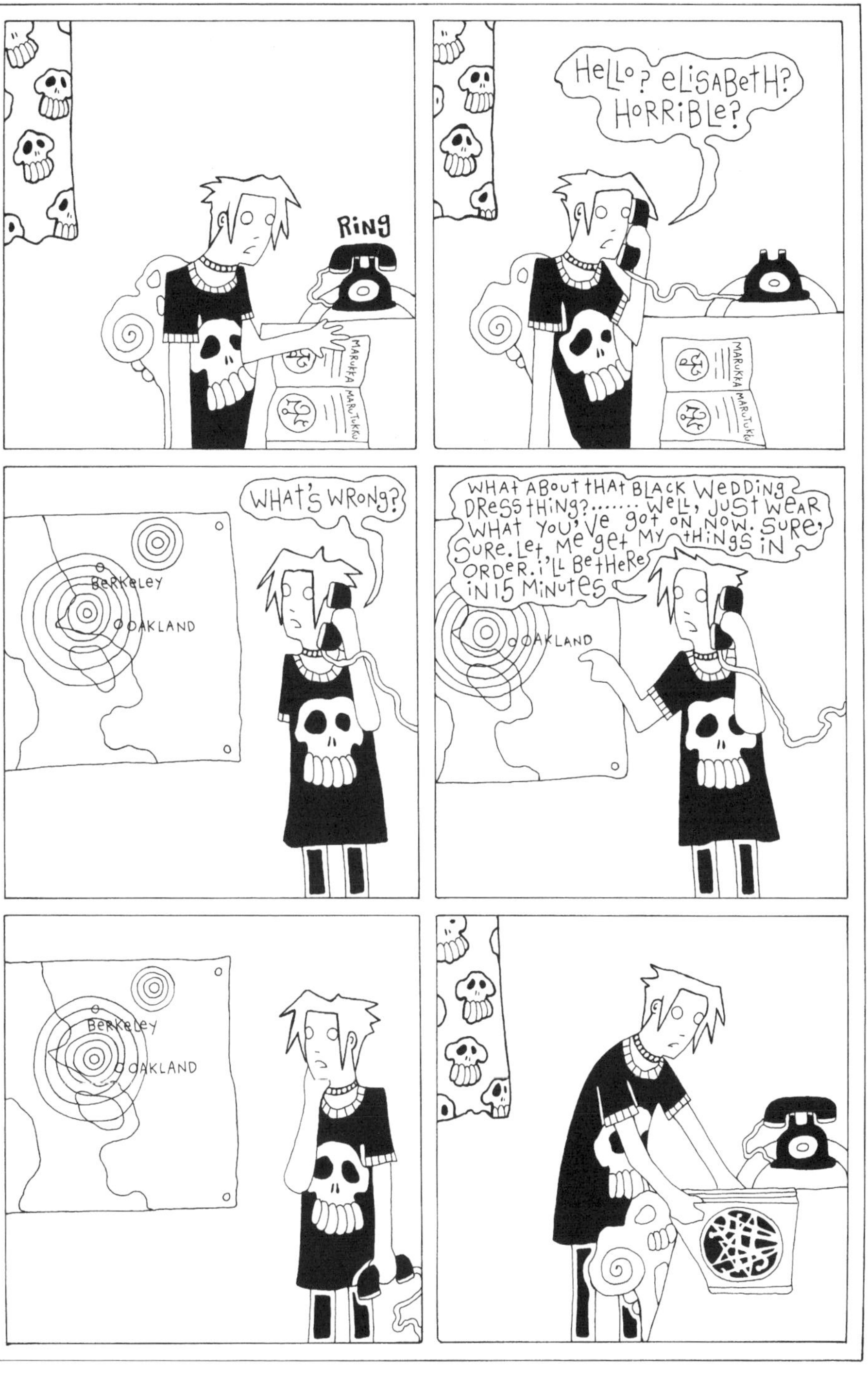
RING
MARUKKA
MARUTUKKU
HELLO? ELISABETH? HORRIBLE?
MARUKKA
MARUTUKKU
WHAT'S WRONG?
BERKELEY
OAKLAND
WHAT ABOUT THAT BLACK WEDDING DRESS THING?....... WELL, JUST WEAR WHAT YOU'VE GOT ON NOW. SURE, SURE. LET ME GET MY THINGS IN ORDER. I'LL BE THERE IN 15 MINUTES
OAKLAND
BERKELEY
OAKLAND

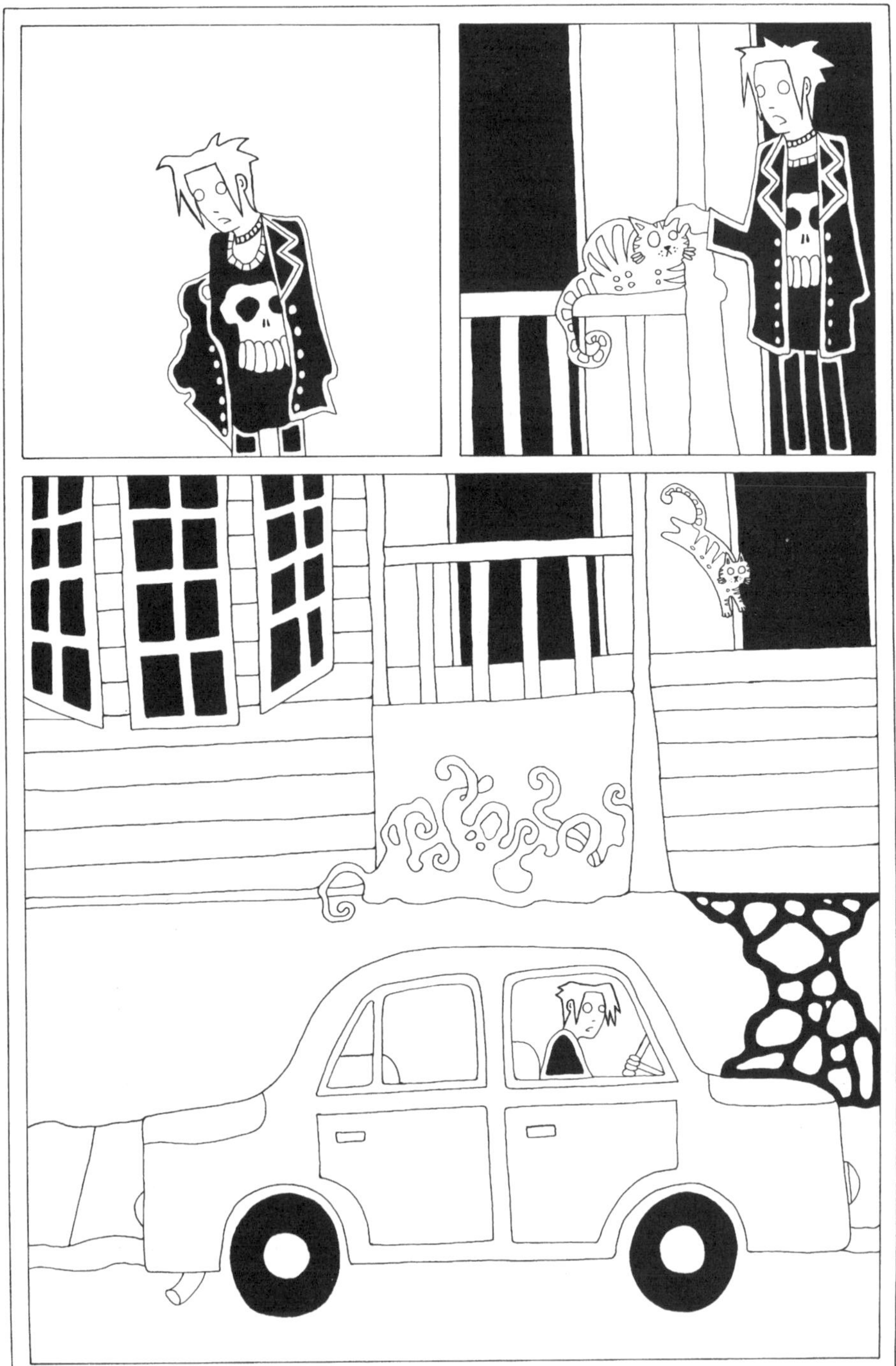

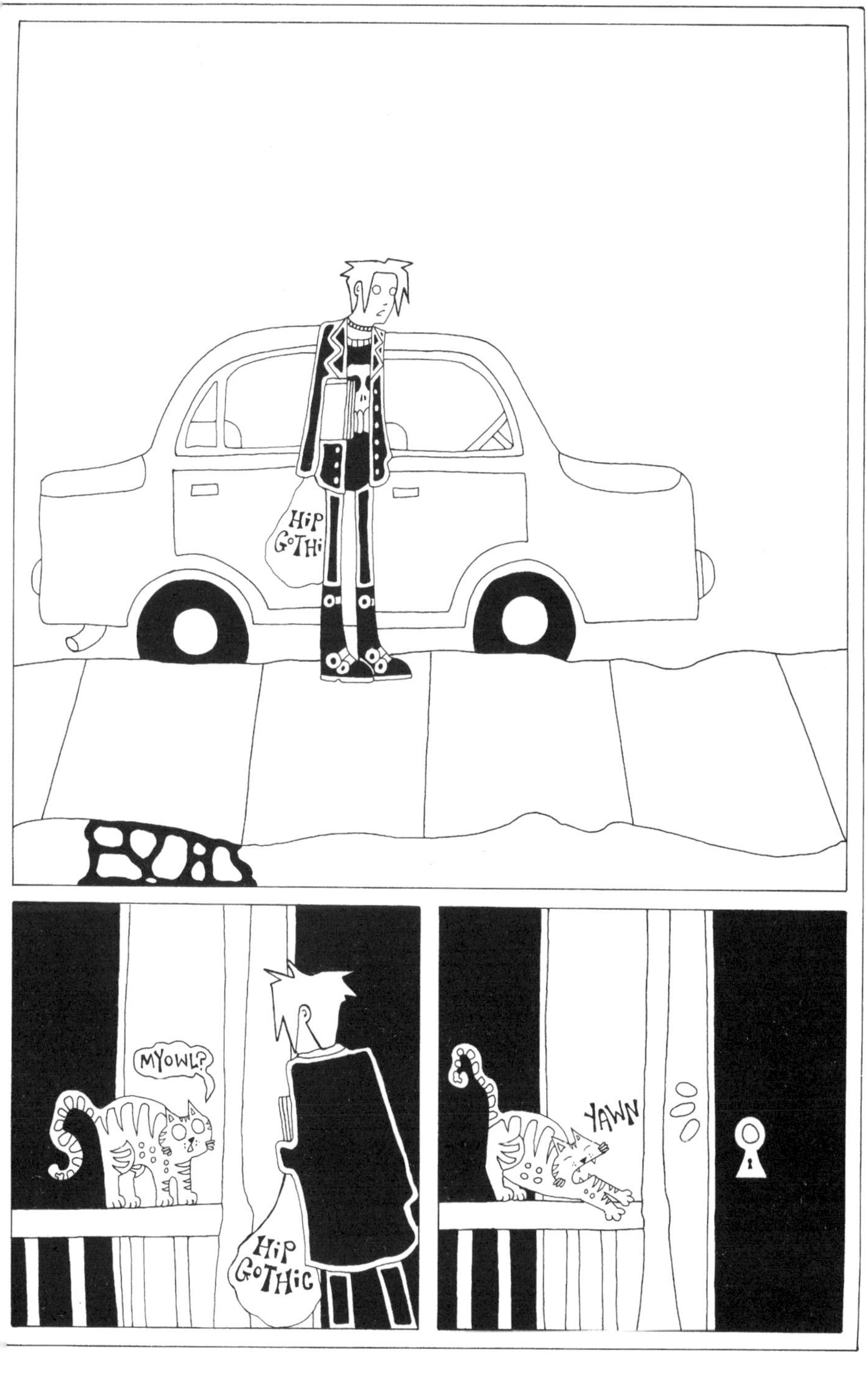
HIP GOTHI
MYOWL?
HIP GOTHIC
YAWN

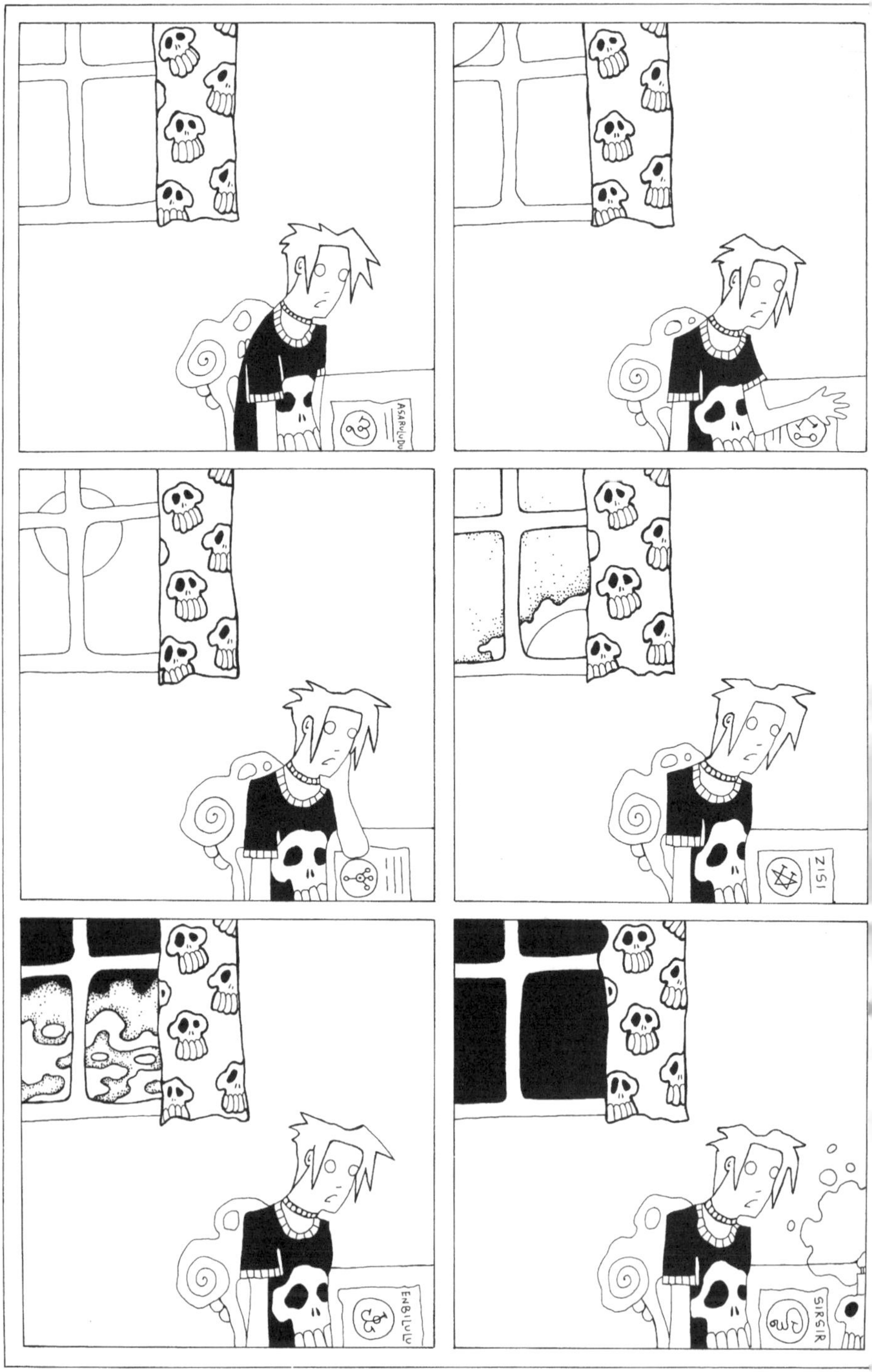
ASARULUDU
ZISI
ENBILULU
SIRSIR

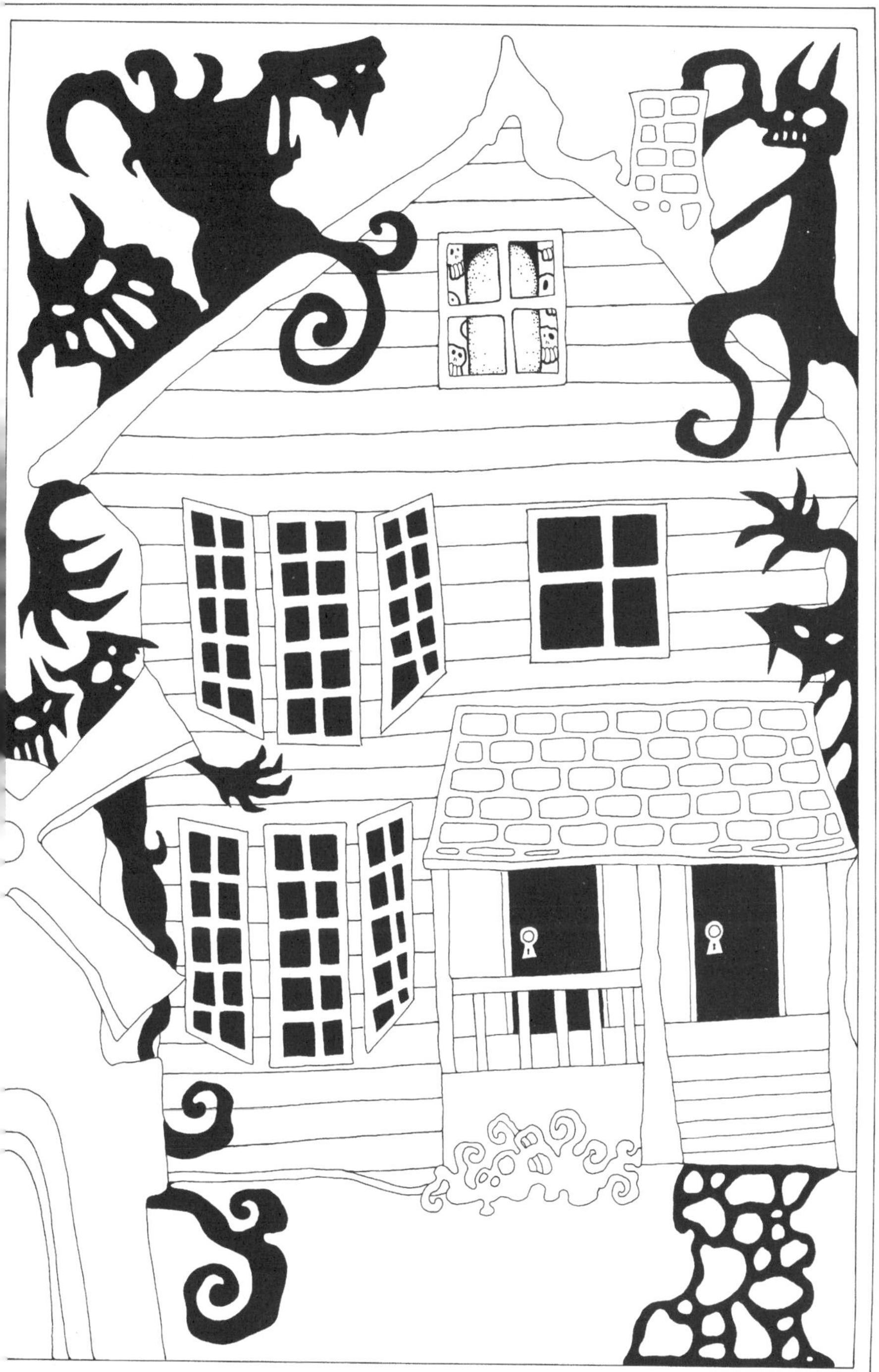

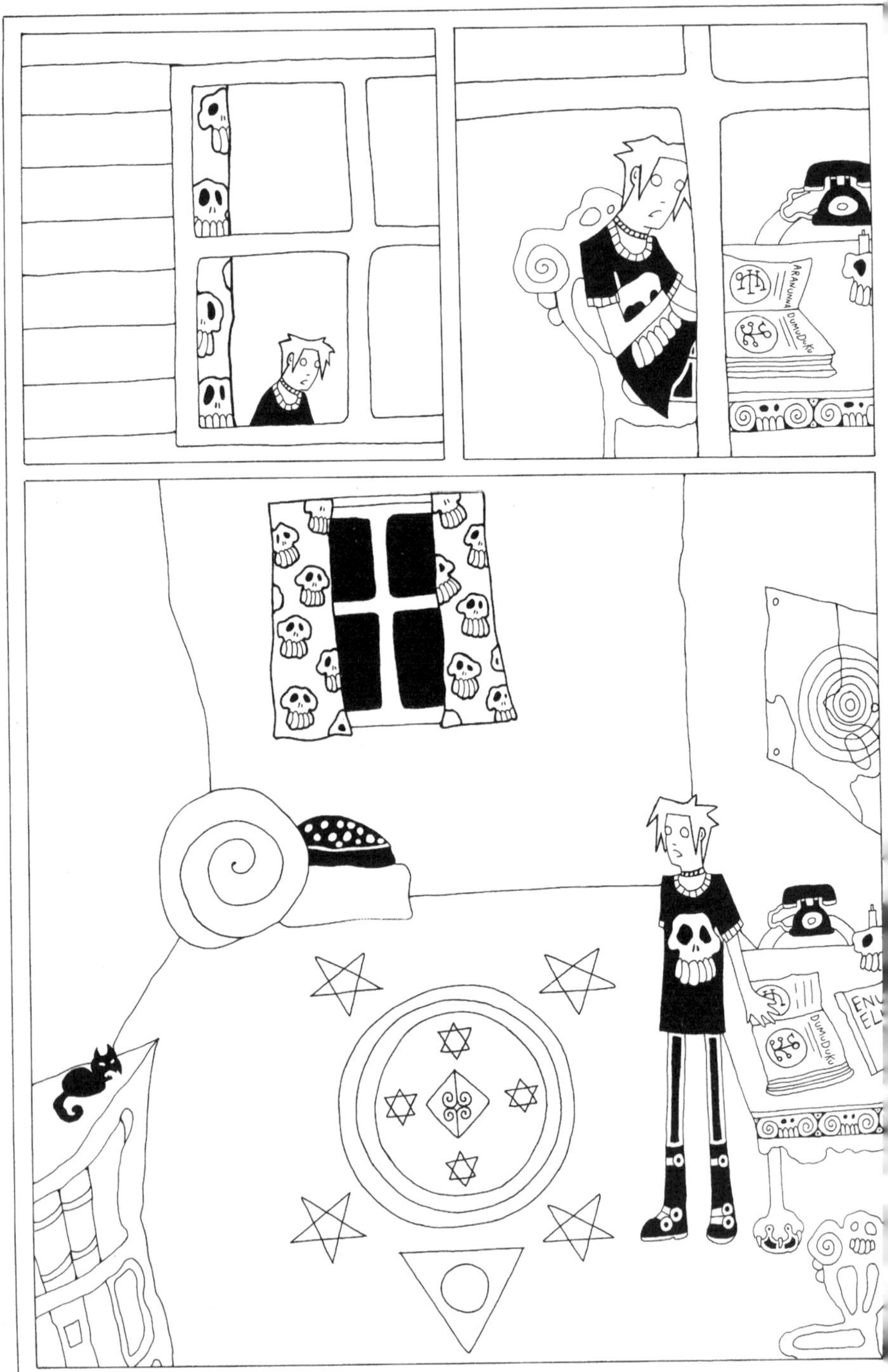
ARANUNNA
DUMUDUKU
DUMUDUKU

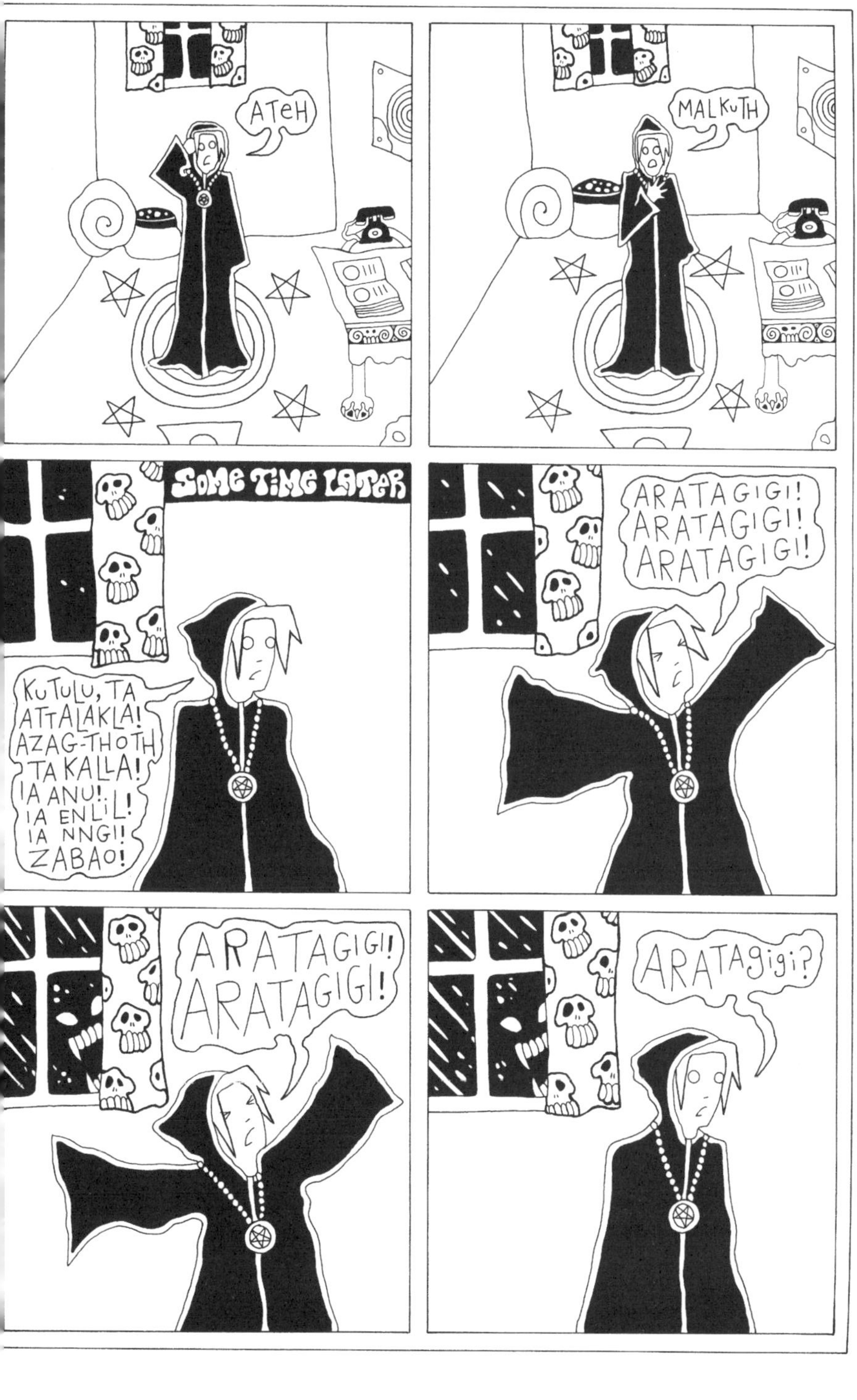
ATeH
MALKUTH
SOME TIME LATER
KUTULU, TA ATTALAKLA! AZAG-THOTH TA KALLA! IA ANU! IA ENLIL! IA NNGI! ZABAO!
ARATAGIGI! ARATAGIGI! ARATAGIGI!
ARATAGIGI! ARATAGIGI!
ARATAgigi?

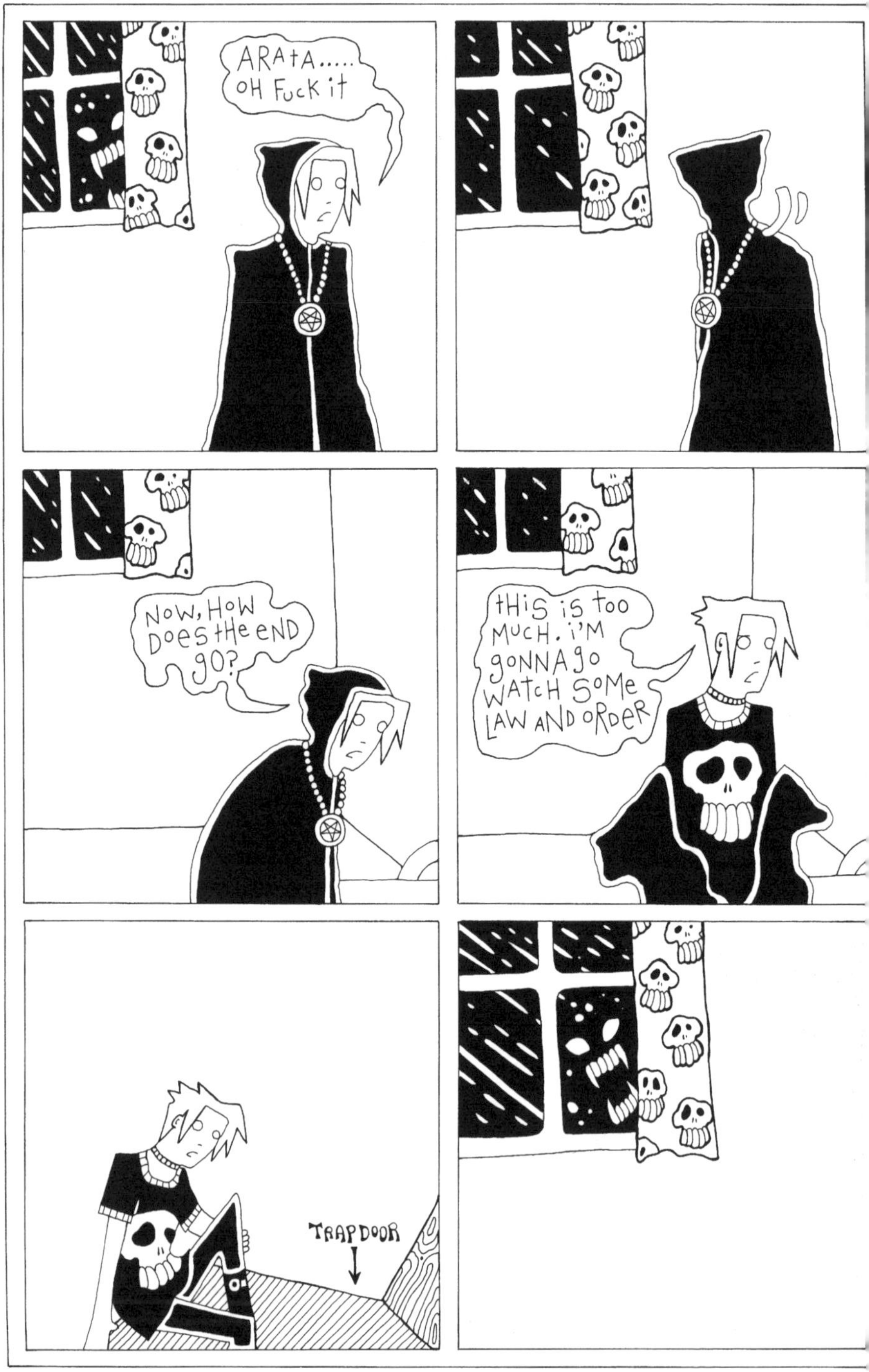
ARAtA.....
OH Fuck it
Now, How Does the END go?
this is too MUCH. i'M gonna go WATCH SOME LAW AND ORDER
TRAPDOOR

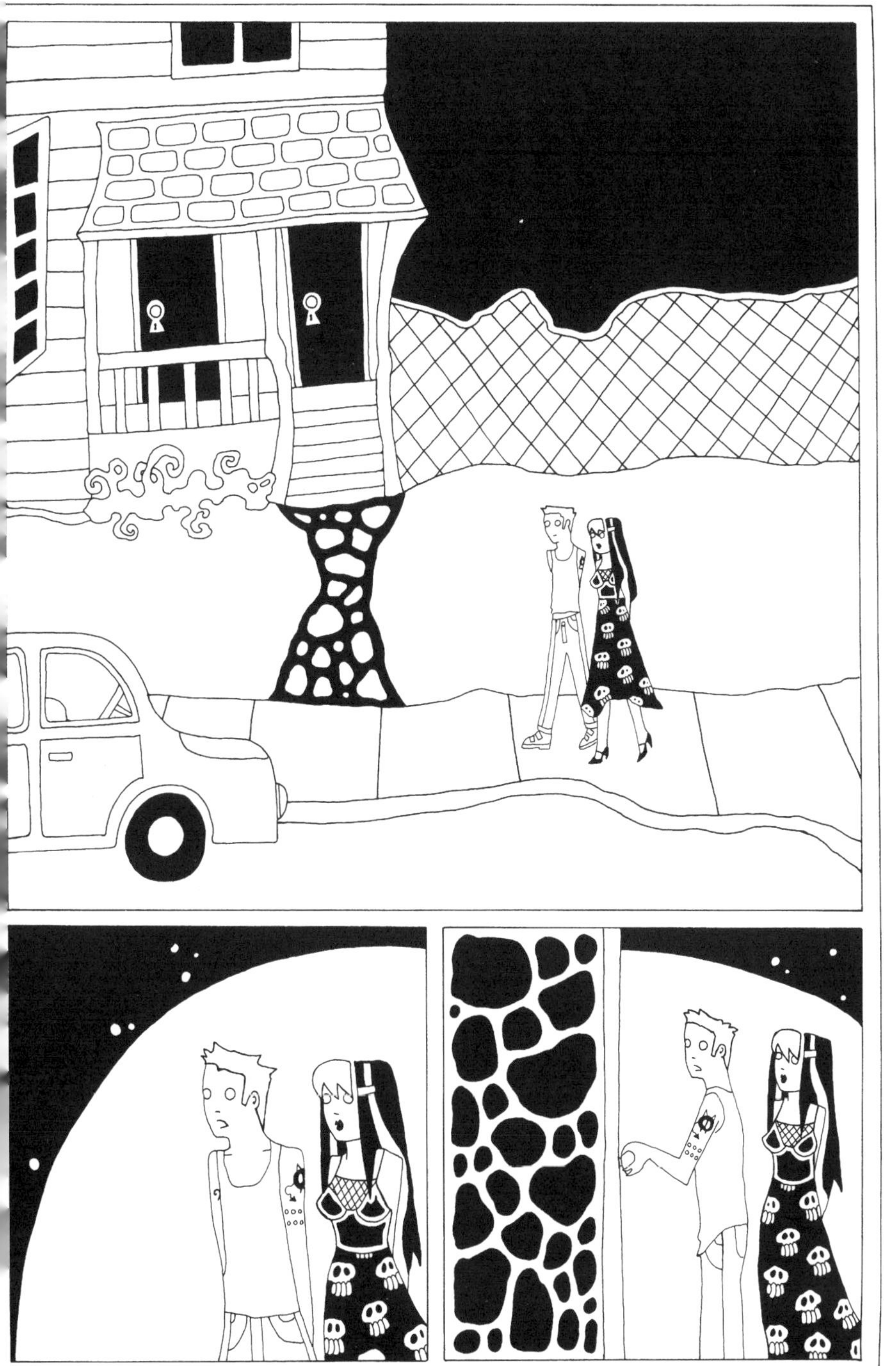

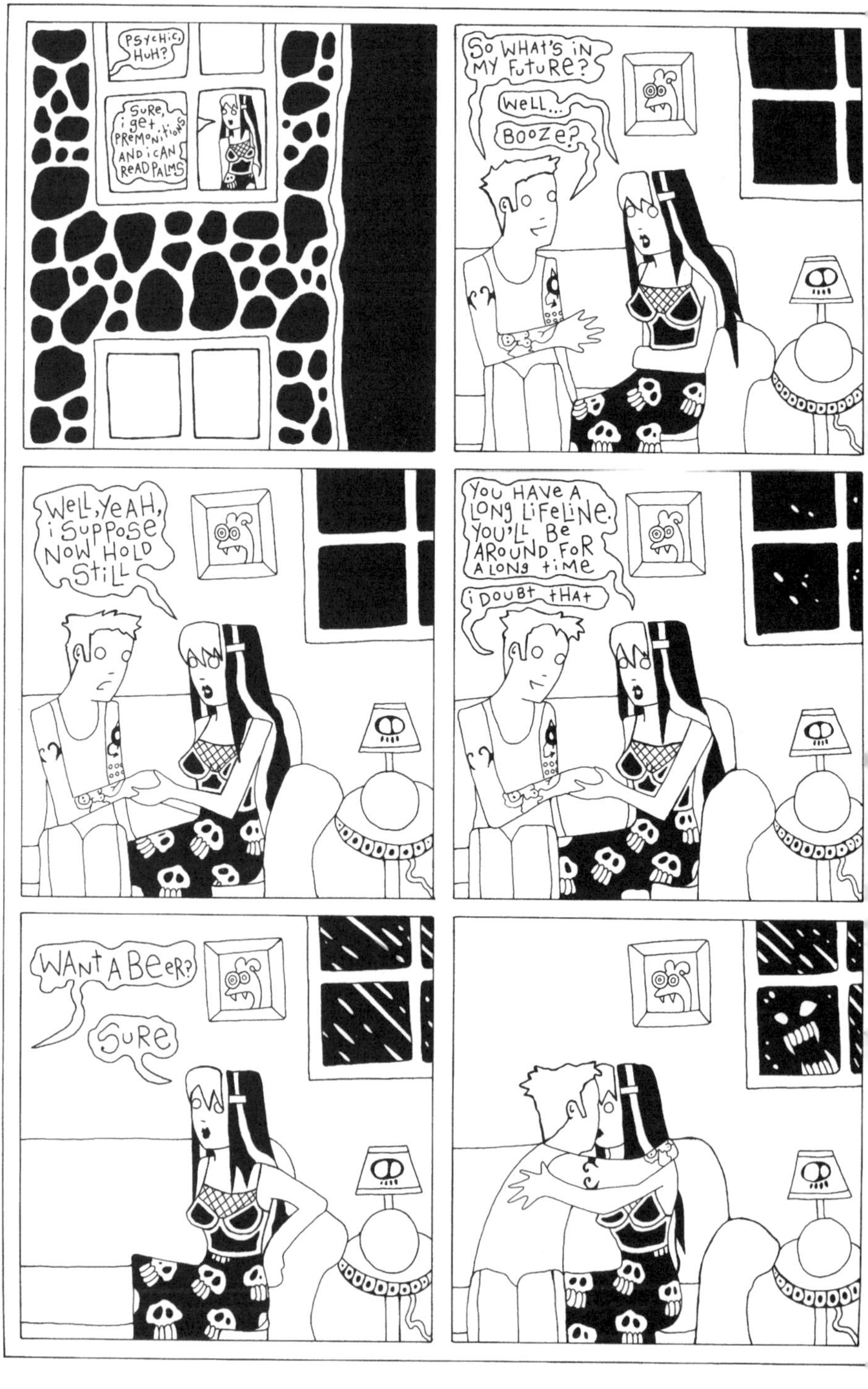
PSYCHIC, HUH?
SURE, i GET PREMONITIONS AND i CAN READ PALMS
SO WHAT'S IN MY FUTURE?
WELL...
BOOZE?
WELL, YEAH, i SUPPOSE NOW HOLD STILL
YOU HAVE A LONG LIFELINE. YOU'LL BE AROUND FOR A LONG TIME
i DOUBT THAT
WANT A BEER?
SURE

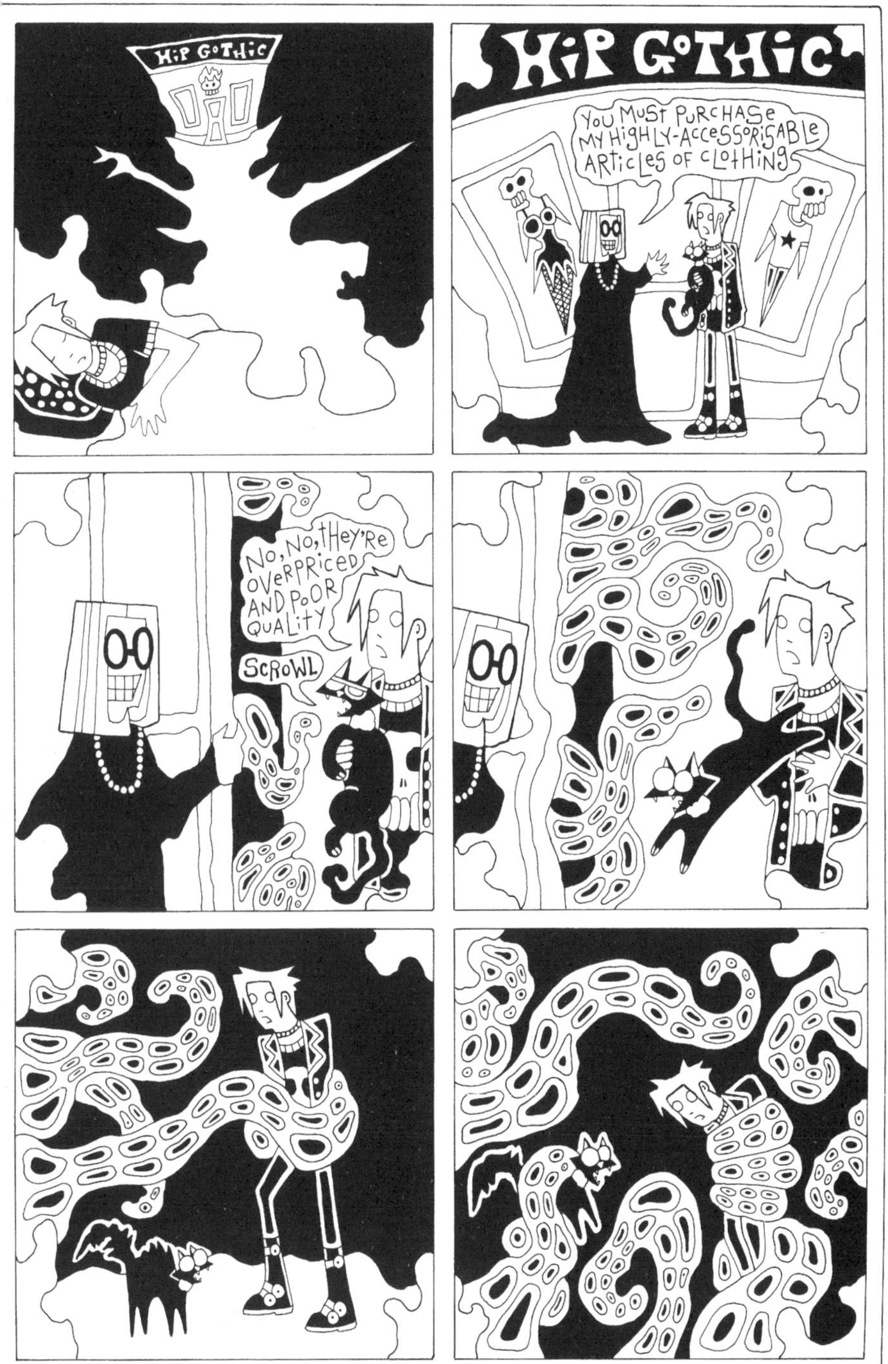
HiP GoTHic
HiP GoTHic
YOU MUST PURCHASE MY HIGHLY-ACCESSORISABLE ARTICLES OF CLOTHING
NO, NO, THEY'RE OVERPRICED AND POOR QUALITY
SCROWL

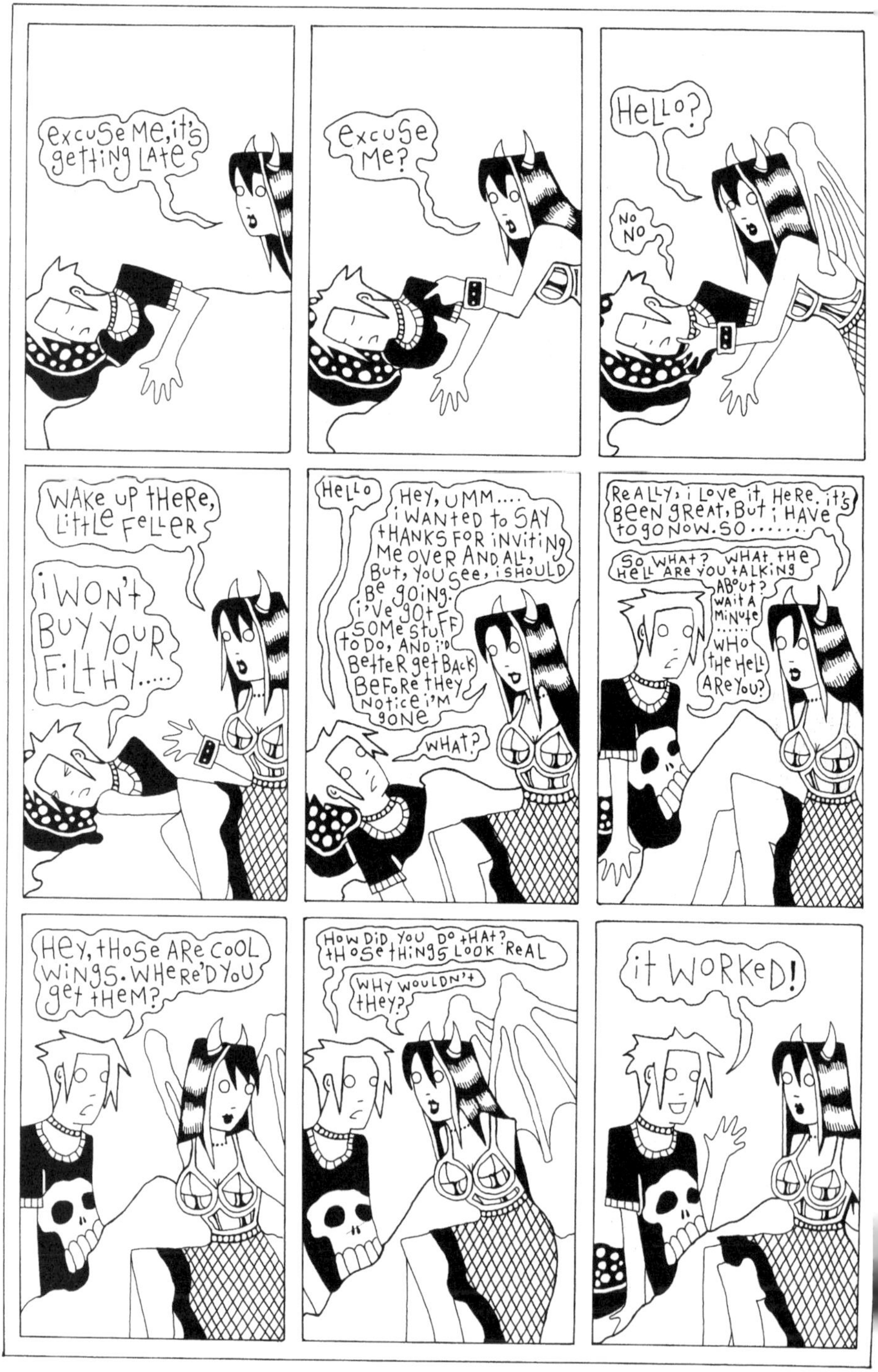

excuse Me, it's getting LATE
excuse Me?
HeLLo?
No No
WAKE UP tHeRe, LittLe FeLLeR
i WON't BUY YOUR FiLtHY.....
HeLLo
Hey, UMM.... i WANted to SAY tHANKS FOR iNViting Me OVER AND ALL, But, YOU See, i SHOULD Be going. i've got SOMe stuFF to DO, AND i'D BetteR get BACK BeFoRe tHey Notice i'M gone
WHAT?
ReALLY, i Love it Here. it's Been great, But i HAVe to go NOW. SO.......
So WHAT? WHAT tHe HeLL ARe YOU tALKiNg ABout? WAit A MiNute...... WHO tHe HeLL ARe You?
Hey, tHose ARe COOL WiNgS. WHeRe'D YOU get tHeM?
HOW DiD YOU DO tHAt? tHOSe tHiNgS LOOK ReAL
WHY WOULDN't tHey?
it WORKeD!

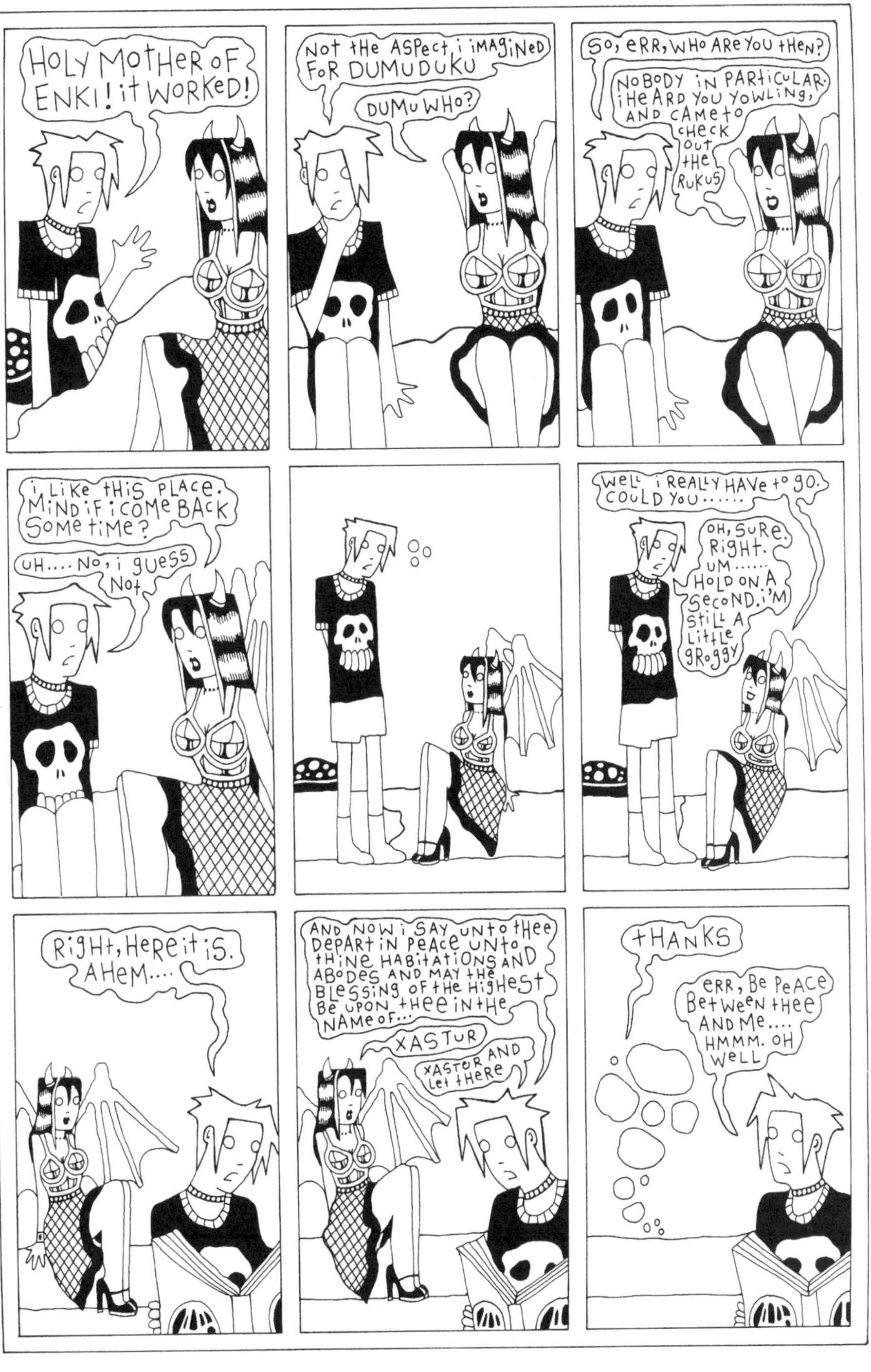
HOLY MOTHER OF ENKI! iT WORKED!
NOT THE ASPECT i IMAGINED FOR DUMUDUKU
DUMU WHO?
SO, ERR, WHO ARE YOU THEN?
NOBODY IN PARTICULAR. i HEARD YOU YOWLING, AND CAME TO CHECK OUT THE RUKUS
i LIKE THIS PLACE. MIND iF i COME BACK SOMETIME?
UH.... NO, i GUESS NOT
WELL i REALLY HAVE TO GO. COULD YOU......
OH, SURE. RIGHT. UM...... HOLD ON A SECOND. i'M STILL A LITTLE GROGGY
RIGHT, HERE iT iS. AHEM....
AND NOW i SAY UNTO THEE DEPART IN PEACE UNTO THINE HABITATIONS AND ABODES AND MAY THE BLESSING OF THE HIGHEST BE UPON THEE IN THE NAME OF...
XASTUR
XASTOR AND LET THERE
THANKS
ERR, BE PEACE BETWEEN THEE AND ME.... HMMM. OH WELL

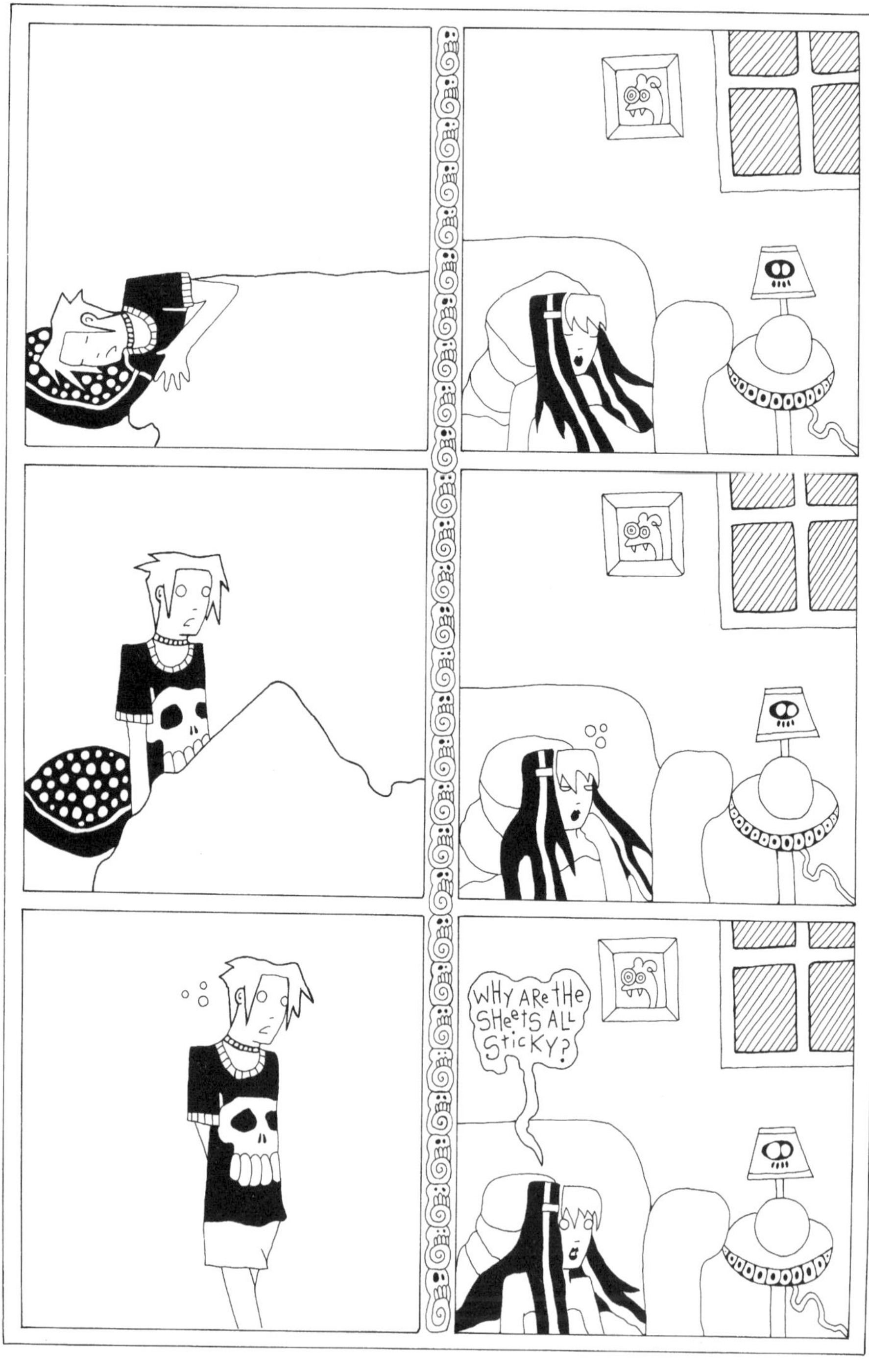
WHY ARE THE SHEETS ALL STICKY?

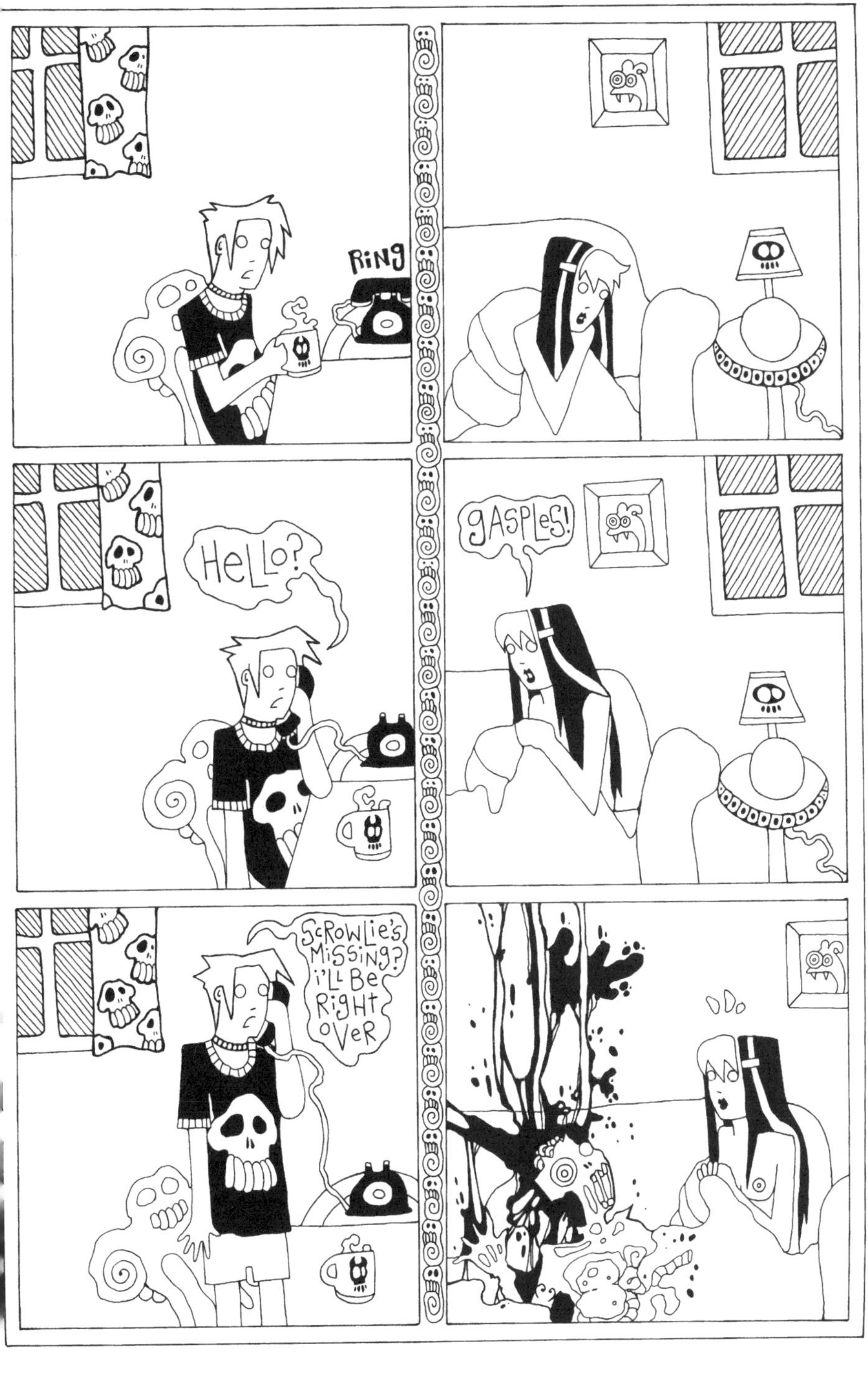
RING
HELLO?
GASPLES!
SCROWLIE'S MISSING? I'LL BE RIGHT OVER

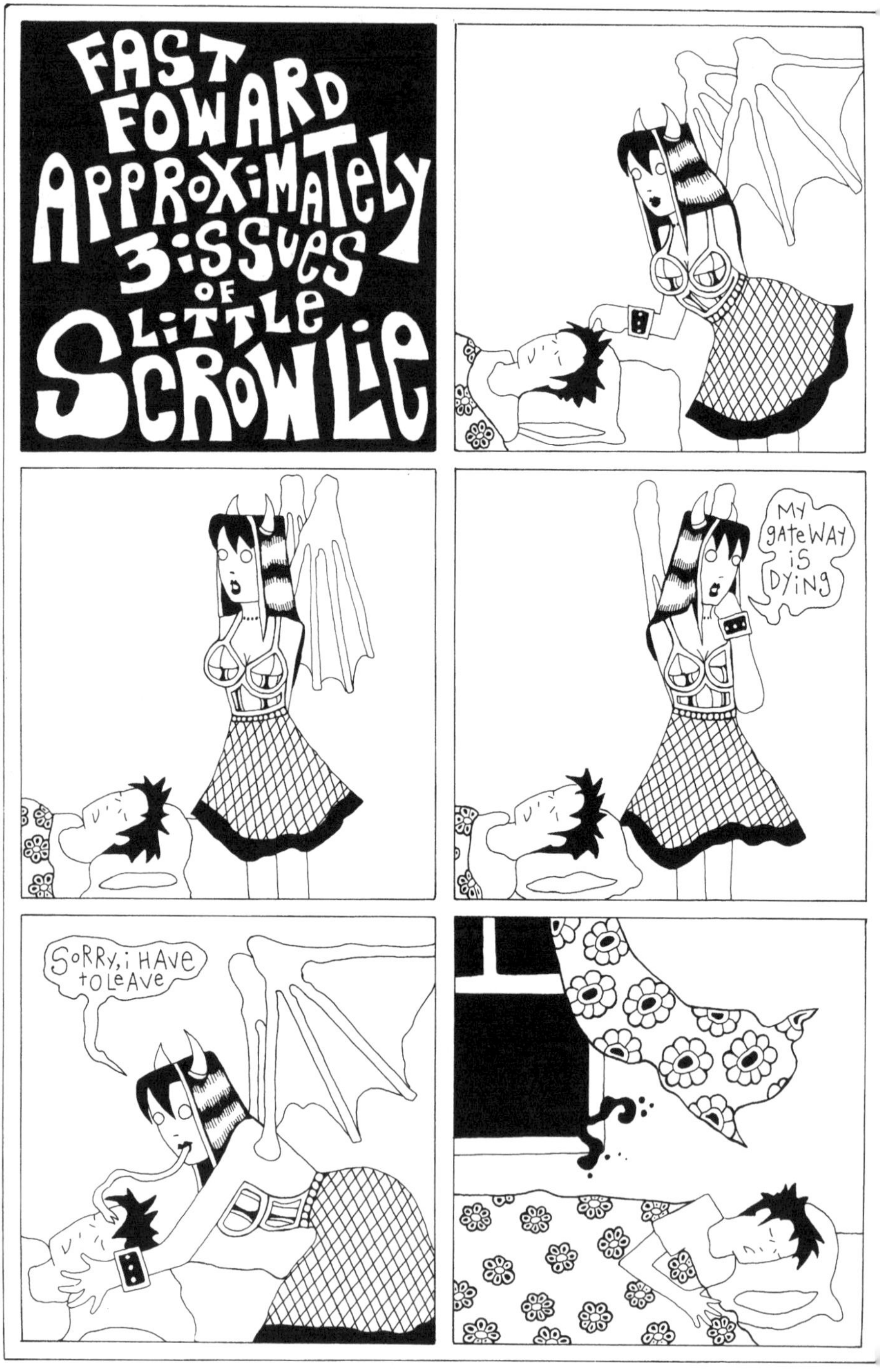
FAST FOWARD APPROXIMATELY 3 ISSUES OF LITTLE SCROWLIE
MY GATEWAY IS DYING
SORRY, I HAVE TO LEAVE

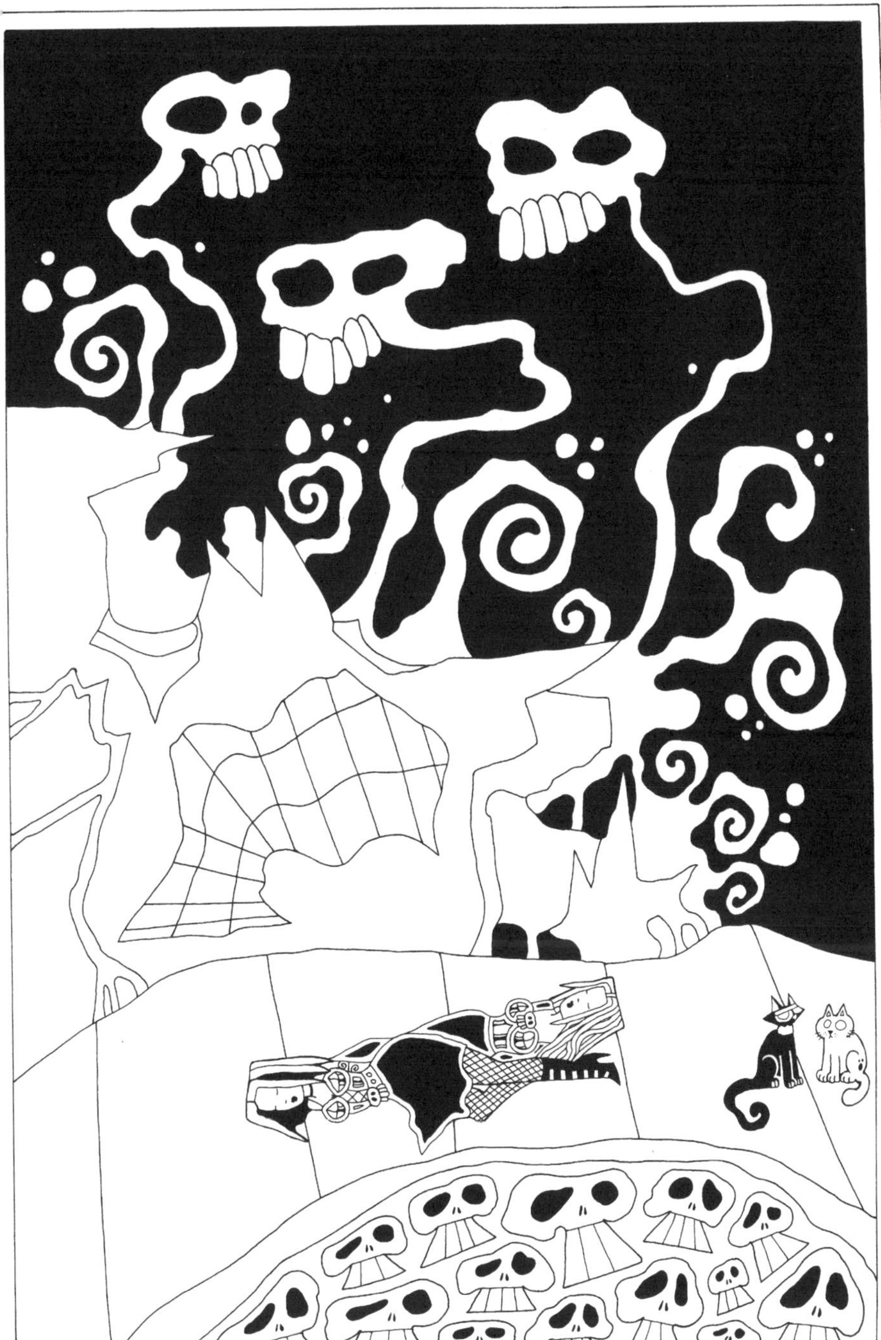

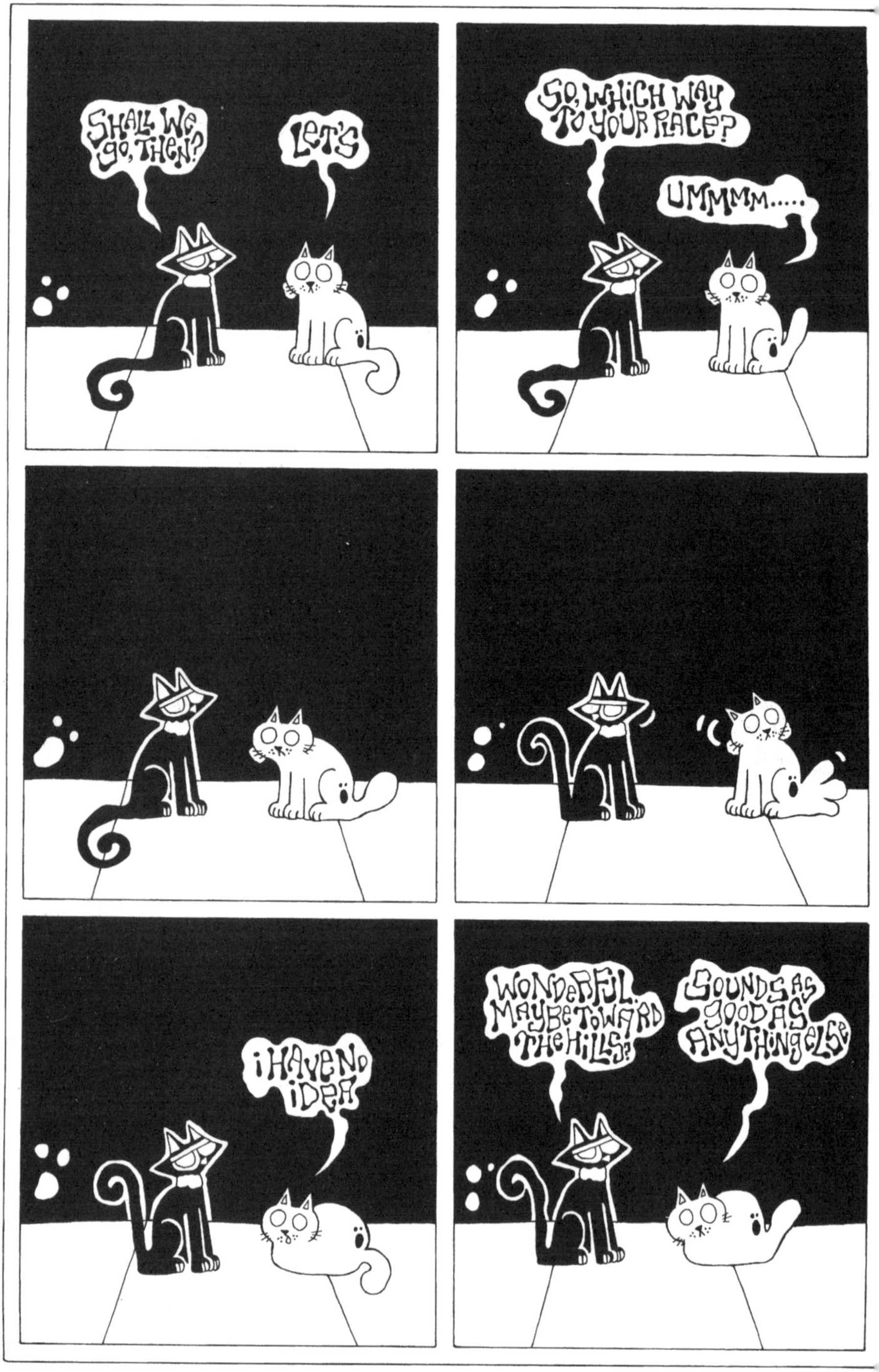
SHALL WE GO, THEN?
LET'S
SO, WHICH WAY TO YOUR PLACE?
UMMMM.....
I HAVE NO IDEA
WONDERFUL. MAYBE TOWARD THE HILLS?
SOUNDS AS GOOD AS ANYTHING ELSE

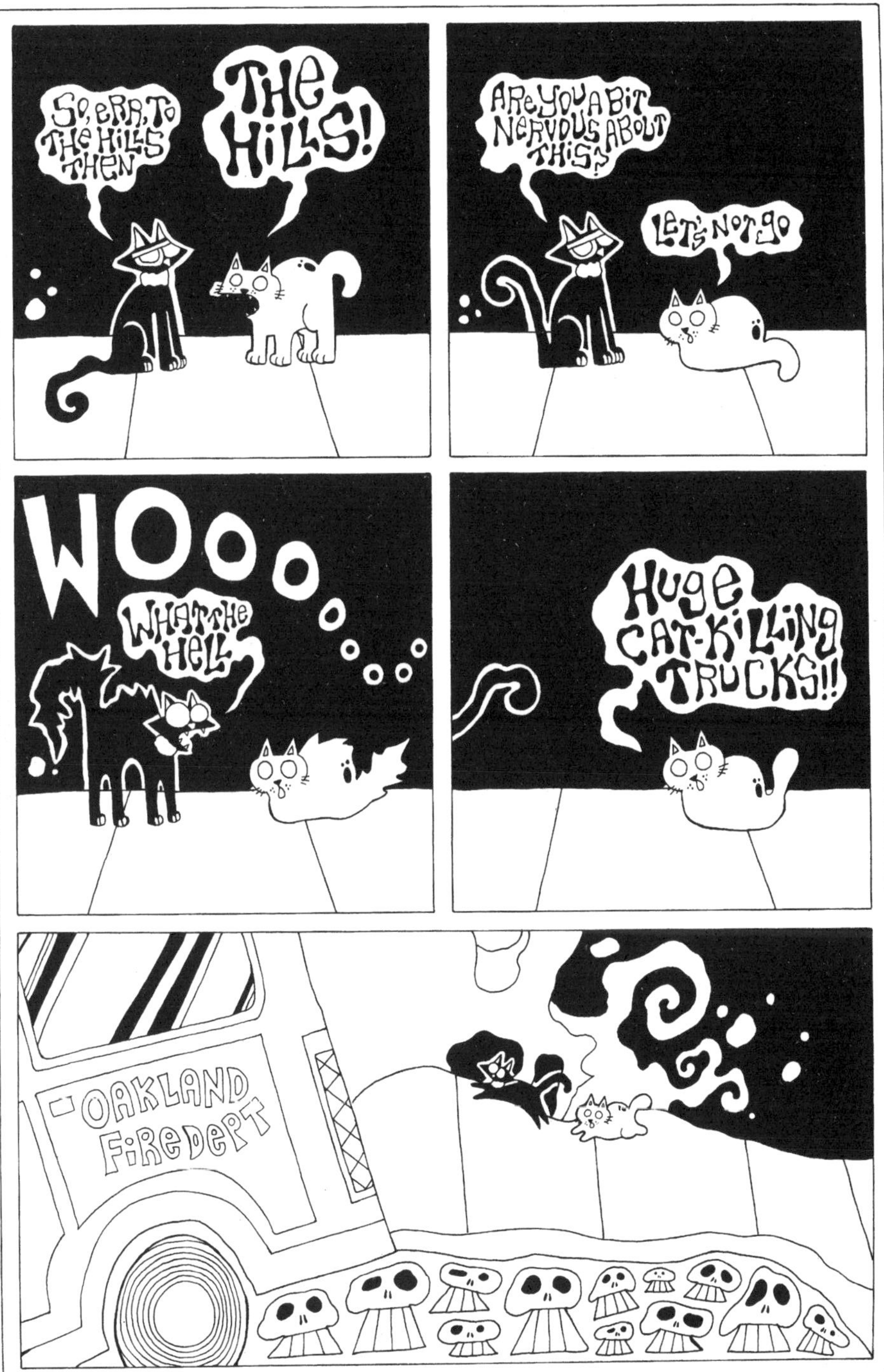
So, erm, to the hills then
THE HILLS!
Are you a bit nervous about this?
Let's not go
WOOOOOOOO
What the hell
Huge cat-killing trucks!!
OAKLAND FIRE DEPT

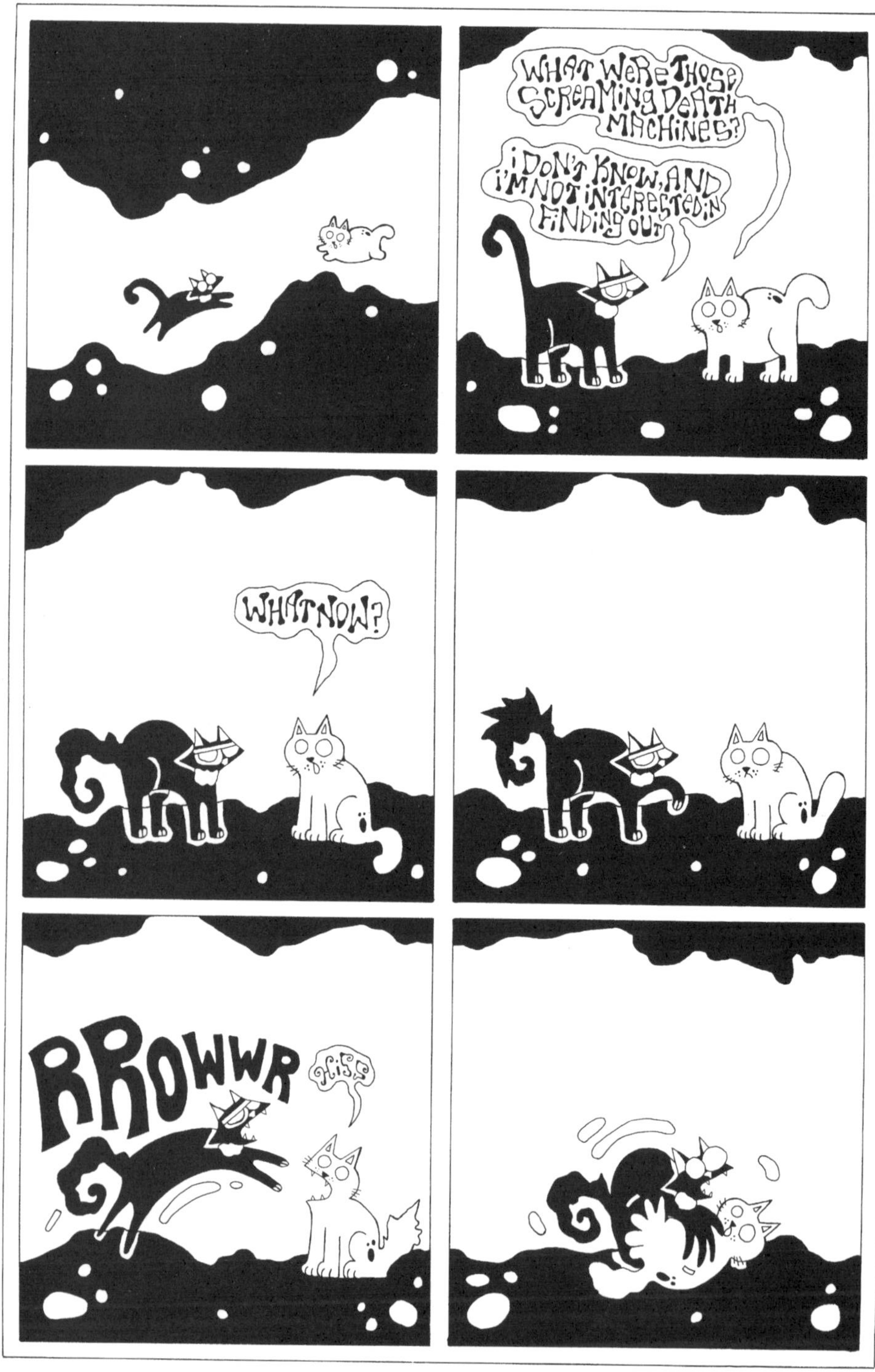
WHAT WERE THOSE SCREAMING DEATH MACHINES?
I DON'T KNOW, AND I'M NOT INTERESTED IN FINDING OUT
WHAT NOW?
RROWWR
HISS

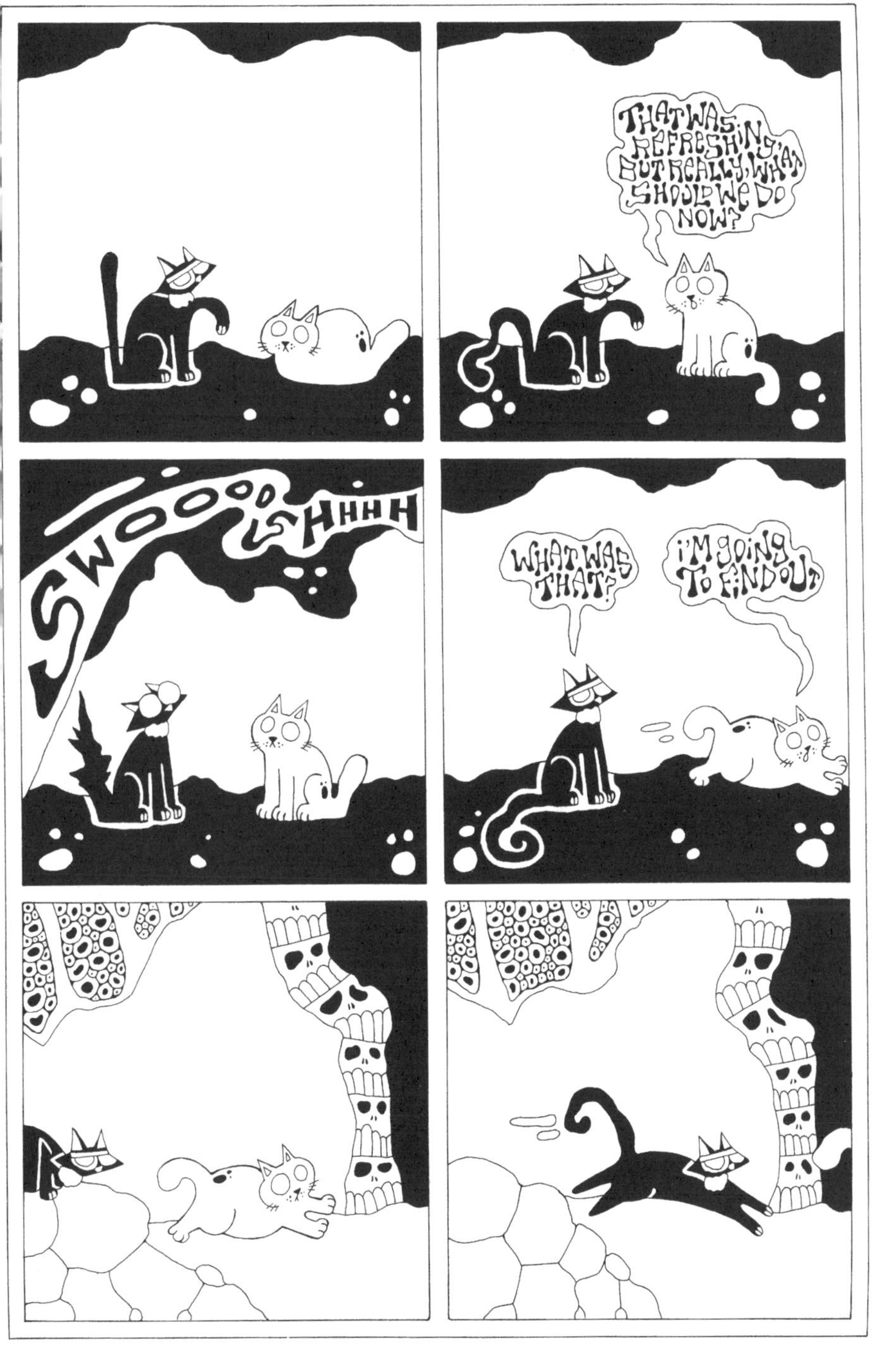
THAT WAS REFRESHING, BUT REALLY, WHAT SHOULD WE DO NOW?
SWOOOOSHHHH
WHAT WAS THAT?
I'M GOING TO FIND OUT

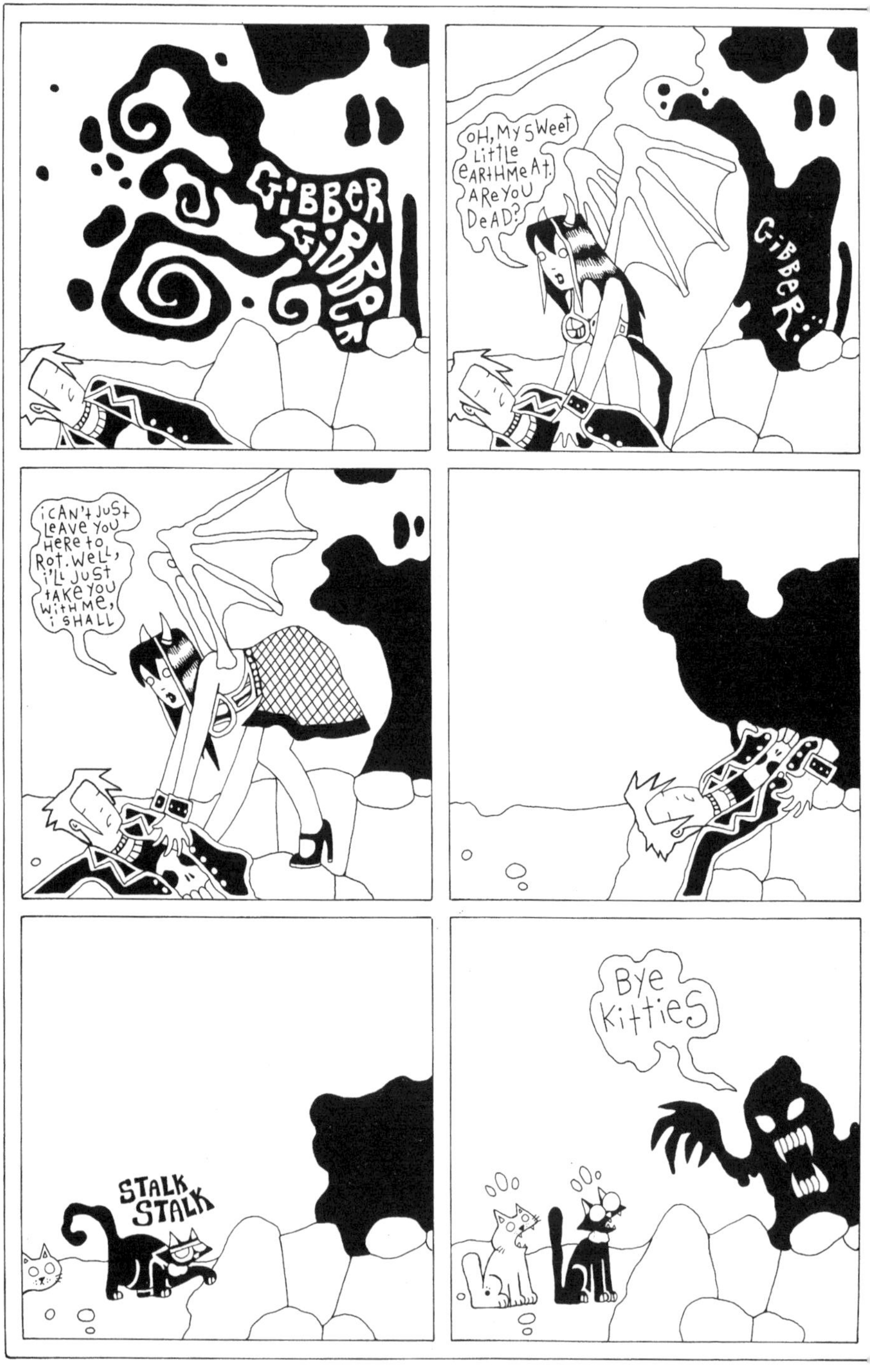
GIBBER GIBBER
OH, MY SWEET LITTLE EARTHMEAT. ARE YOU DEAD?
GIBBER..
I CAN'T JUST LEAVE YOU HERE TO ROT. WELL, I'LL JUST TAKE YOU WITH ME, I SHALL
STALK STALK
BYE KITTIES

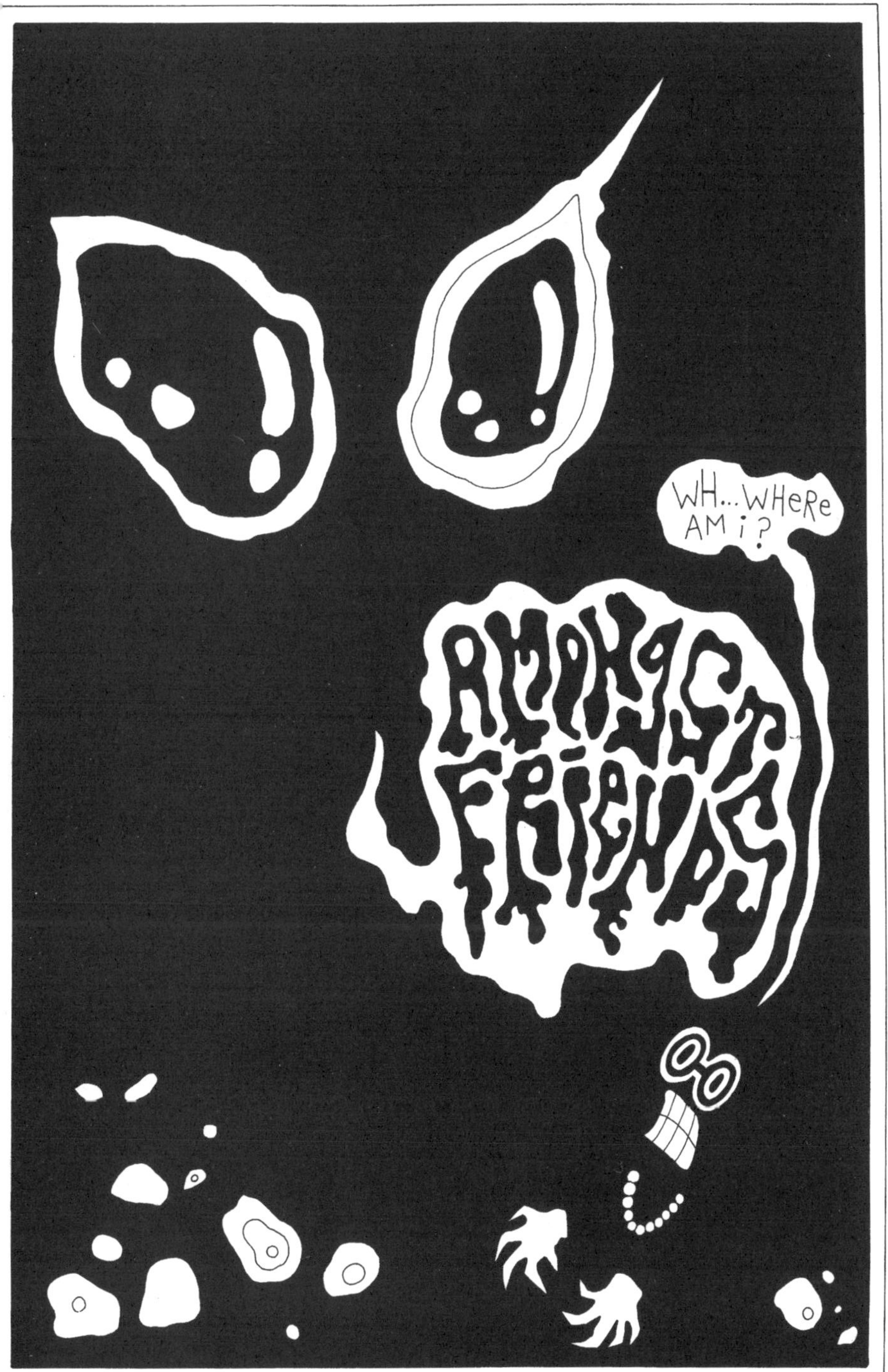
WH... WHERE AM I?
AMONGST FRIENDS

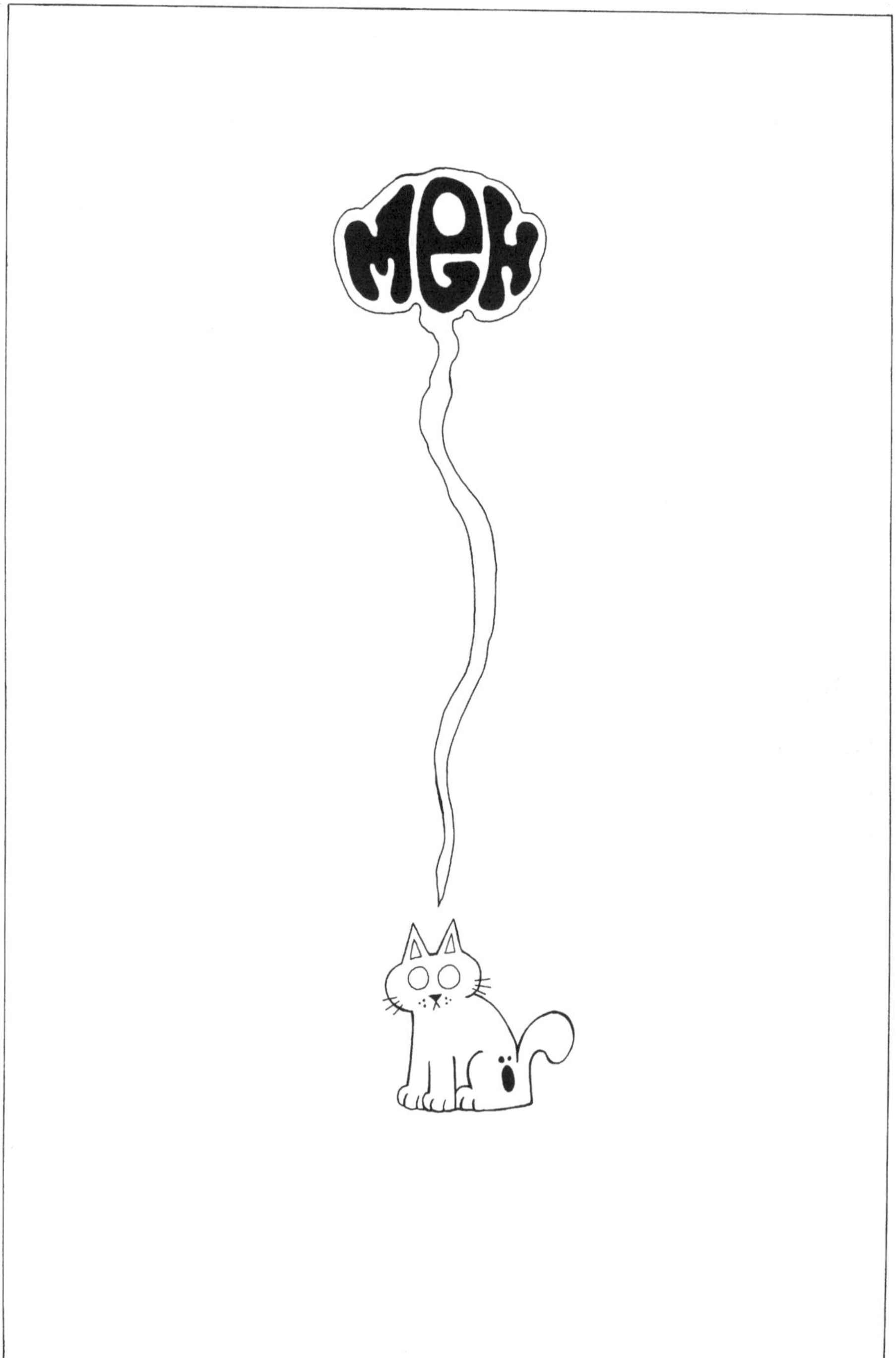
MEH

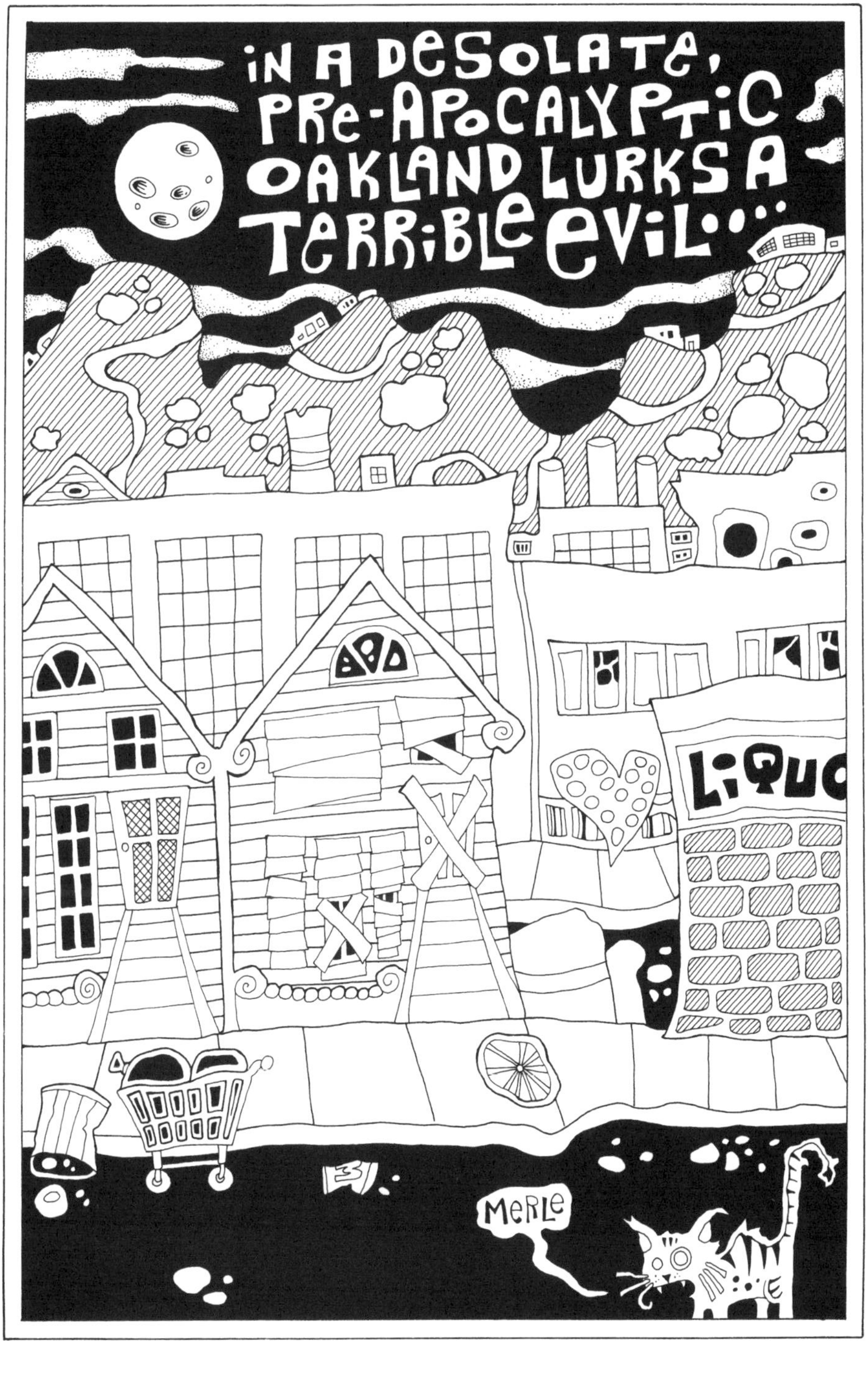
IN A DESOLATE, PRE-APOCALYPTIC OAKLAND LURKS A TERRIBLE EVIL...
LIQU
MERLE

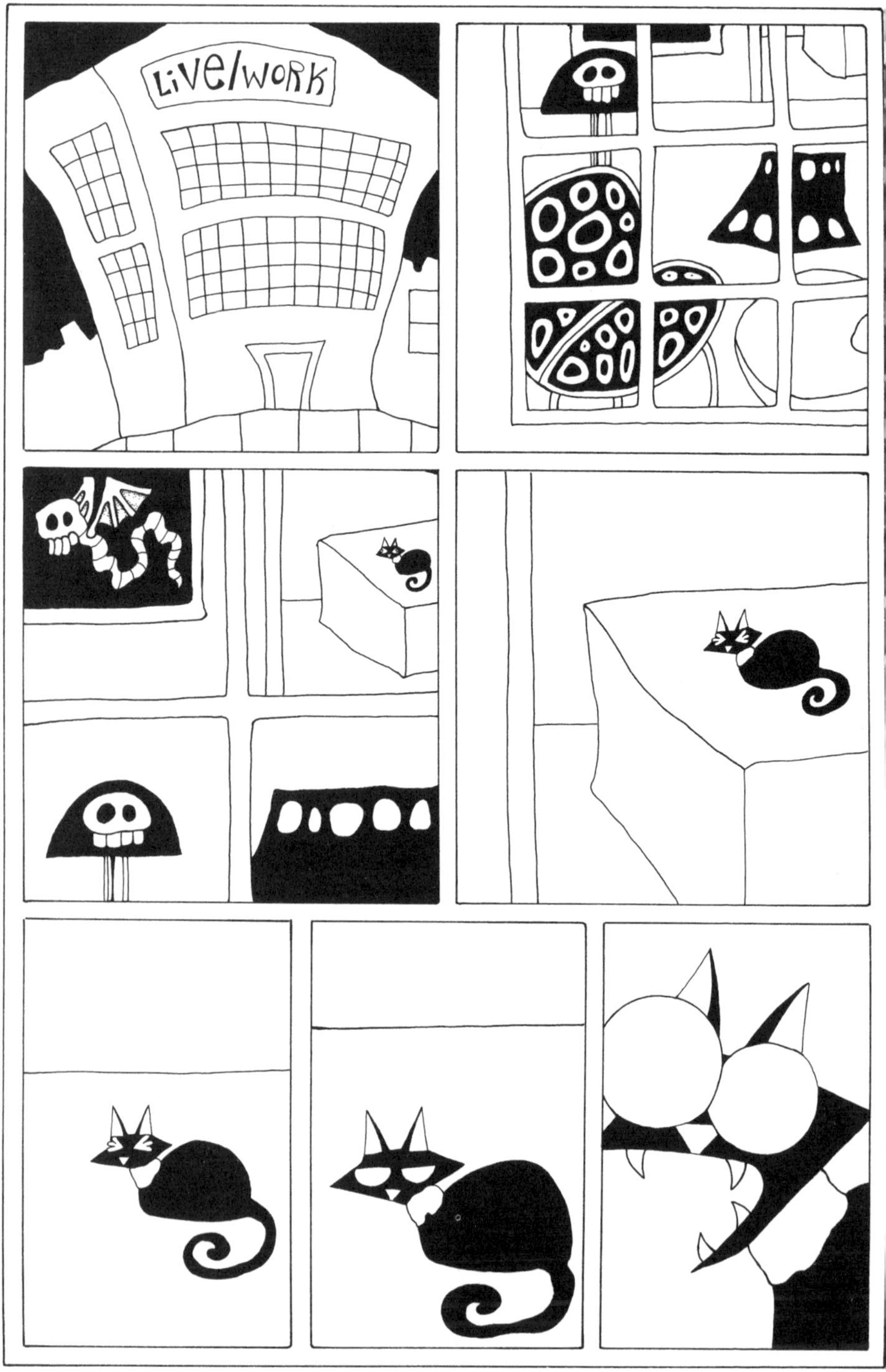
LIVE/WORK

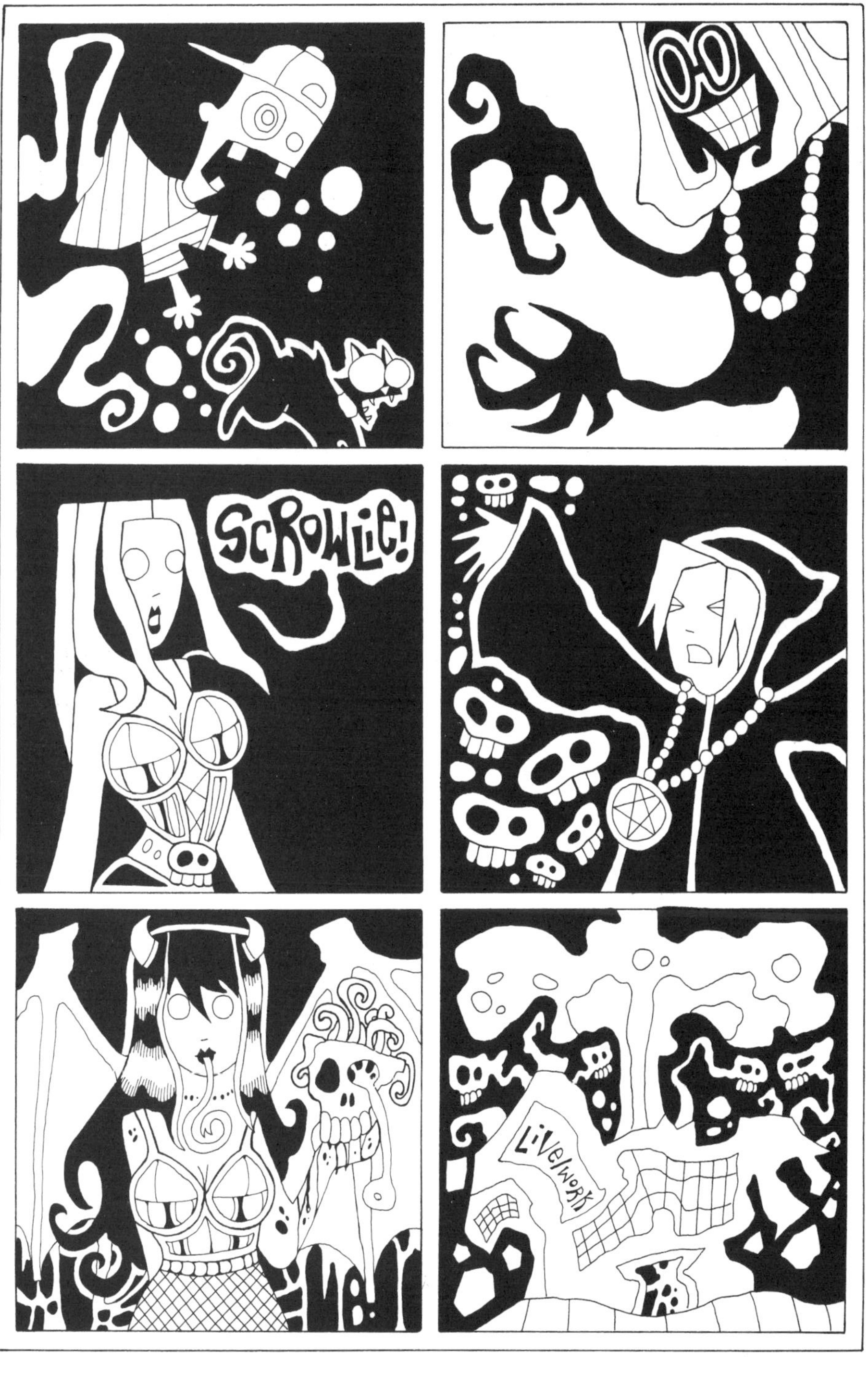
SCROWLIE!
LIVE/WORK

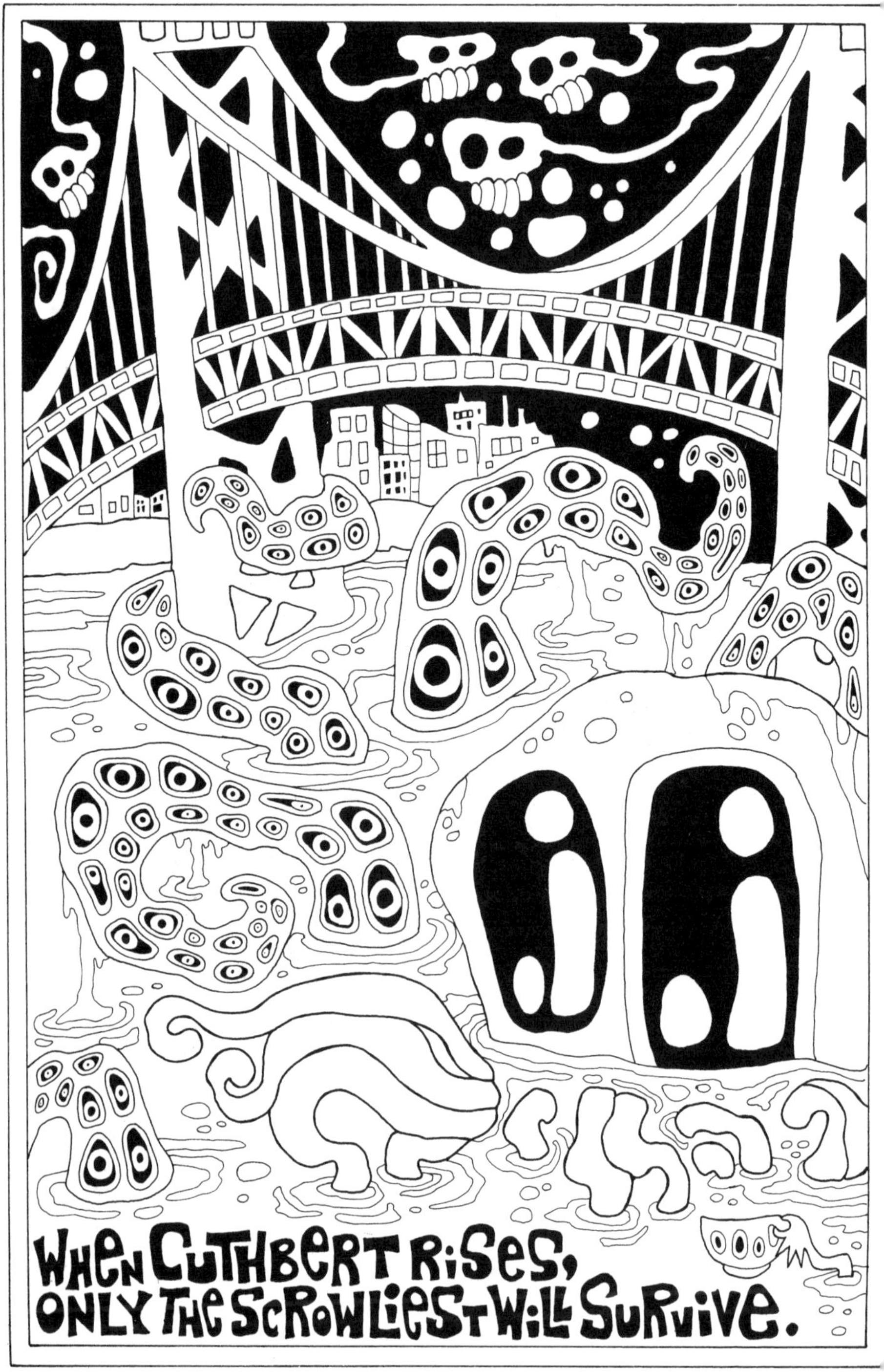
WHEN CUTHBERT RISES,
ONLY THE SCROWLIEST WILL SURVIVE.

PIN-UPS

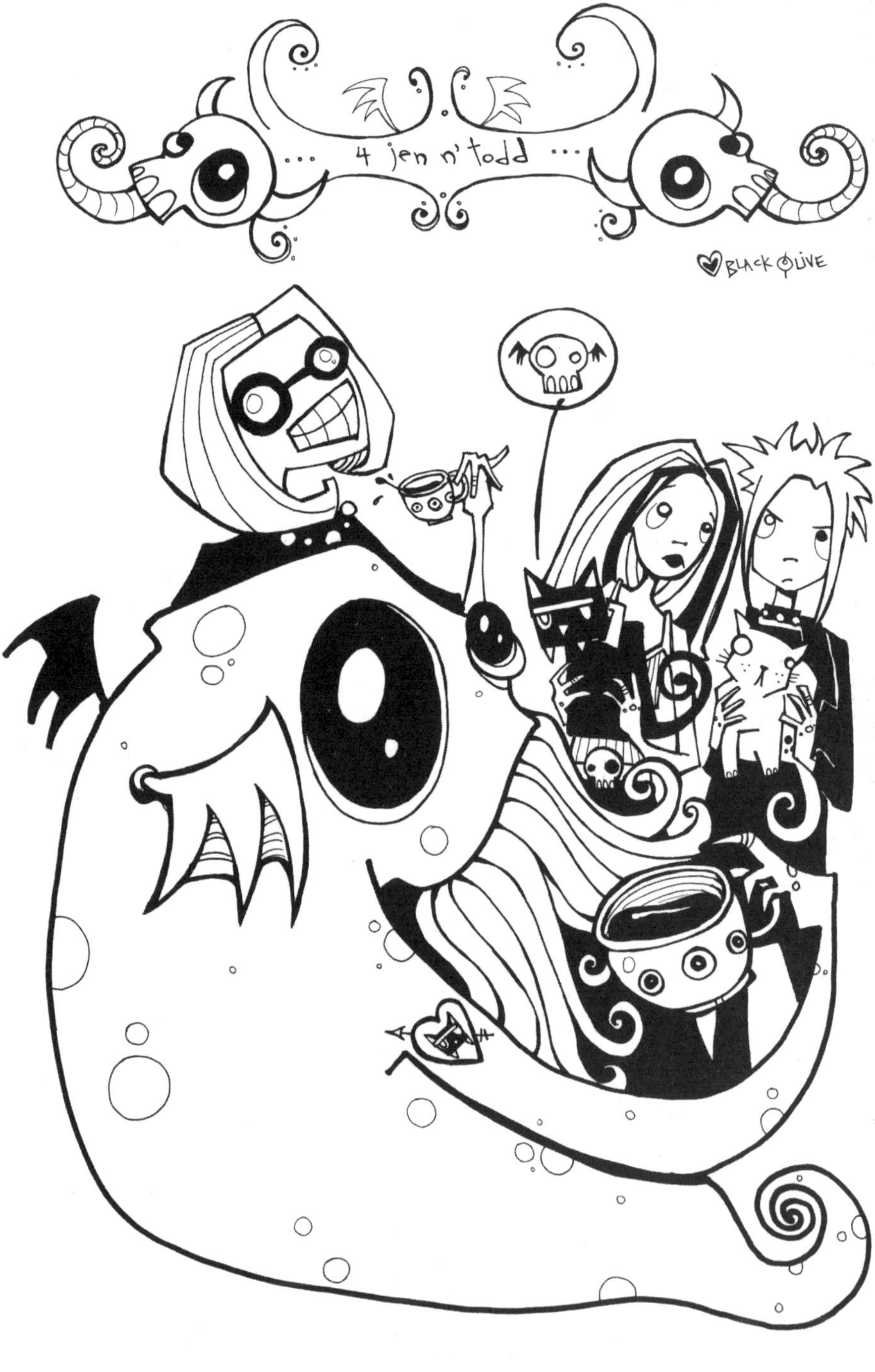
... 4 jen n' todd ...
BLACK OLIVE

Artwork by Black Olive

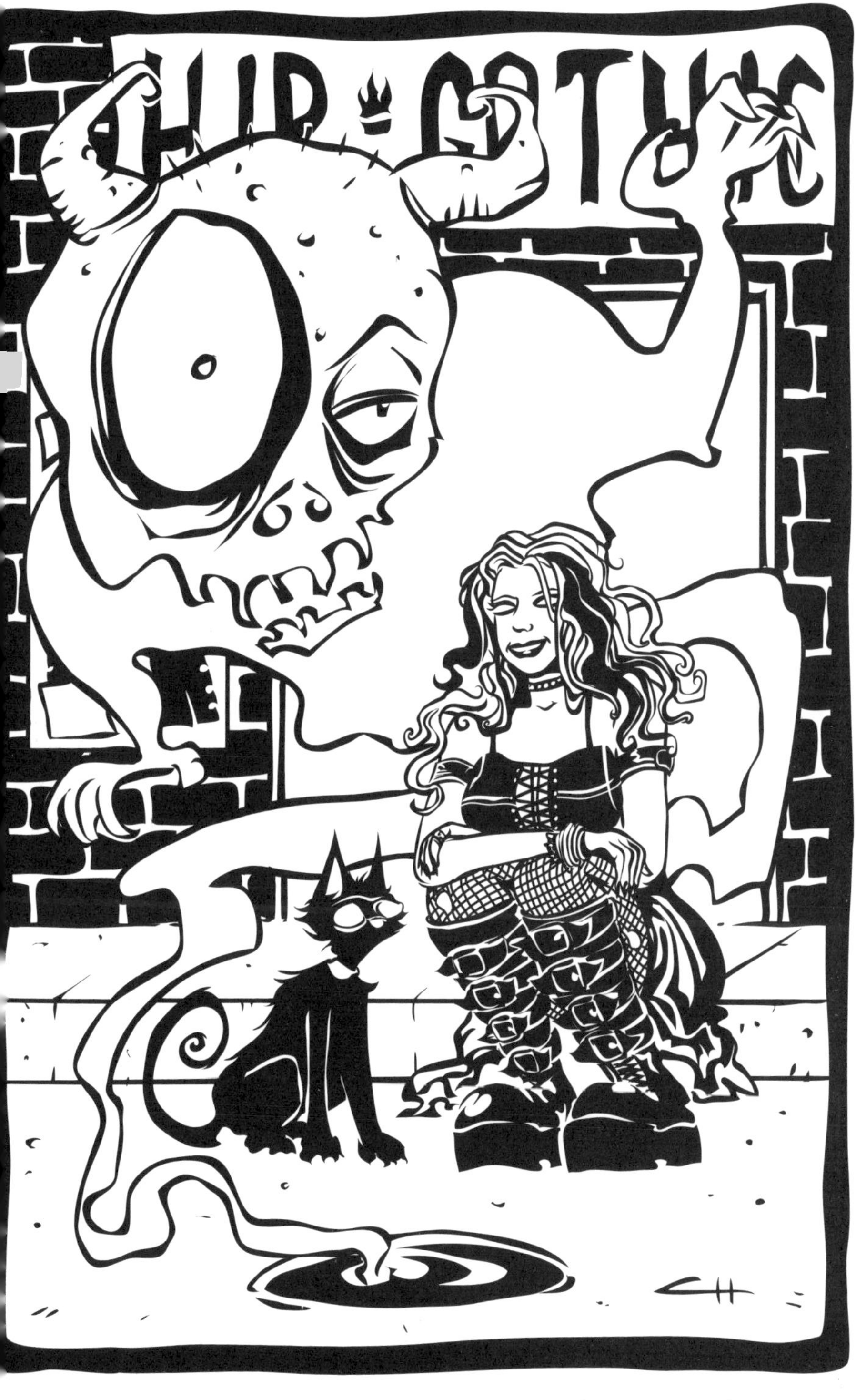

Artwork by Christopher

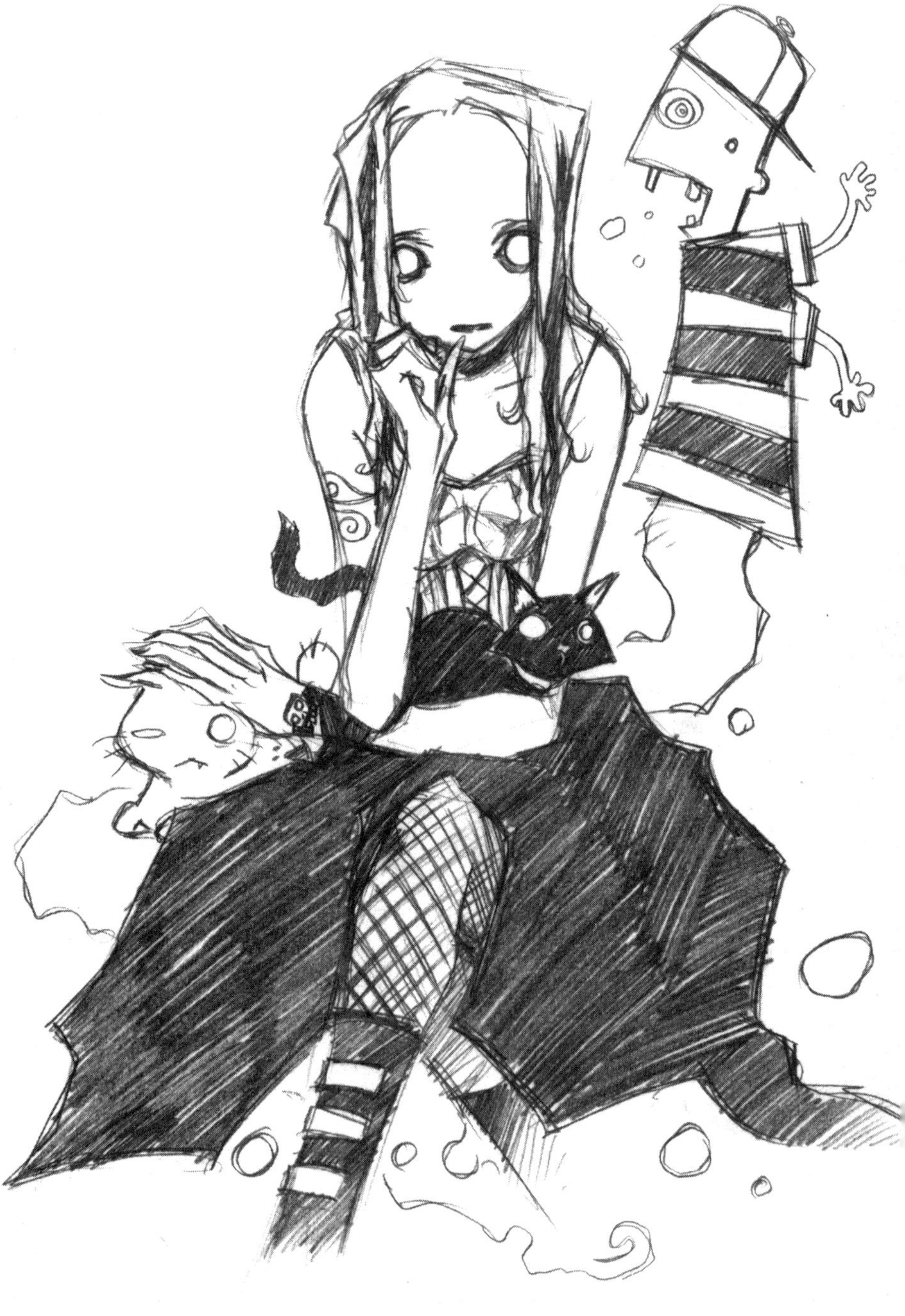

Artwork by FSc

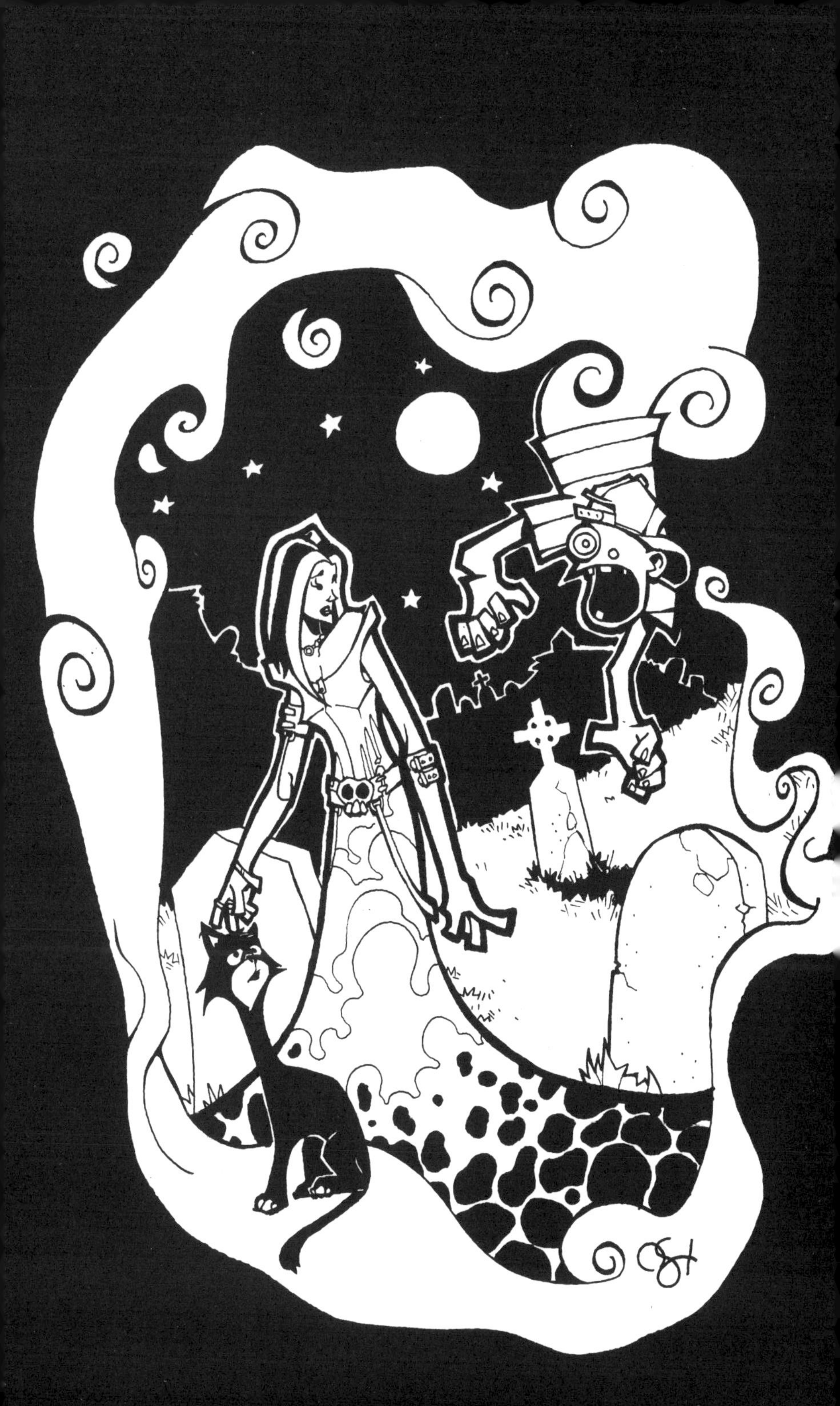

Artwork by Derek Hunter

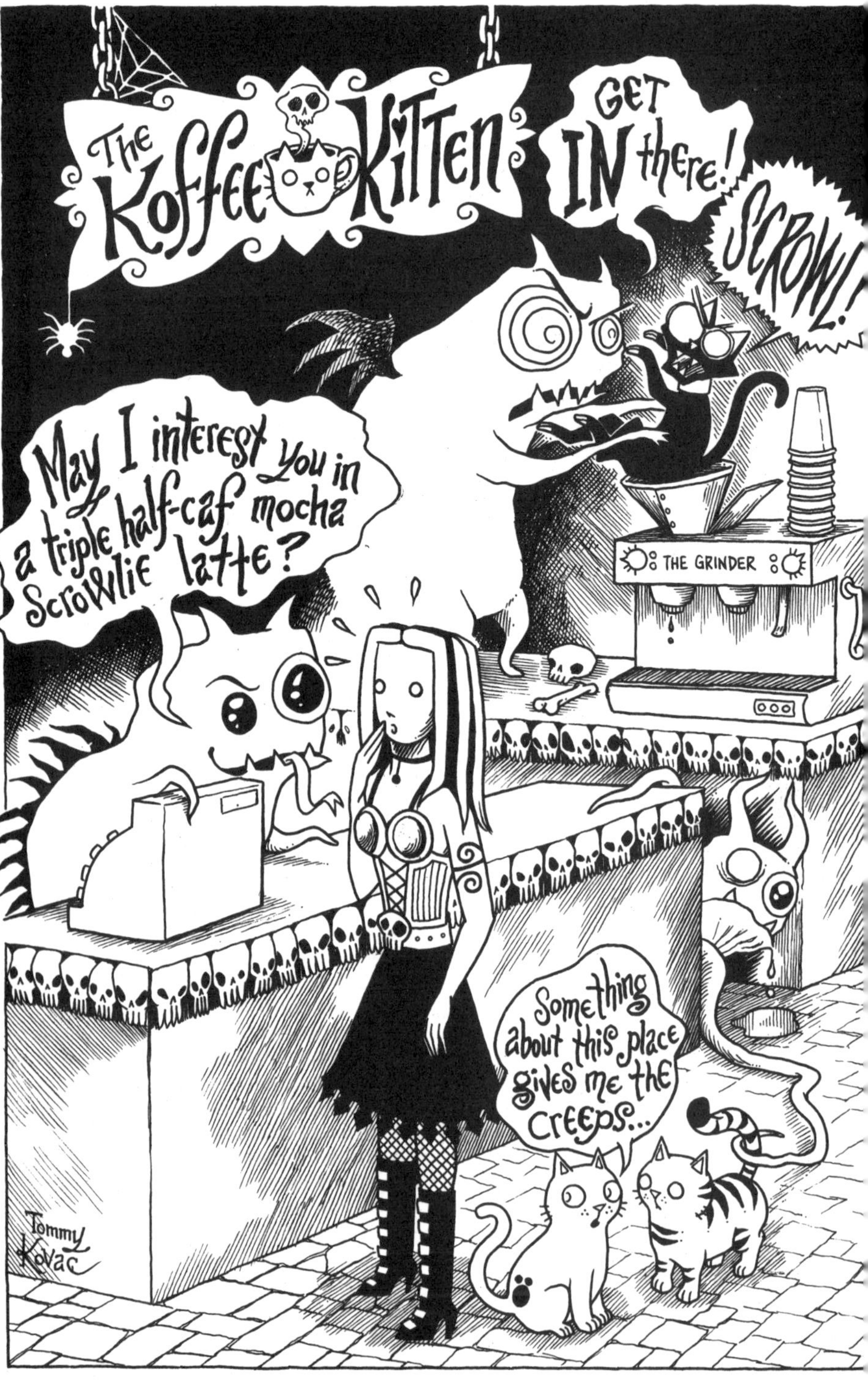
The Koffee Kitten
GET IN there!
SCROWL!
May I interest you in a triple half-caf mocha Scrowlie latte?
THE GRINDER
Something about this place gives me the CREEPS...
Tommy Kovac

Artwork by Tommy Kovac

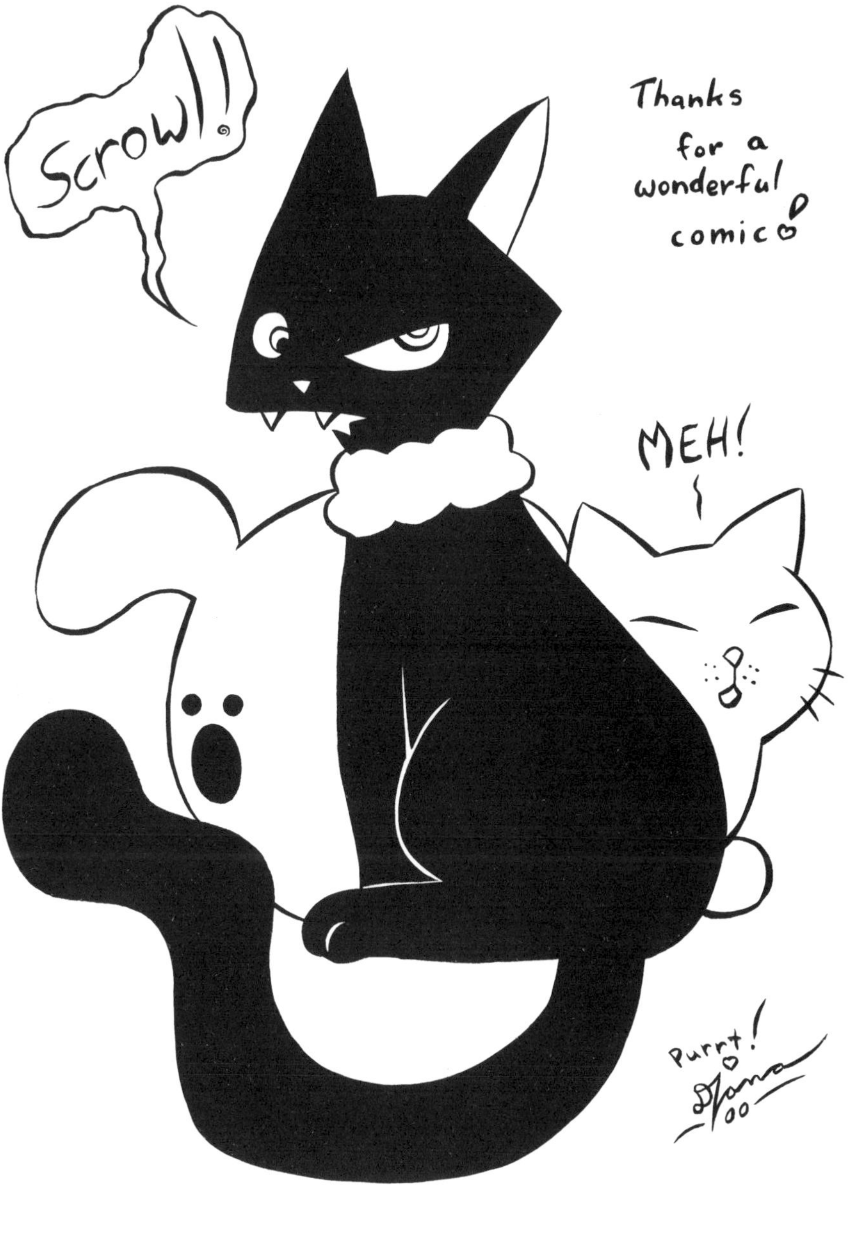
Scrowl!!
Thanks for a wonderful comic
MEH!
Purrt!
Diana 00

Artwork by Diana X. Sprinkle

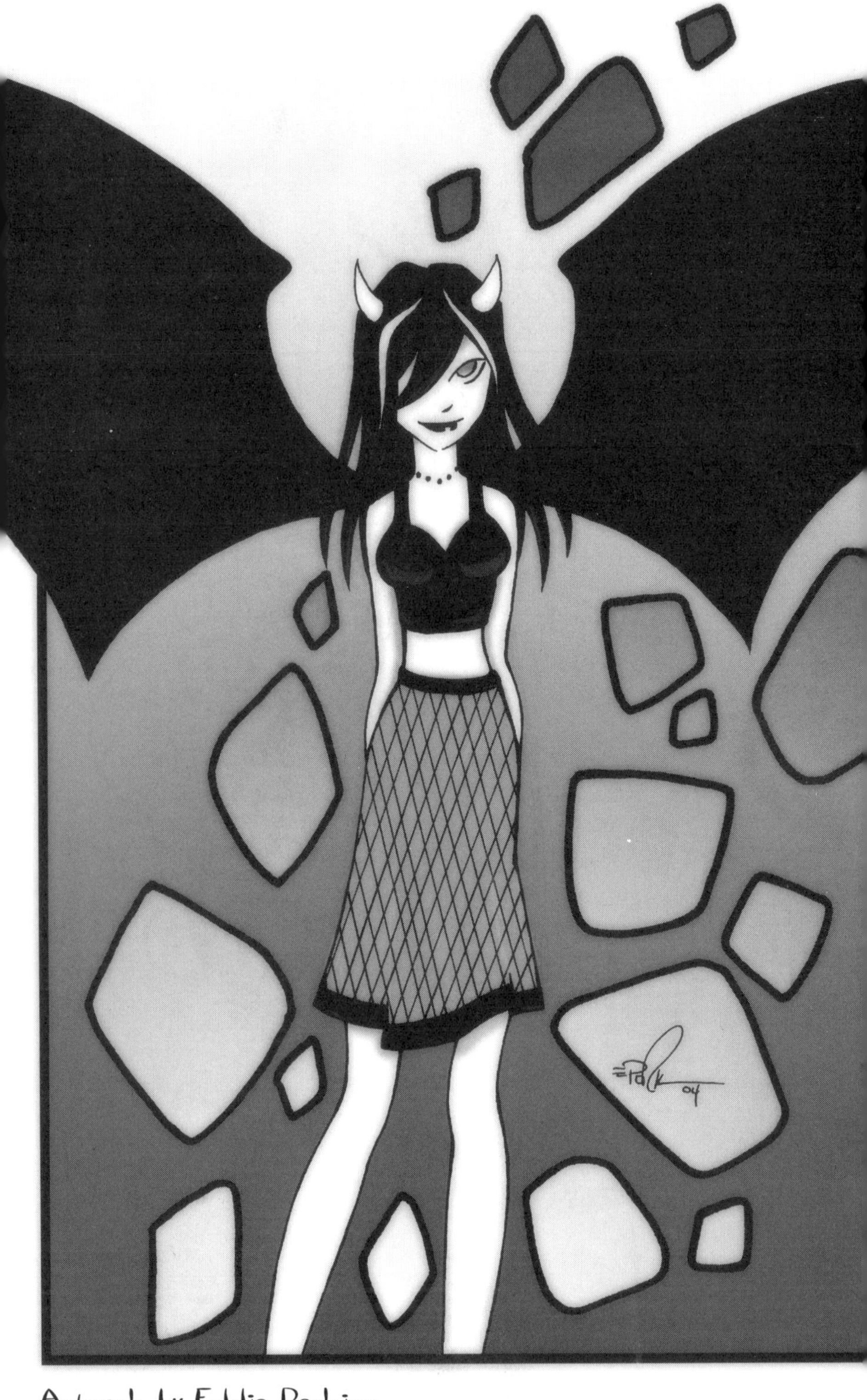

Artwork by Eddie Perkins